BOSTON

INSIGHT *City* GUIDES

Edited by Marcus Brooke
Principal Photography: Marcus Brooke
Editorial Director: Brian Bell

APA
PUBLICATIONS

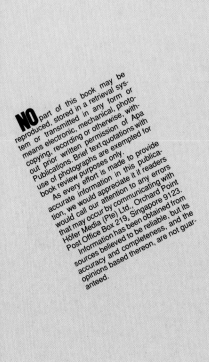
BOSTON

First Edition
Printed in Singapore by Höfer Press Pte. Ltd

ABOUT THIS BOOK

Boston, said Henry Wallsey, author of *An Excursion to the United States of North America in 1794*, "is the Bristol, New York, the Liverpool, and Philadelphia, the London of America." In the intervening two centuries, Bostonians have expanded that sadly inadequate list, transforming their city into nothing less than the "Hub of the Universe." When, therefore, Apa Publications decided to add the city of the Adamses, Reveres, Hancocks and Kennedys to its series of American City-Guides, it turned appropriately to one of its most peripatetic regular contributors, a man who, having lived all over the world, could see Boston clearly for what it is, as well as what it isn't.

Marcus Brooke needed little persuasion to take on the project. A Scot, born and educated in Glasgow, he fell victim to the charms of Boston and Cambridge when, in the 1950s and early 1960s, he was on the faculty of Harvard and, later, Massachusetts Institute of Technology. In recent years, he has traveled constantly, earning his living with his pen and his camera, contriving whenever possible for his journeys to take him through Boston.

"Quite simply, I adore the place," he says. "The changing seasons, the Charles River basin with its scudding sailboats, lilacs at the Arboretum, magnolias on the Back Bay's Commonwealth Avenue, the courtyard of the Public Library, snow upon the Hill (Beacon Hill)... what simple joys, but what pleasures." By taking most of the photographs in this book, Brooke has been able to convey his enthusiasm in images as well as prose, roaming outside Boston itself to survey the impeccable ensembles of colonial architecture that surround the city. In addition, he compiled the fact-filled Travel Tips section at the back of the book, drawing on his years of experience in sampling the food in most of the city's restaurants, window-shopping in most of its stores, and visiting its many world-ranking museums. "I have also sat in all the city's theaters and concert halls," he says, "and have heard and seen the good and the bad – mostly the former."

Working closely with Brooke throughout the book's production was **Brian Bell**, Apa's London-based editorial director. He insisted that Brooke keep *CityGuide: Boston* within a manageable size by reminding him of the words of John Winthrop as the *Arbella* with the Pilgrims aboard sailed towards the New World: "We must be willing to abridge ourselves of our superfluities." He did not, however, promise Brooke, as Winthrop promised the Pilgrims "the admiration of the world." Instead, he offered to contribute an introductory chapter on the Boston character – a subject with which he is acquainted by virtue of being an Irishman. In addition, he is no stranger to the attractions of New England, having married a Connecticut girl.

City of Neighborhoods

John Gattuso, a major contributor to the History and Places sections, is no stranger to the area either. Having majored in English and anthropology – useful subjects for any student of Boston – he has traveled extensively in the US and his many involvements with Apa books include the writing of *Pocket Guide: New York City* and the project editorship of *Insight Guide: Native America*. "The main thing I love about Boston," he

Brooke

Bell

Gattuso

says, "is that it is a city of neighborhoods, villages even, each with its own distinctive character. And, for all its puritanical roots and high ideals, it's still a town that knows how to have fun."

William Schofield, who contributed the Downtown chapter and the Paul Revere and Witches of Salem stories, was born in Providence, Rhode Island. He started his professional life as a reporter with that city's *Journal Bulletin* and entered Boston newspaperdom in 1940; "The Hub" has been his home ever since. His love of Boston is evident from the fact that in 1951 it was he who, single-handed, suggested what is now the Boston Freedom Trail, possibly the most-followed historical route in America. Schofield, a gunnery officer in World War II, had a long career in the Naval Reserve, retiring with the rank of captain. He has written novels, biographies and non-fiction books dealing with history and naval subjects.

Dana Berg, who writes here about architecture and profiles the Emerald Necklace, is an artist and art historian who currently lives in his native Boston. "I love city life and am forever toying with the idea of moving to New York or further afield," he says. "But Boston has many virtues. The human scale of the city, the handsome architecture, good film theaters, bookstores and musical offerings all exist within a manageable, compact area. Temperamental weather patterns create a variety of splendid light effects and the whole place is permeated with the smell of the ocean."

Michael Wentworth, curator of painting and sculpture at the Boston Athenaeum, contributed the chapter on Visual Arts. He likes the generally receptive, intelligent approach to culture in Boston, while deploring a dark New England tendency to turn culture into a lecture – "a kind of intellectual pretension which alone can explain the seats at Symphony Hall." He swears by Filene's Basement, a visit to the Aquarium, and the Gardner Museum. He hates the heat in August and is bored by local politics.

In addition to Marcus Brooke's photography, the book also contains the work of **Jeffrey Dunn**, **Steve Dunwell** and **Gene Peach**. The first two are full-time photographers working out of Boston, while Gene Peach now divides his life between Boston and Santa Fe, New Mexico, and his time between photography and painting.

Rounding off the team who captured the spirit of Boston and its environs on film are the renowned photographer **Brownie Harris**, who is based in New Jersey, **Kathy Tarantola**, who escaped from New Jersey to Boston, **Stanley Rowin,** Boston-born and based, and **Catherine Karnow**, a prolific contributor to Apa titles.

No Arguments

Like all Apa's Insight Guides, this book combines detailed and insightful reporting about what makes a place tick with a daring, photojournalistic style of illustration. In doing so, it has boldly challenged the judgment of Henry Adams, who wrote with Brahmin authority that "only Bostonians can understand Bostonians and thoroughly sympathize with the inconsequences of the Boston mind." To those denizens of the Hub who believe that Adams was right, we can only respond by taking the advice of Rudyard Kipling: "I have learned enough never to argue with a Bostonian."

Schofield   *Berg*   *Wentworth*

History

23 Introduction: The Boston Character
    —by Brian Bell

29 Beginnings
    —by John Gattuso

39 The Road to Revolution
    —by John Gattuso

45 *Paul Revere*
    —by William Schofield

48 Immigration and Renewal
    —by John Gattuso and Marcus Brooke

Features

59 The Education Industry
    —by Marcus Brooke

71 *Medical Trailblazer*
    —by Marcus Brooke

74 Sporting Life
    —by Marcus Brooke

79 *The Boston Marathon*
    —by Marcus Brooke

83 The Visual Arts
    —by Michael Wentworth

Places

—by Marcus Brooke
(*unless otherwise stated*)

95 Introduction

101 Beacon Hill and Boston Common
—by John Gattuso

104 *The Black Heritage Trail*

115 *Music Making*

119 North End
—by John Gattuso and Marcus Brooke

129 Charlestown

137 Downtown
—by William Schofield

143 *The Freedom Trail*

149 *Architectural Hodgepodge*
—by Dana Berg and Marcus Brooke

153 The Waterfront

163 The Back Bay and Fenway
—by John Gattuso

173 *Christian Science*

179 South End

189 The Charles River

195   *Head of the Charles Regatta*

197   **The Emerald Necklace**
      —by Dana Berg

205   **Cambridge**

217   *Harvard's Museums*

231   **Day Trips West**

236   *Relics of the Industrial Revolution*

243   **Day Trips South**

253   *Whale Watching*

257   **Day Trips North**

259   *The Witches of Salem*
      —by William Schofield

Maps

 96   Boston
192   The Suburbs
206   Cambridge
212   Harvard University
232   Beyond Boston
234   Concord
247   Cape Cod
260   Salem
278   "T" Rapid Transit Lines
295   Freedom Trail

TRAVEL TIPS

Getting There
270 By Air
271 By Rail
271 By Bus
271 By Car

Travel Essentials
272 Visas & Passports
272 Money Matters
272 Health Tips
272 Customs
272 Tipping
272 What to Wear

Getting Acquainted
273 Geography & Population
273 Time Zones
273 Climate
274 Weights & Measures
274 Electricity
274 Business Hours
274 Fax Facilities
274 Public Holidays & Events
276 Media

Getting Around
277 Rapid Transit
277 By Bus
279 Commuter Rail
279 Passport Visitor Pass
279 Taxicabs
279 Car Hire
279 Limousine Services
280 Commuter Boat
280 Other Ferries, Buses & Planes
280 Tours

Where to Stay
282 Boston Hotels
284 Greater Boston B&B
285 Hostels & "Ys"
285 Cambridge Hotels
286 Greater Boston Hotels

Food Digest
287 Where to Eat
287 Restaurants

Things to Do
294 High Spots
294 Freedom Trail

Culture Plus
296 Places of Interest
303 Parks
303 Entertainment
305 Theater
306 Movie Theaters

Nightlife
306 Comedy Clubs
307 Dance Clubs
307 Folk Music
307 The Jazz Scene
308 Pubs
308 Gay Scene

Sports
309 Spectator
310 Participant

Shopping
311

Further Reading
314 Non-Fiction
315 Fiction

Special Information
315 Information Sources
316 Essential Phone Numbers
316 Consulates

Arts/Photo Credits
317

Index
318

"Like it? Why, I never thought of it that way. Liking Boston is like saluting the flag." The sentiments are those of a Proper Bostonian, so called because she lives in downtown "Boston Proper," the old "walking city" of the 17th century.

Justifiable pride? Insufferable arrogance? Perhaps visitors' reactions to Boston and Bostonians reveal more about themselves than about the city and its inhabitants, but it is certain that no other American city has provoked so many polarized opinions. Writers in particular have always flocked to Boston, drawn by its strong literary tradition, so the quality of both praise and invective is of an uncommonly high standard.

Boston is "a state of mind," said Mark Twain (or perhaps Ralph Waldo Emerson, or possibly Thomas Appleton, for Bostonians can always find something to disagree about). It's "a moral and intellectual nursery," said (again, arguably) the Spanish philosopher George Santayana. "A museum piece," thought Frank Lloyd Wright. "A hole," wrote Robert Browning.

Hard sell: Maybe Boston simply oversold itself. Even today, when city halls all over America house marketing teams intent on promoting their "product" with the publicity tools once dedicated to breakfast cereals and sun-tan oils, no copywriter would dare claim for the city the status that Oliver Wendell Holmes, author, philosopher and professor of anatomy at Harvard, gave it in 1860: that "it is the thinking center of the continent, and therefore of the planet." To the scholars at Harvard, this seemed scandalously faint praise and in no time at all this small northeastern corner of the new republic had extended its sphere of influence to become nothing less than the Hub of the Universe.

Naturally this red rag, though it wasn't

meant to be taken entirely seriously, infuriated many literary bulls. "Boston prides itself on virtue and ancient lineage – it doesn't impress me in either direction," wrote the philosopher Bertrand Russell in 1914. "It is musty, like the Faubourg St Germain. I often want to ask them what constitutes the amazing virtue they are so conscious of."

In the mid-19th century, the valued virtue was culture, as the New World, a child rapidly approaching adulthood, sought to con-

vey its maturity to the Old. Not that everyone worshipped it: "In Boston," wrote Charles Mackay in 1859, "the onus lies upon every respectable person to prove that he has not written a sonnet, preached a sermon, or delivered a lecture."

Self-esteem was certainly valued even more than sonnets, and the city's establishment readily approved Oliver Wendell Holmes's description of them as "Boston Brahmins." Not only was the alliteration attractive; the term also suggested an ancient lineage, a certain austerity, unquestioned wisdom. No matter that the 19th-century

Preceding pages: stars, stripes and clapboard; afternoon tea at the Ritz; Charles River Basin and Back Bay; Rowe's wharf; Back Bay reflections; magnolias on Commonwealth Avenue. Left, Boston Brahmin. Above, Boston Irishman.

businessmen who ran Boston were often closer in their intellectual interests to Donald Trump than to an Indian ascetic: "Brahmin" was accepted. No J. Walter Thompson copywriter could have done a better job.

The tone had been set even earlier, in 1841, by George Combe, a phrenologist who, having studied the city's inhabitants from 1838 to 1840, delivered the kind of prognosis that court physicians reserved for absolute monarchs: "Here the female head is in general beautifully developed in the moral and intellectual departments, and the natural language of the countenance is soft, affectionate and rational. In the men, also, large

as a race, far inferior in point of anything beyond mere talent to any other set upon the continent of North America," wrote Edgar Allan Poe in 1849. "They are decidedly the most servile imitators of the English it is possible to conceive."

Even the Bostonians' speech patterns and accent came under fire as being slavish replicas of Oxford English. As an anonymous wit put it, if you hear an owl hoot "To whom" instead of "To who," you can be sure it was born and educated in Boston. The Brahmins were impervious to such sneers, of course, and the curious inflections and intonations have remained unmodified so that

moral and intellectual organs are very general, but Benevolence and Veneration are more frequently large than Conscientiousness. The cerebral organization of this people, taking them all in all, appears really to have been enlarged in the moral and intellectual regions by long cultivation, added to the influence of a favorable stock."

But along with the superior stock came stock attitudes. The problem, for many, was that Boston, rather than creating its own distinctive culture, was slavishly imitating the discredited characteristics of its cast-off colonial parent. "The Bostonians are really,

you will be invited, for instance, to *pahk yuh cah* rather than park your car.

Whether you will be able easily to accept such an invitation, however, is doubtful, since traffic congestion is one of the Hub's chronic afflictions. The city center's roads, which remain more faithful in their patterns to 17th-century cow tracks than to anything suggesting a grid, encourage local drivers to be noticably aggressive: they race away from traffic lights, weave in and out of lanes, and tailgate alarmingly. Visitors from Europe find such behavior quite normal; people from other American cities, where driving is more sedate and courteous, think they're in a Hollywood movie. It's not just an impression either: insurers confirm that Boston's drivers are the nation's most accident-prone.

Ever adaptable, Bostonians have responded to the traffic chaos by regarding walking as a virtue. Where a New Yorker would unhesitatingly flag down a cab, the Bostonian, eschewing extravagance, will step smartly towards his or her destination. Given the jams, of course, that's sound common sense; as the joke has it: "Shall we walk or do we have time to take a cab?"

Split personality: But if walking is sometimes a necessity, it is usually a pleasure. It

as well as secretaries boast of the bargains they unearth among the scheduled markdowns. The city is unquestionably America's medical capital; yet in its very center sits the vast concrete bunker of the Christian Science Complex, whose occupants reject many of the tenets of modern medicine.

Academics adore such paradoxes and probably encourage them. Like Oxford or Cambridge, Boston is a factory town whose product is college graduates and each new generation adds its own pinch of quirkiness to the cocktail, sustaining the legend. Also, many find jobs and stay on in the area after graduating, adding fresh blood to the popu-

enables one to savor the strange contradictions of this untypical town. The architecture expresses part of its split personality: the size, color and design of the carefully preserved older buildings convey class, heritage and a human scale, while the gleaming new skyscrapers radiate boldness, modernity, commercial confidence. A spell of window-shopping will quickly indicate that Boston is an expensive place to live; yet here is Filene's Basement, where society matrons

Left, a bevy of colleens. **Above left**, Italian matriarch. **Above right**, the sky is the limit.

lation and keeping urban sclerosis at bay.

And so the debate goes on. For more than two centuries, the Boston character has delighted and infuriated, almost in equal measure, and has defeated most attempts to define it. Such attempts, Bostonians will tell you, are futile in any case, unless you had the good fortune to be born and brought up in the Hub of the Universe. Then, like Charles Francis Adams, they can rejoice: "In the course of my life I have tried Boston socially on all sides: I have summered it and wintered it, tried it drunk and tried it sober; and, drunk or sober, there's nothing in it – save Boston!"

American cities have a way of effacing history. The present is so jammed with information, and reminders of the past are so glibly destroyed, we have trouble remembering what happened last year in our cities, much less last century. It's rare indeed to hear people talking about "old Los Angeles" or "old New York," unless of course it's in the sense of the "old neighborhood," which we all know "ain't what it used to be."

But Boston is different. Here's a city whose identity is still firmly rooted in the past. Every schoolboy knows that Boston is the cradle of American independence. Adams, Revere, Hancock – they are more than historical figures, they are players in a national mythology. Americans look to the patriots for a sense of who they are. And they look to Boston as the birthplace of the nation.

Native Americans: At the time of European contact, the New England coast was inhabited by several loosely affiliated Algonquin tribes, including the Massachusetts in the Boston area and the Wampanoag near Cape Cod. They led fairly settled lives, moving seasonally within tribal boundaries and making their livelihood from hunting, fishing and planting. By the time English settlers arrived, they had already suffered greatly from European diseases introduced by traders. Between 1616 and 1617 a smallpox epidemic wiped out nearly one-third of the native population and put the coastal tribes at the mercy of their inland enemies. The devastation was so complete at some Wampanoag villages that settlers found nothing but bones scattered on the ground because there was no one left to bury the dead.

At first, the Indians and whites managed to sustain reasonably peaceful relations. With the help of Tisquantum (Squanto), who had learned English after being sold into slavery by the Europeans, the Wampanoag sachem Massasoit negotiated an alliance with the

settlers at Plimoth Plantation – the Indians supplying food and instruction, the whites supplying defense against threatening tribes to the east. But, as English settlements expanded, relations between Indians and whites grew hostile.

Finally, in 1675, Massasoit's son Pometacom (King Philip) led a raid against a small settlement on Narragansett Bay, launching a bloody three-year conflict. Although Boston was never attacked, King Philip's War

devastated about 50 other towns in New England. In the end, Pometacom was captured and beheaded, and the Wampanoag were decimated.

City on a Hill: At the time of Pometacom's defeat, Boston was already a bustling seaport and the undeclared capital of New England. Nearly 40 years earlier, John Winthrop came to the site with a group of Puritans determined to create a new society – a "visible kingdom of God." While still aboard the *Arbella*, halfway between the Old World and the New, Winthrop addressed his fellow colonists, laying out for them the terms of their covenant with the Almighty.

"We must be knit together, in this work, as one man," he told them. "We must entertain each other in brotherly affection. We must be willing to abridge ourselves of our superfluities, for the supply of other's necessities... We must delight in each other; make other's conditions our own; rejoice together; mourn together; labor and suffer together." And if they stood by this commitment, Winthrop said, they would be rewarded with divine benefaction and the admiration of the world. "For we must consider that we shall be as a City upon a Hill. The eyes of all people are upon us."

To the small group of gallant colonists gathered on deck, Winthrop's words must have resounded with a comforting sense of purpose. The motherland had long since receded beyond the horizon, and most of them would never see it again. They were alone in unfamiliar waters with nothing but wind and waves in every direction, heading towards a wilderness that must have seemed impossibly remote.

Although many of the colonists didn't know each other before boarding the ship, they held a common body of convictions. They saw themselves as religious reformers, followers of a strict brand of Calvinism that sought to purge the Anglican Church of its "papist" trappings and to free English society from its licentious ways. They wanted to purify the English church and to develop a "holy commonwealth" where they could live and worship as God would wish. But from the time that King James I assumed the throne in 1603, England had grown increasingly oppressive. He scorned the Puritans as non-conformists, charged them with seditious behavior, and promised "to harry them from the land."

By 1629, conditions in England had become so difficult that even men of considerable wealth such as John Winthrop, who was a Suffolk lawyer, were thinking about leaving. Together with several other middle-class Puritans, Winthrop purchased a charter that had been issued by the king a year earlier. The charter entitled the group – known as the Massachusetts Bay Company – to occupy a strip of land between the Charles and Merrimack Rivers and stretching from the Atlantic to the Pacific Oceans. Much to their credit, they also arranged to "transfer the government of the plantation to those that shall inhabit there," which meant that for all practical purposes the company would be self-governing.

As the Puritan leadership planned their migration, they had the benefit of over 100 years of interest in the region. In 1524 Giovanni da Verrazano was the first European to explore the American coast north of the Carolinas, and he was followed in 1525 by Estevan Gomez. Oddly, the European powers didn't pay much further attention to New England until the early 1600s, when several expeditions were launched at once, including the voyage of Captain John Smith in 1614. Smith made a detailed survey of the Massachusetts Bay region, and returned to England enthusiastic about the possibilities of colonization.

After several failed attempts to establish trading posts in the region, the first permanent settlement was founded at Plimoth by the so-called "Pilgrims," a small group of religious dissenters (even more radical than the Puritans) who fled from England to Holland in 1606 and then sailed to the New

World in 1620. The Pilgrims were followed in 1623 by a small party of Puritans who settled north of Massachusetts Bay at a place called Naumkeag. Five years later, John Endicott arrived at Naumkeag with a second group of settlers, and the village was re-named Salem.

When Winthrop set out from England on March 29, 1630, with a fleet of 11 ships and about 750 colonists, there was some talk of joining Endicott's people at Salem. When they arrived more than two months later, however, they found the town in such a "sad and unexpected condition" that they decided to move south to Charlestown and build a

the Indians called Shawmut. Together with 150 settlers, Winthrop moved to the site which, at the first meeting of "freemen" on September 7, was officially named Boston after their hometown in Lincolnshire.

"Aristocracy of Saints": The town grew remarkably fast. There were about 300 people in 1632, 600 in 1635 and 1,200 in 1640 – most living in wood houses huddled around Town Cove or in the market-place near present-day North Square. Although democratic in structure, the government was basically a theocracy. Only male church-members were allowed to vote, and the ministers were consulted on all but adminis-

settlement of their own. This first camp was overcrowded and riddled with disease, and it gradually broke up, a few small groups heading up the Charles River to the sites of Watertown and Newtown, others moving to Saugus, Medford, Dorchester and Roxbury.

For his part, Winthrop took up the invitation of an eccentric minister named William Blackstone who had been living in solitude across the Charles River on a hilly peninsula

Left, 8-year-old Anne Pollard, the first white woman to set foot in Boston (1630). **Above**, Pilgrims at Plimoth Plantation.

trative matters. The Rev. John Cotton, minister of the First Church of Boston, was a major influence on Governor Winthrop, who considered himself a "sacred student" under Cotton's direction. In later years, ministerial power shifted to the "Mather dynasty" (Richard, Increase, Cotton and Samuel) which ruled from the pulpit of the Second Church of Boston for the better part of four generations.

Although many settlers planned to make their living as farmers, it quickly became clear that Boston's future was tied to the sea. By the late 1630s, Boston ships were carrying loads of codfish to England, Spain and Portugal and were returning with much needed manufactured goods. Merchants were also exporting to the West Indies, which, by the late 1600s, was supplying molasses to Boston rum distilleries and slaves to wealthy land-owners.

Life in these early days was rigorous. To the Puritans, people were naturally sinful and required unrelenting discipline. Work, frugality and humility were highly valued, while "harmless" distractions such as dance, music and stylish clothes were scorned as frivolities. Education was considered essential, and within six years of their arrival the

detested sin was also believed to be a good way of protecting the town from divine retribution, and as a result wayward members of the community were often cruelly punished for their deeds.

Even minor offenses like cursing or gossiping could be punished by whipping, branding or being placed in the stocks. Ironically, the stock-maker, upon handing the General Court an inflated bill, was the first to be locked in his contraption. A sailor just returned from a long voyage was whipped for kissing his wife in public. And one poor soul on trial for adultery was found innocent of the crime but nonetheless "guilty

Puritans established a public school for children and a college for ministers – later called Harvard – across the river in Cambridge.

The corner-stone of Puritan theology was the Calvinist doctrine of predestination, a belief that God preordained who was saved and who was damned. The key to acceptance in Puritan society was to demonstrate through pious demeanor that you were, in fact, one of God's chosen people. Because a saint was thought to depise sin in others, much effort was put into reforming those who didn't quite measure up. Making a public display of just how thoroughly they

of very filthy carriage." He was sentenced to stand on the gallows with a rope around his neck for half a hour and then be whipped 39 times. When the poor fellow protested, the court immediately amended the sentence: "For his Contemptuous Carriage Confronting the sentence of this Court he shall stand to the pillory on the morrow at one of the clock his ears nailed to the pillory and after an hours standing there, they to be cut off and he to pay twenty shillings for his swearing or to be whipped with ten stripes."

Although the Puritans were themselves religious dissenters, they showed no tolerance for non-orthodox beliefs. Both Roger Williams and Anne Hutchinson tried to introduce theological innovations, and both were banished from the colony. The unfortunate Quakers who came to Boston were whipped or had an ear cut off, and were then kicked out. A few brave enough to return from banishment, including the heroic Mary Dyer, were hanged from the Great Elm on the Common.

But despite the hardships of Puritan life, settlers continued to pour into Boston, although many were more interested in the condition of their purses than the condition of their souls. In the face of so many outsid-

community getting by as best it could.

"Tyrant Andros": In its first 30 years the Massachusetts Bay Colony enjoyed virtual autonomy from the mother country. With English politics being rocked by Oliver Cromwell, England was much too preoccupied with business at home to monitor its colonial backwaters.

But when Charles II assumed the throne in 1660, this age of benign neglect came suddenly to an end. Among the new monarch's first acts was to rein in the New England colonies, which were not only governing themselves like a sovereign nation, but doing business like one too. There wasn't much

ers, the churches closed themselves off, and it wasn't long before a rift developed between members and non-members, saints and sinners. At its inception, Winthrop envisioned Boston as a town where citizens would be committed to a common purpose by the bonds of "brotherly affection." But by the time Winthrop died in 1649, Boston had become quite a different place, with an "aristocracy of saints" commanding most of the political power and the remainder of the

Left, Pilgrims at Plimoth Plantation. **Above**, trial of George Jacobs, accused of witchcraft, 1692.

sense for a king to have colonies if they didn't produce revenues, so Charles set about putting them on a money-making basis. First, he used the Navigation Acts to force colonial merchants to do business exclusively with England. And then, in order to hamstring the Puritan leadership, he ordered voting rights in Massachusetts be granted to all men of "good estate" regardless of church membership.

Although the Puritans made a fuss over the change in suffrage, most merchants simply ignored the Navigation Acts and continued trading with whomever they wished. When

Charles got wind of just how widespread smuggling had become, he answered the colonists' audacity by revoking the Massachusetts Bay charter in 1684 and transforming the whole of New England into a single royal colony.

Charles died before he could finish this work, but his brother, James II, picked up where he left off by appointing Sir Edmund Andros governor-general of the Dominion of New England. To Bostonians, Andros was a particularly contemptible man. In his first few weeks as governor, he not only converted the Old South Meeting House into an Anglican Church – sacrilege to the Puri-

original charter. The new monarchs were sympathetic, but unwilling to relinquish so much power. They offered Mather a compromise. The colonists would be allowed to elect their own representatives, but suffrage would be extended to all property-holders, irrespective of religion, and the crown would appoint the governor. It was a blow to the authority of the Puritan clergy, but it was the best deal Mather could get.

When Mather returned to Boston, he found a bizarre situation brewing that was to damage the clergy's authority even further. In 1692, in the town of Salem, several young girls fell victim to a strange malady, causing

tan clergy – he also limited town meetings to one a year and forced all property-holders to make new payments on land titles.

The colonists were furious. And when word finally reached them that King James had been ousted during the "Glorious Revolution," they staged an insurrection of their own. Andros was forced out of office, thrown in jail and shipped back to England.

In the meanwhile, Boston's most prominent minister, Increase Mather, was sent off to England to make the Puritans' case against Andros. When William and Mary took over the crown, he begged them to restore the

them to writhe in pain and "make most piteous outcries of burnings, of being cut with knives, beat, etc. and the marks of wounds were afterwards to be seen."

The ministers attending the children declared them to be bewitched, and in the process of finding the culprits, touched off a flurry of accusations that quickly developed into full-blown hysteria. Even the brilliant Cotton Mather (Increase's son) was convinced of the sorcery, and he fanned the flames of paranoia with blistering sermons about the breakdown of Puritan law and the artful designs of Satan.

By the time the new governor arrived in Boston and put an end to witch-hunting, hundreds of people had been accused of witchcraft and 19 had been executed. The credibility of the clergy, and the church in general, suffered irreparable damage. The age of Winthrop's "city upon a hill" came to an inglorious end. Puritan ideals were still very much a part of Boston life, but a new class of men were already rising to power.

Rise of the Merchant Class: With suffrage now open to property-holders, a class of wealthy merchants emerged as an influential force in Boston's affairs. The town had always made its living from the sea, but by the

Faneuil Hall, which was funded by Peter Faneuil and donated to the city.

Although Boston merchants were doing well, the rest of the city was not. The economic slow-down was partly due to competition from other colonial towns, especially New York and Philadelphia, which were steadily creeping into Boston markets. Boston was also taking the brunt of England's colonial battles – the so-called French and Indian Wars which had raged intermittently since the late 1600s and flared again in 1740 (King George's War) and 1754 (Seven Years War).

The wars were an enormous drain on Bos-

early 1700s shipbuilding and codfishing thrived and Boston dominated coastal and international trade. Merchants like Thomas Hancock (John Hancock's uncle), Peter Faneuil and James Otis amassed fortunes on the "triangle trade," shipping fish and crafted goods to Europe and picking up molasses and slaves in the West Indies. Their newly acquired wealth was put into handsome homes like Hancock's mansion atop Beacon Hill as well as into civic projects like

<u>Left</u>, **Cambridge colleges, 1743.** <u>Above</u>, **Long Wharf and part of Boston Harbor, 1764.**

ton. Hundreds of men were killed, ships were destroyed, and the city was overburdened with the care of widows and orphans. As if that weren't enough, an earthquake in 1755 toppled buildings and terrified the populace. And five years later, the town was devastated by the worst fire in colonial history, leaving at least 1,000 people homeless.

By the time the French were defeated in 1763, Boston was a shambles. And just as the town got hold of its bootstraps, the British started all over again with the old tug-of-war over the extent of colonial rights and the power of the Crown.

Engrav'd Pri

ROAD TO REVOLUTION

d by PAUL REVERE BOSTON

With the French out of the way, England turned its attention again to the colonies. And, as always, the job at hand was to get as much money out of them as possible.

In 1763, King George III launched the effort with a battery of legislation that prohibited colonial currency and cracked down on the lucrative sugar trade between Boston and the West Indies. Before New Englanders could mount an effective protest, parliament also passed the Stamp Act (1765) requiring colonists to pay taxes on legal documents.

To the fiesty Bostonians, these restrictions were worse than the old Navigation Acts and smacked of the same arbitrary use of power. The rallying cry went out, "No taxation without representation," as angry mobs took the protest into the streets. They looted the Lieutenant Governor's home and terrorized tax collectors. By the time the stamps actually arrived in Boston there wasn't an official in town brave enough to distribute them.

At the heart of the uproar in Boston was a loose organization of agitators known as the Sons of Liberty, whose membership included Paul Revere, John Hancock, Dr Joseph Warren, and their leader, Samuel Adams. They were as unlikely a collection of conspirators as one could imagine. Sam Adams was a disheveled middle-aged man who, despite a genius for political organization, had managed to squander a sizable inheritance on several failed businesses and spent much of his life in what he called "honorable poverty."

His protégé, John Hancock, on the other hand, was the wealthiest man in New England. He was much younger than Adams, not a particularly deep thinker, and known for his vanity and dandified manners. As one observer described him, his "brains were shallow and pockets deep." The other two members also made an unusual pair. Joseph Warren was an upper-class, Harvard-trained physician. And Paul Revere was a sort of

Preceding pages: Boston, 1855. **Left**, bloody massacre on King Street.

working-class Renaissance man – a gifted craftsmen, a courageous patriot and, with a hand in just about everything, an indefatigable public servant.

While the Sons of Liberty were raising hell in Boston, the hastily formed Stamp Act Congress called for an American boycott against British goods. By March 1766, the boycott had caused so much damage to British commerce that King George relented and lifted the tax.

When news of the Stamp Act's demise reached the colonies, Boston celebrated like it never had before. John Hancock even opened his magnificent Beacon Hill estate

quell the unruly mobs, and a series of skirmishes followed between Redcoats and civilians. For more than a year, the taunting and bullying became an ugly game of brinkmanship that finally erupted into all-out violence. It happened on March 5, 1770, when a group of Redcoats fired into a threatening crowd. The so-called "Boston Massacre" claimed the lives of five colonists and wounded several others. Ironically, the Townshend Acts were repealed in England on that very day. It wasn't a total surrender, however. As a symbol of the "supremacy of Parliament," a nominal tax on tea remained.

The tea tax won no friends in Boston, and

and supplied Madeira wine to the commoners who gathered in the yard.

But George III wasn't a man who took defeat lightly. In 1767 his new chancellor of the exchequer, Charles Townshend, lashed out with a new tax on a variety of imported items including paper, lead and tea. Again, the town reacted with predictable fervor. When the Massachusetts House of Representatives issued Sam Adams' "circular letters" denouncing the Townshend Acts, the governor closed it down – and Bostonians hit the streets!

Four thousand British soldiers were sent to

when the first loads arrived in Boston Harbor, the Sons of Liberty were ready to prevent the cargo from reaching colonial teapots. On December 16, 1773, about 50 townsmen disguised as Indians boarded the cargo ships and dumped the tea into Boston Harbor while a crowd of thousands cheered from the wharves.

The Boston Tea Party was more than the British could tolerate. Parliament immediately lashed out with the Coercive Acts, which closed down Boston Harbor, dissolved the government of Massachusetts, installed General Thomas Gage as military governor and provided for the use of private homes to quarter British troops. Thousands of people moved out of Boston, and the town ground to a halt.

In September 1774, the First Continental Congress met in Philadelphia and voted in favor of forming a colonial army. In Boston and the surrounding towns, colonials began stockpiling guns and ammunition in preparation for war. When word reached General Gage of a weapons cache in Concord, some 20 miles west of Boston, he dispatched 800 Redcoats to capture it.

While the troops prepared to move out, Paul Revere was already paddling across the Charles River to warn the countryside of the British march. He arranged for a friend, Robert Newman, to place lanterns in the steeple of Christ Church as a signal of the soldiers' direction: one lantern if the Redcoats marched by land over Boston Neck, and two if they crossed the Charles River to Cambridge. When Revere reached Charlestown he borrowed a horse and rode into the countryside warning villagers that the British were on their way.

At Lexington he found Sam Adams and John Hancock hiding out together, hoping to evade capture before attending the Second Continental Congress. Revere also met William Dawes, another messenger dispatched by Joseph Warren, and together they rode toward Concord until they ran into a British patrol. Dawes escaped into the woods, but Revere was captured, only to be released a few hours later.

By the time the British regulars reached Lexington green en route to Concord, 70 local "minutemen" – armed civilians pledged to fight at a minute's notice – were assembled on the field. The rebels were ordered to lay down their weapons, but refused to budge an inch. The British fired, the rebels scattered, and all hell broke loose as the Redcoats chased after them with muskets and bayonets. When the smoke finally cleared, eight minutemen lay dead and 10 had been wounded.

The British marched on to Concord, destroyed the few weapons they found there, and tried to return the same way they came. But by then rebels were hidden along the road and peppered the Redcoats with musket fire all the way back to Charlestown. By the time the troops returned to Boston, 73 Redcoats had been killed and 200 wounded.

As news of the confrontation at Lexington spread out from Boston, thousands of colonials poured into the area, forming an arching line of siege between Charlestown and Boston Neck. On June 17, 1775, 2,600 Redcoats attempted to break the siege by storming a rebel position on Breed's Hill (adjacent

to Bunker Hill). British artillery flattened Charlestown as the colonials repelled two attacks, and then running out of ammunition, retreated on the third. It was a technical victory for the British, but with over 1,300 casualties, and an enormous boost in American spirits, it was hardly decisive.

Less than a month after the Battle of Bunker Hill, General George Washington arrived in Cambridge and took command of the colonial forces. The siege of Boston continued through the bitter winter of 1775–76, until Washington forced the evacuation of the British with a clandestine placement of artillery on Dorchester Heights, overlooking the British flotilla in Boston Harbor. On the morning of March 17, 1776, nearly 9,000 Redcoats and 1,000 Tories boarded 78 vessels and sailed from Boston while American militiamen re-occupied the town.

The Revolutionary War raged for seven more years and, although Boston was spared its horrors, the population was reduced from 20,000 to 6,000 residents who survived as best they could.

Bulfinch and Brahmins: In the spring of 1787, a young man of means by the name of Charles Bulfinch returned to Boston after two years abroad. The town he surveyed

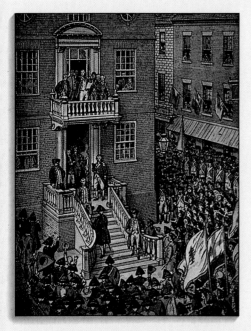

upon his arrival was in many respects still the colonial seaport of his boyhood – a cluster of narrow streets and wooden buildings gathered haphazardly around the waterfront. Since the Revolutionary War, Boston had put itself back on its feet and returned to business as usual. Wealthy merchants were still in control of local affairs, and they still earned their riches from the sea, although many were now engaging in the China trade, sailing around the tip of South America to lucrative Asian markets.

During his European travels, young Bulfinch acquired a taste for architecture,

and he began offering "gratuitous advice" to friends who were building new homes in the West End. Although no one could have guessed from so humble a beginning, it was the start of a career that would ultimately change the face of Boston.

Between 1795 and 1818, Bulfinch launched an architectural renaissance that, perhaps more than anything else, expressed the ambitions of Federalist Boston and solidified the ascendency of the ruling class. Although an early failure in the South End caused him financial troubles throughout much of his career (he even spent a month in debtor's prison), he worked with extraordinary energy. In addition to designing churches, homes and public buildings, he rehabilitated Faneuil Hall, nearly tripling it in size, and spearheaded the development of Beacon Hill. His crowning achievement, however, was the magnificent domed State House, which, from its perch overlooking the Common, is something of a Boston icon.

In 1818 Bulfinch was commissioned by the federal government to design the new capitol in Washington, DC. He left Boston, not as he found it, but a transformed place, no longer an 18th-century town of wooden houses and crooked lanes, but a 19th-century city of cobblestone and brick.

Bulfinch's work gave Boston a new sense of gravity that was immediately appealing to upper-class families, many of whom moved out of the North End into prestigious homes on Beacon Hill. In many respects, Boston's bluebloods were the heirs of the Puritan "aristocracy of saints," and, in fact, many of them claimed to be descendents of New England's "first families." More telling than the jealously guarded bloodlines, however, was the prominence of Puritan virtues like modesty and frugality, not to mention a sense of self-importance.

Politically, the Brahmin class was wedded to the Federalist notion of government by "the wise, the well-born, and the good," a policy near and dear to their pocketbooks as well as their conceits. Since the Revolution, Massachusetts Federalists had played a major role in crafting the new government, and they had always kept a firm grip on the reins of city politics. But when Thomas Jefferson was elected President in 1800, all that seemed to change. Jefferson was a classic democrat, and his belief in the principles of equality were anathema to the Brahmins.

Worse yet was his foreign policy. In 1807, hostilities with England led to the Embargo Act, which nearly strangled the lucrative China trade. "Jimmy Madison's War" with England (the War of 1812) only made a bad situation worse, and once again, Boston ships were left to languish in the harbor while merchants scrambled for new opportunities in which to invest their capital.

Always enterprising, several high-ranking Brahmin families, including the

that were necessary to get this enterprise off the ground were forged with wedding vows. By the 1850s, a number of new family names were added to Boston's social register, and a sub-class of *nouveaux riches* manufacturers was planted in the loam of Brahmin society.

Spirit of reform: The infusion of fresh blood into Brahmin veins not only secured a new source of capital, but a wealth of new ideas. From the days of the Puritans, Boston's ruling class acknowledged its obligation to improve the conditions of their less fortunate brethren, if not by actual material assistance, then by the power of example.

But in the early years of the new century

Lowells, Appletons and Amorys, began diverting their money into small textile plants that had been established some years before as a sort of entrepreneurial experiment. Their timing was impeccable. With European trade impaired by the war, Americans were clamoring for manufactured goods. Factories were built in outlying towns, and within several years the Brahmins were making a killing in the textile industry.

As was customary, the financial alliances

Left, first Declaration of Independence in Boston.
Above, State House and State Street, *circa* 1801.

Brahmin paternalism took on a more ardent quality. The first breath of this new personality was the growing popularity of the Unitarian church. As it was defined by the Rev. William Ellery Channing, Unitarianism did away with the old Calvinist notions of predestination and original sin, stressing instead the benevolence of God and the potential for human perfectibility. The road to salvation, he argued, was through the exercise of conscience, rationality and tolerance.

The Unitarian spirit was driven to its loftiest heights by a school of thought known as Transcendentalism, espoused in its most beautiful and stirring form by the "sage of Concord," Ralph Waldo Emerson. Emerson contended that truth wasn't to be found in the scriptures but in the workings of the natural world; salvation wasn't to be achieved by blind obedience to the social and religious hierarchy, but by taking an active part in the battle against oppression and poverty. It was Emerson's vision that set the stage for the intellectual renaissance that swept through New England in the mid-1800s, nurturing the genius of writers such as Henry David Thoreau, Henry Wadsworth Longfellow and Nathaniel Hawthorne.

Within official circles, the reform movement was advanced by Mayor Josiah Quincy, who engineered a major overhaul of city services. On the fringes, however, the new activism took on a more radical edge. To the shock of Brahmin society, women began taking a leading role in temperance, health care and prison-reform movements. Early feminists like Margaret Fuller and Lydia Maria Child took up the cause of womens' rights, demanding a full stake in educational, political and economic opportunities.

But the most significant movement to be launched in Boston at this time was William Lloyd Garrison's crusade against slavery. In 1831, Garrison began publishing an anti-slavery newspaper called the *Liberator* from a tiny office on Washington Street. Obscure at first, Garrison's blistering diatribes inflamed Southerners as well as Brahmins who were dependent on Southern cotton for their textile mills.

On one occasion Garrison was yanked out of a meeting by a mob, tied up, and nearly trampled. He speculated later that the assault "was planned and executed not by the rabble, or the workingmen, but by 'gentlemen of property and standing from all parts of the city'." As a fellow abolitionist described it, the attack was made "in broadcloth and broad daylight."

The abolitionists stirred even more controversy when they turned their attention to discrimination against blacks within Boston itself. The polarizing issue, then as now, was the segregation of public schools. Encouraged by Garrison's work, Benjamin F. Roberts sued the Boston School Board for

denying his daughter admission to a white school. Although unsuccessful, the suit revitalized the drive for legislative action, and in April 1854 – after five years of intensive lobbying – a law was passed prohibiting the segregation of schools on the basis of "race, color, or religious opinions."

Meanwhile, Garrison's movement was beginning to have national repercussions. Hostility over slavery continued to mount between North and South, and even conservative Yankees joined the protest against its expansion into western territories. The underground railroad routinely smuggled slaves through "safe houses" in various parts

of the city, and when a black Bostonian named Anthony Burns was captured by a slave-catcher, the whole town turned out to watch him being marched to the docks while 2,000 troops guarded against a riot.

In November, 1860, Abraham Lincoln was elected president without a single Southern electoral vote. Five months later Fort Sumter was bombarded by Confederate artillery. The Civil War was on, and New England responded dutifully to Lincoln's call for men.

<u>Above</u>, "Freedom to the slave."

PAUL REVERE

Paul Revere's name is so firmly fastened to Boston's history that it's scarcely possible to rate one without citing the other. In many respects, he symbolizes the transition from outraged colonialism to visionary independence.

It was a lucky day for the Bay Colony when Paul's father, Apollos de Revoire, left his home in the Channel Islands and set sail for Boston. Apollos was a talented craftsman who produced goldware and silverware of exquisite and extraordinary design. And on January 1, 1735, he and Mrs de Revoire produced an extraordinary Boston baby who became Paul Revere.

Paul inherited the family business, improved on his father's craftsmanship, and, from his shop in the North End, quickly won the reputation of being the best silversmith in colonial America. That might have been sufficient distinction for the average Bostonian, but not for Revere. Early in life he took off on a career that embraced enough sidelines, specialities, diversions, adventures and excitements to satisfy a dozen men. He was an expert horseman, a skilled man-at-arms, and an authority on explosives. As a young man, he served as a worthy artillery lieutenant in the French and Indian Wars.

Through the years, Paul also excelled as an artist, inventor, merchant, mechanic, politician, engineer, orator, dispatch rider, leading bell-ringer for Old North Church, share-holder in the privateer *Speedwell*, operator of a gunpowder mill, maker of copper sheathing for the *USS Constitution*, designer of whale-oil chandeliers for the Massachusetts State House, metallurgist skilled in casting cannon and bells, maker of false teeth for General Joseph Warren, participant in the Boston Tea Party, artillery colonel in defense of Boston Harbor, printer, publisher, propagandist – and assorted other occupations.

Meanwhile, he found time to marry and to sire eight children; then, when his first wife died, he re-married and fathered eight more. For relaxation, he would drive his cows all the way from the

North End to Boston Common and tether them there for grazing. And, from time to time, the Committee of Safety kept him galloping in and out of Boston on inter-colonial messenger duties.

This, then, was the man the Committee of Safety summoned in haste on the night of April 18, 1775. There was work to be done and a critical message to be delivered. Somebody must mount up and ride post-haste to Buckman's Tavern in Lexington. John Hancock and Sam Adams would be there, entertaining Hancock's fiancée, the beautiful Dorothy Quincy. They should be warned that 800 Redcoats would be moving out from Boston to capture Hancock and Adams, and would then march on to Concord to destroy a store of rebel guns and ammunition. That was the situation; and, as usual, Paul Revere was the designated rider.

Once he was ashore in Charlestown, Revere "went to git me a horse" from his friend Deacon John Larkin. Then Paul galloped to Medford where he stopped at the home of Captain Isaac Hall who was commanding officer of the local minutemen.

Beside being a soldier Hall was a well-known distiller of Medford rum and a most generous host. Thus it is worth noting that Paul hadn't bothered to wake up anybody between Charlestown and his stop-off at Isaac's. "After that," he wrote in his journal, "I alarmed almost every house till I got to Lexington." This was around 12.30 in the morning. Perhaps history owes a nod of recognition to Isaac Hall and his midnight rum.

At Buckman's Tavern, Revere joined with the alternate dispatch rider William Dawes, who had made the run from Boston via another route. Neither Revere nor Dawes ever got to Concord that night. En route, they joined up with Dr Samuel Prescott of Concord, heading home from a date with his Lexington girl friend. The Redcoats nabbed all three horsemen in a roadside ambush but Prescott escaped in time to alert the colonial militia at Concord. And the war was on.

As for Revere himself, the tireless old patriot was still handling enough tasks to keep 10 normal men busy when he died in 1818 at the age of 83. His oft-visited, much revered grave is in the Old Granary Burial Ground.

By the time Robert E. Lee surrendered at Appomatox, Bostonians were tired of war. Like most Americans, all they wanted was to return to the old way of life and to get back to the business of running their town.

But Boston was no longer the city it had been a generation earlier. For one thing, the balance of national power was shifting away from New England to New York City, where an up-and-coming breed of capitalists like the Vanderbilts, Astors and Carnegies were

modest port town had blossomed over the last 50 years into a rambling metropolis. The city had not only grown in population to 314,000 (1875), but in overall dimensions from its original 780 acres to 24,000 acres.

In 1857, the most ambitious of several landfill projects was launched in the Back Bay, a development that would eventually replace Beacon Hill as the city's most prestigious neighborhood. The job took more than 30 years, and created some 450 acres of

beginning to stake their claim to the Industrial Age. The old combination of textiles and shipping, while lucrative in its day, was no match for the steel and railroad empires.

These new industrialists were more aggressive and materialistic. Unpleasant though it was, Brahmins got a whiff of their own obsolescence. The virtues of good breeding, frugality and civic-mindedness seemed a pallid anachronism in the face of the new regime of "social Darwinism" – a philosophy posited on the most "unlovely" credo, "survival of the fittest."

Boston was changing physically, too. The

"made land." But to Bostonians, the Back Bay was more than a real estate development; it was a symbol of a new age – of a modern, cosmopolitan city.

Unlike the cramped quarters of the old city, Arthur Gilman's design called for broad, Parisian-style boulevards and generous public spaces. The lavishly styled homes that went up along Beacon Street and Commonwealth Avenue were complemented by the grandeur of H.H. Richardson's Trinity Church and the splendid Public Library designed by McKim, Meade and White, both on Copley Square.

The former was built because of the destruction of the first Trinity Church, the most historic building lost in the Great Fire of 1872, which leveled more than 65 acres of downtown and destroyed 765 buildings. It was mainly a commercial disaster: most buildings were crammed with raw materials and manufactured products. Bankrupted insurance companies added a melancholy postscript to the story. Impressive new buildings arose from the rubble and stricter laws

ment houses of the North, West and South Ends. The tide was so overwhelming that by 1855 there were 50,000 Irish in Boston alone, nearly one-third the total population.

Bostonians were suspicious of the Irish not only because they were foreigners but because they were Catholics. Anti-catholicism in New England went all the way back to the Puritans, who viewed "papists" as a loathsome brand of heretic. Until the late 1700s, anti-catholicism was even part of

encouraged safer construction methods.

The Irish: The physical expansion of Boston was in some respects a reaction to the changes going on in the older parts of town. Since the late 1820s, Boston had undergone a huge increase in its immigrant population. Most newcomers were Irish, driven from their homeland by the Potato Blight of 1845–50. Uneducated, desperately poor, and often weak or ill after months of hunger, they came by the thousands and huddled into the tene-

Boston's "Pope Day," when gangs of young men from the North and South Ends met for a brawl on the Common, the North Enders burning the Pope's effigy on Copp's Hill if they emerged victorious, the South Enders doing the honors on the Common.

By the early 1830s, local ministers were sounding the alarm against the "Catholic menace." In 1834, a mob burst into the Ursuline Convent in Charlestown and burned it to the ground. Three years later, the "Broad Street Riot" involving some 10,000 people broke out after a Yankee fire brigade accidentally collided with an Irish funeral

Preceding pages: Boston harbour in the 19th century. **Left** and **above**, Boston wharves.

procession. In the political arena, resistance against immigrants took shape in the highly secretive American Party – the so-called "Know-nothings" who responded to every question about the organization with the same annoying answer, "I know nothing." By 1860, the frenzy had reached such a fever pitch that almost every state office, including the governor's, was occupied by a Know-nothing candidate.

The Civil War proved to be something of a reprieve for the Irish, as Bostonians turned away from inflammatory Know-nothing rhetoric and focused their attention on the larger issues of slavery and the South. Some

that was due to modernization of the city. The installation of electric wires, the construction of the country's first subway and the expansion of city bureaucracy created a demand for civil servants and utility workers. Just as the Irish started to move up the economic ladder a new wave of immigrants from southern and eastern Europe arrived to fill the void. By 1890 the Irish were sharing their neighborhoods with about 45,000 Italians, 4,000 East European Jews and a scattering of Poles, Portuguese and Greeks.

Once again bigotry reared its head. In 1894, three Harvard graduates founded the Immigration Restriction League of Boston

immigrants joined the Union army or took jobs in war-related industries, proving once and for all that they weren't conspiring against the Yankee way of life. But for the most part, the conditions of Irish neighborhoods continued to be appalling. Housing was overcrowded and unsanitary, and work places were often dangerous. Crime was particularly bad in the North End, where Anne Street (now North Street) was notorious for its bordellos, gambling halls, and roving bands of sailors.

It really wasn't until the 1880s that the Irish began to break out of the slums. In part

and even persuaded Congressman Henry Cabot Lodge to stand behind their cause. By then, however, the tide could not be stemmed. By 1910, 30,000 Italians and 40,000 Jews were firmly entrenched in the North and West End.

And now the Irish discovered they had a flair for politics: to coax, to buy and, on occasion, to conjure votes from the grave. Hugh O'Brien, in 1884, became the first Irish mayor and since then, for all but six years, Boston's mayor has been of Irish origin. It is as if an invisible sign "ONLY IRISH NEED APPLY" was hung on the Mayor's door.

However, unlike in New York City, there was no political machine to recruit the Irish vote. Rather, Irish neighborhoods fell under the control of homegrown bosses such as Martin "Mahatma" Lomasney and John F. Fitzgerald, the charistmatic "Honey Fitz," so-called because he would sing "Sweet Adeline" at the drop of a shillelagh.

"Honey-Fitz," a spellbinding blarney-dispenser, became mayor in 1905 and proceeded to conduct one of the city's most corrupt administrations. He lost his seat in the following term, but reclaimed City Hall in 1910 after promising voters a "Bigger, Better, and Busier Boston." And, he did give

ambitious man of poor immigrant parents and with no formal education beyond grammar school. However, he devoured books on law, politics, literature and the fine arts and had a remarkable photographic memory.

By the time he was a public figure he dressed impeccably, attended banquets, held forth on oriental jade, quoted the classics and cited appropriate passages from Shakespeare and Tennyson when the occasion provided an opportunity for him to display the trappings of a learned Bostonian.

With biting wit, personal charm and an uncanny ability to make political friends, Curley did what others could not. He

them a zoo, locally established Mothers' Day, and led Red Sox rooters to New York for the World Series.

After him, from the same mold, came James Michael Curley who dominated Boston politics from 1920 till 1950, serving now as mayor (four times), now as governor and now as congressman, and who in 1943, won an election from a jail cell. Curley was an

Left, vote recount in Fitzgerald-Storrow mayoral contest in 1910. Above left, "Honey Fitz" hands out Christmas baskets. Right, young Italian immigrants, 1911.

thumbed his nose at both Republicans and Democrats and created a city-wide patronage system, the "Curley Machine." He considered the bosses petty (the Democratic City Committee was a "collection of chowderheads") and the Brahmins "gabbing spinsters and dog-raising matrons in federation assembled." The day after his election he sent the Yankees into fits of apoplexy by proposing to sell the Public Garden for $10 million and placing a water pumping station under the Common.

With Curley firmly at the helm, Boston headed into the difficult years of the Great

Depression and, like many American cities, was devastated. But with a healthy cut of Roosevelt's New Deal and, after 1941, a piece of the war industry, the city survived intact, even if somewhat shaken. Ironically, it was Curley's success at attracting federal projects that helped to lead to his downfall. With the US government supplying jobs and money, the "old pol's" patronage system – and powerbase – was pulled from under him.

In addition, the Boston Irish and the Boston Brahmins were beginning to discover each other. The latter, taking a good look at the former after almost half-a-century of inattention, found that not infrequently the Irish had become more Brahmin than the Brahmins themselves. Why should the two groups not combine to work together in financial and political affairs? Curley, always hated by the Brahmins, no longer needed by the Bullyboys, was eased out.

The Kennedy years: Boston politics underwent a change after World War II. The days of cigar-chomping bosses and wholesale patronage seemed to have run their course. During the war, a new electorate came of age that was more interested in economic progress than stale ethnic rivalries. Second- and third-generation immigrant families were now part of the middle-class, and they wanted leaders who represented mainstream values and good clean government. Indicative of this change is the fact that since World War II three of the Speakers of the House of Representatives have been Boston Irish and, in 1946, Bostonians sent a young man to Congress who seemed to epitomize those qualities. His name was John F. Kennedy, grandson of "Honey Fitz." He was handsome, charming and idealistic. And he came to symbolize, both for Boston and the nation, the hope of progressive politics.

In Boston itself, the search for "non-political" leaders turned up John Hynes, who handed James Curley a stunning defeat in 1949. An unassuming, soft-spoken bureaucrat, "Whispering Johnny" showed remarkable ambition as mayor, launching in 1957 the Boston Redevelopment Authority

which, over the next 15 years would carry out urban renewal projects covering 11 percent of Boston's land. This exceeded those in any city of comparable size. The program was implemented mainly during the tenure of Mayor John F. Collins (1960–1968). He cajoled prominent business people to help finance his revitalization plan and also brought to Boston Edward J. Logue who had a genius for guiding projects through the rocky terrain of federal bureaucracy.

Meetings of White, of the Vault, as the group of businessmen was called, and of "Ed the Bomber" as Logue was called by his detractors, led to the New Boston in the

shape of such buildings as the Government Center, the Prudential Complex and the Charles River Park. Private enterprise announced its presence with the John Hancock skyscraper and the Christian Science Complex. I.M. Pei, a Harvard- and MIT-trained architect, was heavily involved in several, both public and private, of these projects.

The program got off to a somewhat shaky start when, as the result of bureaucratic vandalism and insensitivity, Scollay Square was razed to the ground, a well-established community of Italian, Irish and Russian Jewish immigrants was evicted and the Government

Left, Curley, the people's choice. <u>Above</u>, Ted Kennedy, part of an American dynasty.

Center built. However, by the 1970s, under Mayor Kevin White who held continuous office longer than any other mayor in the city (1968–84), the thrust changed from bulldozer mega-development to recycling with serious attempts to utilize the city's physical and social resources. Faneuil Hall was one of the first and most successful of these projects and just as *Jiminey Cricket* (the weather vane on the roof of that building) was the symbol of Boston so has the Hall become a symbol of the recycled and revitalized Boston.

But while resources were being lavished on the city center, trouble was brewing in the neglected outer neighborhoods. Since the

for a long overdue share in city services, housing and education. On the other, working-class whites felt themselves being pushed out of their old neighborhoods and in competition for the same limited resources.

As the civil rights movements gained momentum in the 1960s, the situation grew more volatile. In 1974 the National Association for the Advancement of Colored People sued the Boston Board of Education, claiming it was not in compliance with anti-segregation laws. It was true that blacks and whites went to different schools, the Board replied, but that was only because blacks and whites lived in different neighborhoods. The

war, middle-class families had been moving out to the suburbs with the city losing 100,000 residents in the 1950s, a further 56,000 in the 1960s and 78,000 in the 1970s. Population then leveled off at today's figure of approximately 580,000 which was about where it had stood at the turn of the century.

Busing brouhaha: Poor blacks and Hispanics filled the void created by this exodus and as minority populations swelled in neighborhoods such as Roxbury, the South End and Mission Hill, a whole new set of racial tensions started bubbling to the surface. On the one hand, blacks were calling

federal court didn't agree. Intentional or not, ruled Judge Garrity, Boston was guilty of segregation, and he ordered a program of busing to integrate blacks and whites.

The riots that surrounded the busing crisis turned Boston upside-down and shocked the nation. Every day the evening news telecast images of racial hatred: school buses surrounded by police cars, children threatened by protestors, a crowd of whites beating a lone black man with an American flag on the steps of City Hall. Americans wondered what was happening to Boston, one of the country's most liberal cities, the birthplace of abolition, the very crucible of democracy.

Leading the anti-busing movement was school committee-woman "You Know Where I Stand" Louise Day Hicks and City Councillor Ray Flynn who, however, since being elected Mayor in 1983, has shown himself to be a friend of blacks and other minorities.

In spite of the turmoil, Boston in the 1980s was the hub of the Massachusetts Miracle which was based largely on high tech and venture capital and which launched the governor of the Commonwealth, Michael Dukakis, to the Democratic presidential nomination in 1988. Skycrapers and office

lems than Boston. After 350 years, this is still a city of ideas – "The Athens of America." Its universities attract some of the best minds in the world; its artists hail from a long and inventive tradition; its religious communities are vital and committed.

The Puritans are long gone, but John Winthrop's vision is still very much a part of what this city is all about. "We must love one another with a pure heart," he said aboard the *Arbella*. "We must bear one another's burdens." Over the years Bostonians have learned and relearned how to make that idea a reality. There have been dramatic changes since Winthrop first stepped ashore, but

towers began to be constructed as if there was no tomorrow. Yet the city became the victim of its own success and by the late 1980s had started to run into economic problems. The sure winners – financial services, minicomputers and armaments – all went into recession. By 1990 the Massachusetts State bond rating was the lowest in the country.

Looking ahead: There are, perhaps, fewer cities better equipped to tackle these prob-

Left, school busing brought its problems in the 1970s. **Above,** the new City Hall and its Plaza.

Boston has always been able to pull through.

After all, there is a reason why, in poll after poll, Boston is voted one of America's most livable cities. This is a town that refuses to give up. There are problems today, every city has them, but Bostonians have an advantage. They know that, given enough time, they can make their city better. Maybe that's the reward of a long and rocky history, a certain confidence that bad is followed by good. In the end, Bostonians will find their solutions where they always have, in "the fatherhood of God, the brotherhood of man, and the neighborhood of Boston."

Stroll through the Back Bay, especially on Newbury and Boylston Streets, on a fall weekend and many fellow strollers will be young adults. For, come September, Boston's populace is swollen by about 250,000 students from throughout the world who have come to study at the 50 colleges and universities which are within a 30-mile radius of the city center. Boston, it has been said, "beds down more students per square civic inch than any other metropolis in the world." Many, smitten with Boston, remain.

Such a large body of students, not all of whom are young and impecunious, add much to the élan of Boston and to its social life – students are responsible for the enormous success of the city's comedy clubs – and they, and those who visit them, pour literally billions of dollars into the coffers of Boston and Cambridge stores, restaurants and hotels. Conflicts between town and gown are rare, although occasional hullabaloos erupt when Harvard or Massachusetts Institute of Technology (MIT), both of which are in Cambridge and not in Boston proper, purchase a piece of land.

However, since the late 1960s both make in-lieu-of-tax payments to Cambridge based on a nominal charge for every square foot of property kept off the tax rolls. (These payments for the two institutes now exceed $1.6 million a year.) Cambridge also knows that the revitalization of East Cambridge in recent years was spawned by MIT; that Harvard is its largest employer and that it and MIT's payroll and purchasing activity are responsible for adding well over $100 million to the economy of the city.

Relations are also smoothed by about 14,000 members of the Greater Boston community enrolling annually in nearly 600 courses offered at the Harvard Extension School while MIT's Lowell Institute School, established in 1903, offers tuition in areas of

Preceding pages: studying in Boston University Library. Left, commencement at Boston University. Right, Harvard and MIT masterminds.

modern technology not readily available at other evening institutes. Yet, town and gown relationships are not at their best at Waltham, where Brandeis University is located, in spite of Brandeis students being involved in tutoring and Big Brother/Big Sister programs. Harvard, through its Philipps Brooks House Association, has nearly 40 similar programs such as House and Neighborhood Development, which involve more than 1,000 students.

Rivalry is limited: So many colleges and universities suggest intense rivalries and yet they scarcely exist. On occasion, eggheads may argue as to whether Harvard or MIT has more Nobel laureates, and the students of Emerson, a relatively young and small liberal arts college, may crow because they defeated Harvard in a nation-wide debating competition; but, by and large, each institution is proud of its own achievements and to hell with the others.

Lack of rivalry is also because, especially at the graduate level, it is not uncommon for students enrolled at one school to attend classes at another. MIT graduate students can attend Harvard Medical School, and MIT and Wellesley share programs with students from the latter able to graduate with two degrees – one from Wellesley and one from MIT. Boston University undergrads can take classes at the New England School of Music: Simmons girls can take classes at Hebrew College: Babson students can attend Brandeis and Wellesley: hybird vigor abounds.

Sport is that one area where one might expect much jingoism but, especially in the major sports, the different schools seldom compete against one another and, even among students of others schools, most en-

Also, it boasts more Nobel prize-winners (33) , more Pulitzer winners (30) and more US presidents (six) than any other university and is governed by the oldest corporation in the New World. The story, probably apocryphal, is told of the visitor to the President of the University who was told matter-of-factly: "I'm sorry but the President cannot see you: he has gone to visit Mr Taft." At that time Taft was President of the US.

Harvard has more than 100 libraries, some as far afield as Washington, DC and Florence in Italy, and its University Library, founded in 1638, is the oldest library in the US and the largest university library in the

thusiasm appears to be engendered by Harvard-Yale contests. A significant exception is ice-hockey, at which several Boston teams are invariably ranked nationally. They meet annually in Boston's Beanpot Tournament and then at least some undergraduates from Boston College, Boston University, Harvard and Northeastern find something to shout about.

Harvard: Pride of place of these institutes of tertiary education must go to Harvard, not only because it was the first and is the oldest College in the land, but because it is the richest: endowment in 1990 was $5.1 billion.

world. No other university in the land boasts such a large number of outstanding museums (they are open to the public, see page 217) and collectively the University buildings constitute an impressive, living museum of architecture.

Harvard began in 1636 when a dozen students under one master met in a single-frame house in the College Yard in New Towne which would later be called Cambridge. In 1638, John Harvard, a young minister, bequeathed half his estate and his library to the inchoate shool which was then named Harvard in his honor. (Boston Latin

School, founded in 1635 and still functioning, is even older than Harvard.) Today, in addition to its college, Harvard has 10 graduate and professional schools, some of which (Business, Medical and Dental) are in Boston rather than Cambridge, and the university has about 18,000 students and a faculty of about 3,500. The college enrolls about 6,500 undergraduates, of whom one-third are minorities, and the entire Harvard community is in the region of 40,000.

Harvard is proud of its college admission policy which is "need blind," meaning that candidates for admission are judged only on merit and not on ability to pay. If you are

Cambridge in England. Mather was contrasting the English system, in which students live together in college buildings in close contact with their teachers, with the system practised on the continent, in which students fend for themselves in town. Nearly 250 years would elapse before the government of New England would have its wish.

In 1919, Edward Harkness, a Yale graduate, donated $13.8 million to Harvard with which to institute its house system. This consisted of seven – now increased to 13 – residential houses and one non-residential house. Each house is a separate entity with its own administration, its own library and its

good enough the school takes care of you: in 1989–90 it did this to the tune of $36 million in outright assistance and loans.

In 1684, Cotton Mather of the Harvard class of 1678, wrote that "the Government of New England was for having their Students brought up in a more Collegiate Way of Living." The word "collegiate" was used to refer to the system of education in small, residential colleges followed by Oxford and

own dining hall. Each house has a phalanx of tutors – although the tutorial system is not as intensive as at Oxbridge – and each house has its own societies and its own sports teams. The student body in each house is about 400. What makes a house different from the dormitories of most colleges, in which students simply eat and sleep, is that the house is an important part of the students' intellectual life.

Radcliffe College: No longer can the loyal Harvardian sing "10,000 men of Harvard want victory today" or "Fair Harvard, thy sons to thy jubilee throng" for, since 1975,

Radcliffe College, a prestigious women's school whose physical plant is adjacent to and even interwoven with Harvard's, has become an integral part of Harvard University. Not content with the equality they have attained, Harvard women demand more: the diplomas they receive on graduation are Harvard diplomas but are countersigned by the president of Radcliffe.

Radcliffe started life in 1879 when Harvard teachers were employed to instruct 27 young ladies. Then, during World War II, Harvard and Radcliffe classes were combined as a temporary measure which became permanent in 1946. Today, all the residential

However, no matter the field in which an undergraduate majors, the degree he receives is the Bachelor of Science.

The charter for a school to be known as MIT was awarded by the Commonwealth of Massachusetts in 1861 but the opening was delayed because of the Civil War. Even before the school could open the governor of Massachusetts gave his enthusiastic support for a merger with Harvard which would create "a great university in Cambridge." Such a marriage has frequently been muted but has never occurred, although students at either school may attend classes at the other.

Matters finally got under way when, in

houses are co-ed and one no longer speaks of Harvard men and "Cliffies" but rather of Harvard students.

Massachusetts Institute of Technology: Still in Cambridge, but nearer to Boston and with many of its buildings alongside the Charles River, is MIT which, in spite of claims to the contrary by Caltech, is generally recognized as the premier school of science and engineering in the country. MIT is also no slouch in other fields such as architecture, urban studies and economics, and several of its liberal arts departments, such as history, literature and music, are well respected.

1865, 15 students and six professors sat down in a room in Copley Square to aid, in the words of William Barton Rogers, the first president, "the development and practical application of science in connection with arts, agriculture, manufactures and commerce." Not until 1916, and then only after several moves, did the school occupy its present site.

Slightly more than half of MIT's approximately 10,000 students are graduates. The faculty numbers about 1,000 and currently includes 12 Nobel laureates. (Over the years 23 MIT faculty members, staff and alumni have received this coveted award and 15 past or present members of the faculty have been awarded the National Medal of Science. Harold D. Edgerton, the much-loved father of high-speed photography who "froze" drops of water, was awarded the National Medal of Technology.)

The curriculum is demanding but not all the student's time is spent "tooling" (MIT jargon for studying). MIT was rated 25th in the country in a 1987 *Playboy* survey of "party-schools" and it has more listed varsity teams (24 for men and 13 for women) than practically any other school in the country. And what could be more pleasant than sail-

most significant in New England. Like Harvard, MIT can claim to be a living museum of architecture – although only from 1916, rather than colonial times, to the present.

Tufts University: This college, a couple of subway stops from Harvard Square, straddles a windswept hill, 5 miles northwest of Boston, on the Medford-Somerville boundary. It was formerly said that students at Tufts, a non-sectarian university founded largely under the aegis of the liberal Universalist Church in 1859, were those who had failed to gain admission to Ivy League schools: not any more. Tufts, which started as a college, became a full-blown

ing on the Charles at lunch time?

Ubiquitous and omnipresent at MIT is Project Athena which integrates computers throughout the campus and which has more than 800 work stations located in 16 public clusters as well as in libraries, laboratories, hostels and academic facilities. Also ubiquitous is the outdoor public art; it is part of a permanent collection of more than 1,600 items of contemporary art which is one of the

Left, Presidents George Bush and François Mitterrand receive honorary degrees at Boston University. **Above**, science lab at Boston College.

university in 1953, and is probably more famous for its graduate schools than its undergraduate. Jean Mayer, internationally renowned nutritionist and president since 1976, likes to think that "either we are the smallest complex university or the most complex small university in the country."

The school, whose elephant mascot Jumbo evokes memories of Barnum and Bailey's circus – the former was a trustee – has about 5,000 undergraduates and more than half that number of graduate students. As the result of an Experimental College program which has been running for more than 25 years and in which not only faculty but also undergraduates teach, the regular undergraduate curriculum has been enriched and includes courses in sign language, jazz and ethnomusicology. Yet students claim that music is one of the weaker departments on campus. Offsetting this, the school has joint degree programs with New England Conservatory of Music. It also has a joint degree program with the School of the Boston Museum of Fine Arts.

Most famous of Tuft's excellent graduate schools is the Fletcher School of Law and Diplomacy which enjoys reciprocity with Harvard. Many of its graduates enter the

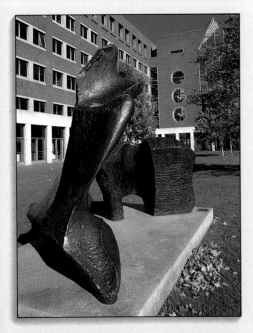

diplomatic service of the US and other countries. Tufts medical school and even more its dental school, both of which are part of the New England Medical Center, located in the city across from Chinatown, enjoy an enviable reputation. So does the School of Nutrition, the only such school in the country. Tufts School of Veterinary Medicine, one of only two private veterinary schools in the country and the only veterinary school in Massachusetts, is in Grafton, 40 miles to the west of Boston.

Boston University: Back in Boston, across the river from MIT, sprawls the campus of Boston University (BU), the fifth largest independent institute of higher education in the country. This is a genuine city school with tram-tracks passing the main entrance. Yet students eager to live on campus should consider BU which claims to have a more internationally diverse student body than any other college or campus in America. More than 8,000 of its 28,000 students reside in more than 200 residences which range in size from charming 12-story brownstone houses to a 1,500-person tower complex.

BU was founded in 1839 as a Methodist Institute. In the 1860s it received a Commonwealth of Massachusetts charter for a school modeled on European universities that would include undergraduate, graduate and professional schools. Until 1967 its president was invariably a Methodist clergyman but then, in 1971, along came John Silber, a layman, who turned the school around until, in 1989, it received more than $110 million in federal funding for research.

Today, BU's 17 schools, the most renowned of which is the College of Communications, include Dentistry, Medicine, Law and Theology at which Martin Luther King Jr. obtained his PhD. In 1873 BU granted leave of absence and an advance of salary to Alexander Graham Bell to permit him to work on his invention: the result was the telephone.

BU can pride itself on many other firsts. These include being the first institute of higher education to open all its programs to women and to minorities, and the nation's first school of music. It was also the first to take a liberal arts program – not a vocational program – to prisons and in 1989 took over the management of the entire school system of Chelsea, a town in greater Boston which is plagued by low funding and poor academic achievement. Another innovation is its College of Basic Studies which permits students with low test scores and grades to transfer into BU after a two-year program.

The University's Mugar Memorial Library has several collections of manuscripts and rare books and contains the personal papers and memorabilia of 300 great 20th-century figures. These include Theodore Roosevelt and Martin Luther King Jr.,

George Bernard Shaw and H.G. Wells and Bette Davis and Ella Fitzgerald.

Boston College: A university in all but name with 11 schools, colleges and institutes offering 13 degree programs, Boston College (BC) is one of the largest Catholic universities in the nation. However, clergy constitute only about 7 percent of faculty and, although most of the students are Catholics, the ethos is not especially religious. The College was founded in 1863 by the Society of Jesus and opened with three faculty members and 22 students sharing a building with Boston College High School in the city's South End. Times have changed.

tournaments. Athletic scholarships abound, with the money for these coming from the large crowds who roll up to cheer the Eagles at the college's magnificent football stadium and basketball-hockey arena. Yet, the College is no academic slouch; it accepts only one in three of those who apply (they have a SAT/ACT average score a tad under 1200) and in the 1990 *US News & World Report* College rankings was placed in "Quartile Two."

Northeast: Closer to the center of the city and also alongside the tram-tracks is Northeast. In spite of attempts to mellow its campus, which has been called an asphalt jungle, it is the quintessential city university.

Now, the schools' approximately 15,000 students, of whom more than half are women, study at campuses at Chestnut Hill and Newton, two affluent suburbs immediately west of Boston proper. The major campus, with its Gothic architecture, is at Chestnut Hill.

BC fields by far the best major sports teams in the region and its football and basketball squads are sometimes ranked nationally and invited to post-season bowls and NCAA

Left, sculpture enlivens the MIT campus. **Above**, studying in Radcliffe Yard.

Northeast, with nearly 36,000 students, is the largest private school in the nation and is the acknowledged leader of co-operative education. Students, many of whom are mature and many of whom are the first of their family to attend college, usually receive their undergraduate degree after five years, having alternated between working and studying for three- or six-month periods. Only about 10 percent live on campus.

Northeast began in 1896 as the "Evening Institute for Young Men" (about 40 percent of today's students are women) in the YMCA which still adjoins the campus. After a gradual evolution the University was formally established in 1922 and now has nine undergraduate and 10 graduate and professional schools, the best known of which are the law and criminal justice schools. Nearly all who graduate from these two schools enter public rather than private service.

Northeast prides itself on being a city school with a profound concern for the social issues which affect Boston. Yet, the school is not parochial and is deeply involved with a variety of projects at universities in Egypt, India, Romania and other countries.

Suffolk: A private university whose fees are about half those at other universities in has a college of liberal arts and sciences, a school of management and a marine biology station in Maine. Its major claim to fame is that it is the home of the National Board of Trial Advocacy, which certifies attorneys throughout the nation as trial specialists in civil and criminal trial advocacy.

Wellesley: Three excellent but disparate schools are situated about a dozen miles west of the city. Wellesley, founded as a women's college in 1875 by Henry Fowle Durant, has remained just that, even although other members of the "Seven Sisters" (the name given to seven New England women's colleges) have become co-educational. Under-

and around Boston, Suffolk is truly a city university, having no dormitory accommodation. Its campus is within a stone's throw of the State House, making it a university upon a hill. It is one of the youngest of the region's universities, having gained that status only in 1937. However, it had already existed since 1906 as a renowned law school open to those denied access to a legal education because of social class, religion or income. Not surprisingly, the majority of students were part-time, as are nearly 50 percent of today's 5,500 students.

In addition to its law school, Suffolk now graduates number about 2,300, of whom about 10 percent are foreign, coming from countries ranging from Argentina to Zimbabwe, and of whom about 25 percent are minorities. About 70 percent of the students, most of whom have been described as "well dressed, politically active and liberal," receive financial aid through an aid-blind program which accepts students without reference to their ability to pay.

In addition to traditional liberal arts courses, students may major in such fields as electrical engineering, psychobiology and urban psychology. However, whatever the subject, the degree awarded is a Bachelor of Arts. Wellesley enjoys reciprocity with MIT and eager beavers can graduate with two degrees for the price of one – a BA from Wellesley and a BS from MIT. However, the school's forte is the arts and it has been said that no student should go through Wellesley without taking a course in arts history and availing herself of the superb materials in the Jewett Arts Center and College Museum.

The school has an extensive complex of greenhouses, a 22-acre arboretum, an observatory and a contemporary science center that was deemed by the Boston Society of Architects to be "the most beautiful piece of

work do not make a woman of Jill" and Wellesley has a well-earned reputation for serious study and research.

Brandeis: A university which boasts one of the best collections of contemporary American art in the nation; a university whose Gordon Public Policy Center is the nation's first interdisciplinary multi-university center for studies of public policy; a university proud of its beautiful chapel, church and synagogue, each built so that none casts a shadow over its neighbors. This is Brandeis, founded in 1948 by members of the American Jewish community and named after the distinguished supreme court judge,

architecture, building, monument or structure within the limits of the city of Boston or the Metropolitan Parks District."

No one can deny that Wellesley has the most beautiful campus in the Boston area. Focal point of its peaceful 500 acres is Lake Waban with its bathing beach, sailing dinghies, canoes and crew shells. This, plus a 9-hole golf course and 24 tennis courts, has resulted in Wellesley being compared to a country club. However, "much play and no

Left, studying at Brandeis University. **Above**, playing at Brandeis University.

Justice Louis Dembitz Brandeis, who was a Bostonian. Although about two-thirds of its 4,000 students are Jewish and although classes are not held on major Jewish (nor on Christian) holidays, Brandeis does not have a religious ethos, and non-kosher as well as kosher food is served.

Although small, Brandeis prides itself on being a research university where undergraduates, who constitute about 75 percent of the student body, are given individual attention (the ratio of faculty to students is 1 to 8) and opportunities for research. Best of its more than 30 fields of undergraduate concentration are probably biochemistry, politics, English and Near Eastern and Judaic studies. The Brandeis libraries contain special collections of international importance in the study of Jewish history and in the history of science, while its Vito Volterra Cultural Center includes a collection of 24,000 rare books and manuscripts in the fields of mathematics, astronomy, physics and the history of science.

Babson College: The name of the game at Babson, whose verdant 450-acre campus with attractive red-brick buildings is in the same neck of the woods as Wellesley and Brandeis, is business. When the college was

ness experience, as has had all the faculty.

The graduate school, which enrolls about 2,000 students, offers an MBA and attracts students from literally hundreds of US colleges and a score of foreign institutes. Nearly all are part-time students who are employed by virtually every major corporation and financial institution in the Boston area. Not unexpectedly, the school has computer network capabilities to and from all on-campus offices, rooms in residential halls and the majority of classrooms.

Emerson College: Back in the city most of those students who, in term time, stroll about the Back Bay in the vicinity of the Public

founded in 1919 by investment adviser and entrepreneur Roger Ward Babson, he urged students "to pull the cart instead of riding it." And so it is today. How well they succeeded is reflected in Babson being ranked Number 1 out of 24 business colleges surveyed by *US News & World Report* in 1990.

The vast majority of Babson's 1,500 undergraduates, most of whom are middle-class, conservative New Englanders dressed in Brooks Bros suits, proceed directly from college into business, accounting and law and already many, through internships in their junior or senior years, have had busi-

Garden are not taking a day off from classes but attend Emerson, whose campus, which consists largely of beautiful brownstone houses, is mainly in this part of the city. Emerson, which was founded in 1880 by Charles Wesley Emerson as an elocution school, has burgeoned over the years and is now the only four-year college in the nation totally oriented to the communication arts and sciences. It proudly boasts that it was the first school in America to offer a program in children's theater (1919) and the first to offer professional training in speech pathology and audiology (1935).

Today Emerson, which has more than 2,500 students, the majority of whom are women, awards undergraduate and graduate degrees and is renowned nationwide for its departments of mass communication, theater arts and communication disorders. Its WERS-FM radio station, although entirely student operated, frequently wins awards as the best radio station in Boston, while the College's glorious 800-seat Majestic Theater in the Boston theater district is used not only for student productions but presents outstanding performances by well established international companies.

New England Conservatory of Music: "Oboe," training academies for performing and teaching musicians. Here, 700 students, many from overseas, can study for a bachelor or master of music degree or, for those interested only in performing, for a graduate or artist diploma. The last, a tuition-free program, is open only to unusually accomplished soloists, usually young professionals who have already begun their career.

More than a dozen large ensembles, numerous small jazz and third stream groups, an extensive music program and new music concerts all provide regular opportunities for students to perform. Add to this many solo performances and a total of about 300 con-

murmured the conductor, "I believe you came in one beat late at 98." "Yes," concurred the embarrassed player. Such incidents occur daily at the New England Conservatory of Music (NEC) which is situated just across the road from Symphony Hall and next door to Northeastern University. Founded in 1867, it is the oldest school of its kind in the nation and with a handful of other such schools ranks as one of America's top

Left, a stillness at Brandeis University. **Above left**, Brandeis professor. **Right**, Harvard's Widener Library.

certs a year. Many are held in Jordan Hall, one of the NEC's three concert halls, generally recognized as one of the most acoustically perfect halls in the country. NEC graduates are found – and often occupying first chairs – in major orchestras, not only in America but throughout the world. Nearly half the players in the Boston Symphony, which supplies many of the NEC faculty, were trained at the Conservatory.

Berklee College of Music: Not too far away from the NEC, a dozen musicians practise paradiddles, flams and press rolls on the carpet: 400 ensembles, among which are traditional concert bands, chamber groups and groups playing music which ranges from folk to funk, swing to salsa, and ragtime to rock, rehearse. This is the Berklee College of Music, often said to be the best school of contemporary music in the nation and which, when founded in 1945, was known as the "jazz school." Today, its 2,500-strong student body, of whom about 25 percent are from overseas with nearly 200 coming from Japan, attend courses not only on jazz, but also on rock, fusion, pop and Latin music which lead to a degree or a diploma.

Berklee's campus has no playing fields but rather has three large recital halls and a

dents on campus but would probably be relieved to learn that they are attending classes at the graduate schools which attract about 1,300 students.

Recently Simmons students, who are from diverse backgrounds, were indignant when it was rumored that the school intended to go co-educational: a few score of male graduate students on campus is quite enough, thank you. These graduate schools offer programs leading to masters and doctoral degrees in library and information sciences and in social work. Masters degrees are also offered in a variety of other fields, including communications management, health care ad-

seven-studio recording complex. Applaud Quincy Jones, Steve Smith, Gary Burton or Sadao Watanabe and you are applauding Berklee alumni.

Simmons College: Still in this neck of the woods is Simmons College, founded in 1899 by John Simmons as an all women's college with a curriculum that would enable women to grasp the breadth of the liberal arts and sciences while developing expertise in professional fields. At Simmons both theory and application are integrated into one program. Mr Simmons might be surprised to see a fair number of men among the 2,800 stu-

ministration and children's literature.

About two-thirds of the undergraduates live on campus and can study in 38 departments for a BA or a BS degree. Internships are a major feature at the college, which also has a strong foreign study program. Many students are in pre-professional programs and many go into teaching and nursing.

These, then, represent just a sample of Greater Boston's tertiary schools of learning. Fees (tuition and board) at most of them exceed $20,000 a year.

"George M" being performed at Emerson College.

A MEDICAL TRAILBLAZER

"Gentlemen, this is no humbug." So announced Dr John Collins Warren in 1846 to those who had observed Mr Gilbert Abbot undergoing surgery at the Massachusetts General Hospital (usually known as the MGH, sometimes "Man's Greatest Hospital" or Mass General or, to medical students, the "massive genital"). Mr Abbot, who was operated on for a tumor, had just announced to the entranced gathering that he had "suffered no pain." This was because here in Boston, for the first time in the world, ether had been used to anaesthetize the patient.

Today, at the MGH, the visitor can see the Ether Dome, the work of Bulfinch, and the operating theater where ether was first used. (Public tours on Tuesdays and Thursdays at 2 p.m.)

In the same way that Boston is *numero uno* in education, it is the leader in medicine in the United States. Today, the hub boasts 17 major hospitals and Greater Boston has nearly 100 facilities. Harvard, Boston University and Tufts each has its medical school and the Massachusetts Institute of Technology has a medical program with Harvard. In the past 50 years more than a score of doctors and scientists working at Boston's hospitals and medical schools have won Nobel prizes in physiology and/ or medicine.

Among these is John Enders who, with Frederick Robbins and Thomas Weller, won this illustrious award in 1954 for their work in developing the poliomyelitis vaccine which effectively eliminated this scourge. (Later, Jonas Salk in Pittsburgh developed the mass production of this vaccine which would wipe smallpox from the face of the earth.) Almost 150 years before this, Dr Benjamin Waterhouse of Harvard Medical School (HMS), who constantly lectured on the "ruinous effects of smoking tobacco," had been the first to introduce smallpox vaccination in the country.

Boston's latest Nobel laureate in medicine (1990) is Joseph Murray who, in 1954, at the Peter Bent Brigham Hospital, was part of a team

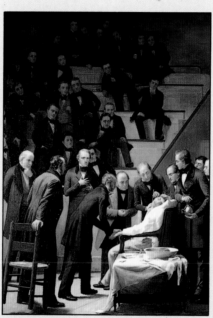

that successfully performed the first human kidney transplant. And, next time open heart surgery is mentioned you might remember that it was first performed at the Boston Children's Hospital by Professor Robert Gross in 1967. Then there was 12-year old Danny Everett who, in 1962, while hitching a ride home on a train after pitching in a Little League baseball game, had his arm shorn off. Dr Ronald Malt and his emergency room team at the MGH succeeded in putting humpty-dumpty together again – the first successful replantation of a human limb.

The list of firsts is long: abdominal surgery (1886); creation of the Drinker respirator (iron lung) in 1928; artificial kidney (1945); clinical reports on efficacy of birth control pills (1959); techniques for freezing and thawing blood (1964); abdominal electrocardiography for monitoring the foetus during labor (1973) and development of artificial skin for burn victims (1981).

Less dramatic, but just as important, Boston national medical firsts include Linda Richards, the first trained nurse; the first medical school to admit women (Boston University); the first city to establish a municipal water supply; and the first Board of Health. On an international level, the much respected, oft-quoted *New England Journal of Medicine*, founded in 1812 by Dr John Collins Warren and James Jackson, is the oldest continuously published medical journal in the world.

It might be thought that Boston is a good place to take ill because the ratio of doctors to residents is nearly 50 percent above the national average. Yet it may be that the care patients receive here is no better than in other parts of the country because many physicians are possibly more interested in curing than caring.

The greatest concentration of hospitals is in the Longwood area in Brookline. This houses not only HMS but also the Brigham and Women's Hospital which receives more funding than any other independent hospital in the US, the Children's Hospital, the Dana-Farber Cancer Institute and, just a short distance away, the Beth Israel Hospital and the Deaconess Hospital. The region qualifies as a mini-city, with a population of more than 20,000.

At the start of the 1978 baseball season Mark Starr, who headed the *Newsweek* bureau in Boston, was on assignment in Jerusalem. He visited the Wailing Wall whose fame – dare it be written? – is challenged only by the "Green Monster," the left field wall at Fenway Park where the Red Sox baseball team plays. After writing a supplication on a piece of paper, he inserted it between the cracks of the Wall. He begged God to let the Sox win the World Series that year. Starr still believes that it was this sacrilegious behavior which denied the Sox the American League pennant when, in the ninth inning of their decisive play-off game with the New York Yankees, Bucky Dent hammered out a three-run homer.

Such sports fanaticism among Bostonians, especially when it comes to baseball, is not unusual. Come summer and, if the Sox are on a roll, then all is well and all Boston walks tall. Let the September Swoon come – as it almost invariably does – and all are dejected and life is scarcely worth living.

Staid, cultured, educated Bostonians invariably turn to the sports pages of the morning newspaper before checking their investments and then reading the world news. Starr believes that this is because tragedies are more enjoyable than comedies and substantiates this theory with the works of Shakespeare.

Still, for much of the time, Red Sox followers are presented not only tragedies but are simultaneously entertained with comedies. How else can one describe the sixth game in the World Series, in 1986, when the Sox were within a heart-beat of clinching the title until a grounder trickled through the legs of first baseman Bill Buckner?

Some suggest that Beantown's infatuation with sport has a regional basis and results from an inferiority complex *viz à viz* New York. Others say that it is the result of immigrant groups (especially the Irish) and student groups seeking a cause to follow. But no: the reasons are arcane, obtuse and complex and the best that can be said is that Bostonians consider their teams, especially the Sox, to be their patrimony and they simply inherit their devoted loyalty.

The latter was seen when, in 1976, the Bruins, the Boston ice hockey team, traded Bobby Orr, their star defenseman, to the Chicago Blackhawks. Many who held life-long tickets to the Garden, where the Bruins play, simply tore them up and vowed never to enter the Garden again – and they have kept their word. Finally, the Boston sports

fan is knowledgable, and the media, whose coverage of the teams exceeds that found anywhere else in the country, cannot, try as they will, pull the wool over his eyes.

A city of firsts: Boston's infatuation with sports is reflected in – or is it the result of? – the fact that here, as in so many other fields, it has known so many firsts. A commemorative stone on the Boston Common informs that "On this field the Oneida Football Club of Boston, the first organized football club in the United States, played against all comers from 1862 to 1865. The Oneida goal was never crossed." Would that the Patriots, who disillusioned fans attempt to dismiss by saying that they do not play in Boston but at Foxboro, could approach that record in one game, let alone four seasons!

On the other hand, Bostonians embrace Springfield, 90 miles to the west. There, in 1881, James A. Naismith hung peach baskets at either end of a local YMCA hall and thus gave birth to the game of basketball. This was a somewhat pedestrian affair until Naismith decided to remove the bottoms of

mask when catching at baseball. Even before this, in 1875, Charles W. Waite, while playing first base in Boston, donned a baseball glove, the first of the "kid glove aristocracy."

The Sox: To most Bostonians, sport is synonymous with the Red Sox, their beloved baseball team which, year after year, raises them to heady heights and plunges them into stygian depths. It is as if the Puritan or Catholic blood surging through Bostonian veins insists that they must bear a cross. The

the baskets. Then, in 1895, in Holyoke, 90 miles from Boston, William Morgan introduced the game of volleyball.

Before this, in 1874, the first grass tennis court in the nation was inaugurated at Nahant (part of Greater Boston). This was also the year when the nation's first football goal posts appeared on the playing fields of Harvard and, two years later, F.W. Thayer, a Harvard man, astonished all by wearing a

Preceding pages: Boston Celtics in the Boston Garden. **Left**, Red Sox slugger. **Above**, Fenway Park, home of the Sox.

Sox – no need to bother with the adjective Red, for what other are there for Bostonians? – have homered, bunted and fumbled at small, cosy, intimate Fenway Park with its terrifying left-field wall, the Green Monster – ah, there lie a thousand stories – since 1912.

Even before that, in 1903, they had won the very first World Series and by 1918 had been crowned world champions five times. Since then the Sox have never won another World Series, although on several occasions they have seen – even practically touched – the Promised Land. Could it be because of the curse of the Bambino, or did Harry

Frazee, the owner of the Sox from 1917 until 1923, sell his soul to the devil: the damned Yankees?

The Bambino or the Babe, christened George Herman Ruth, arrived in Boston from Baltimore in 1914 and, with incomparable pitching and then superman hitting, was the toast not only of Boston but of all America. And then the unthinkable happened: in 1920, Harry Frazee sold the Bambino to the New York Yankees who, for the next half-century, dominated the American League. This was not only because of the Babe who, when he set his record in 1927 with 60 homers, hammered eight of them at

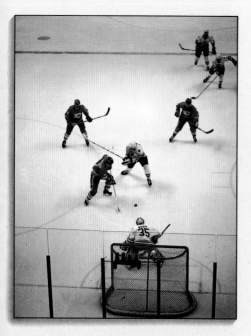

Fenway Park, but because of the steady stream of other top Sox players who Frazee kept trading to the Yankees.

Frazee's problem was money – or rather the lack of it. In addition to owning the Sox, he was a failed theatrical impresario who was always in debt. (In 1925, however, two years before he died, he backed the enormously successful musical *No, No, Nanette* with its show-stopping *Tea for Two*.)

The tormenting of the Sox by the Yankees did not cease with Frazee's death. In both 1949 and 1978, when the teams met on the final day of the season, the result would decide the American League championship. You've guessed it: on both occasions the Yankees won. Glorious retribution occurred in 1990 when Bucky Dent, the Yankee's manager, was fired after a game with the Sox at Fenway Park: Dent's ninth inning homer in the 1978 game had been the hit which destroyed the Sox. (A similar decisive game had been played in 1904 when, because of a wild pitch by the Yankee's Jack Chesboro, the Sox won.)

In 1935, Tom "Mister" Yawkey, for whom money never was a problem, became owner of the Sox and buying rather than selling became the order of the day. Yet the faithful were not immediately rewarded but had to wait until 1946 when the Sox won the pennant, a feat which they repeated in 1967 and 1975 and then, under the reign of Mrs Jean Yawkey, who had assumed control of the club on her husband's death, in 1986.

Four times the Sox were led toward the Promised Land, but it was not to be: each of these four World Series went the full seven games and each time the Sox left empty-handed. This, in spite of the fact that their teams included the mighty Ted Williams, six times American League batting champion and the last player in the majors to hit over 400; Carl Yastrzemski, who had more than 3,500 hits; and Most Valuable Player and two times Cy Young winner Roger Clemens, who, in a memorable 1986 game, threw 20 strike-outs.

On the other hand, Sox teams also included players who, in one game in 1990 against Minnesota, succeeded in hitting into two triple plays in one game – a major league record – and yet winning that game. Statisticians claim that one triple play in a game should occur once in every five years: two – ugh! The same team was then involved in a game with which featured 10 double plays (the Sox hit into six of these). Amends soon followed when, in a game against Detroit, they had 12 two-base hits – another American League record.

In 1959, with the signing of infielder "Pumpsie" Green, the Sox became the last club in the majors to be integrated. One wonders if some Macchiavelian scheme was behind this signing for, it has been said,

"Green was the most inept player ever to play in the majors." At the start of the 1990s, the club had still only one black player on its roster, but the racial imbalance was improved with the signing of Elaine Weddington – not only a black but a woman – as assistant general manager. Also, in 1990, the Sox added play-by-play in Spanish to their regular broadcasts, becoming the tenth team in the majors to offer such a service.

Victory Garden: The accusation of racism has also been leveled against the Celtics, Beantown's beloved basketball team, although Chuck Cooper, who was signed in 1950, was the first black player in the Na-

been the most successful team in any major sport in the country. Unlike the Sox, who began at the top and then went into decline – will they ever win another World Series? – the Celtics started disastrously when the 11-team Basketball Association of America (later to become the NBA) was founded in 1946. Then, coached by Arnold (Red) Auerbach and with such basketball immortals on the floor as Larry Bird, Bob Cousy, Dave Cowens, John Havlicek, Tom Heinsohn, K.C. Jones, Sam Jones and Bill Russell – the list is never-ending – they started winning until the rafters at the Garden had scarcely space for another pennant. Be-

tional Basketball Association (NBA) and, in 1966, the Celtics made history by becoming the first major league team in *any* sport to name a black head coach, Bill Russell. Yet, in the 1990s, when the NBA is dominated by black players, the Celtics are the only team which can field an all-white starting five. On the other hand, during the 1963–64 season they became the first NBA team to put five blacks on the floor at the same time.

Black or white, the green and white has

<u>Left</u>, the Bruins in Boston Garden. <u>Above</u>, they start 'em young in Boston.

ginning in 1959, the Celtics won an unprecedented eight championships on the trot, and, since that year, have won the NBA championship a total of 18 times.

Auerbach, first coach, then manager and finally president of the Celtics, small in stature and a mere Lilliputian among his Brobdingnagian players, has been honored by the city to which he brought so much pleasure and such distinction with a bronze, life-sized statue, clutching his inevitable cigar. It sits in the Faneuil Hall Marketplace.

The basketball pennants on the rafters of the Garden are joined by five Stanley Cup pennants won by the Bruins, who, in 1924, were the first American team to receive a franchise in the National Hockey League. In terms of success and ability to frustrate fans, the Bruins occupy a position somewhere between the Sox and the Celtics. A winning record for 23 years in a row is the longest of *any* professional team and scarcely a season passes when they do not reach the play-offs. Yet, so often, as exemplified in 1990, they just fail to grasp the Stanley Cup.

Greatest of all Bruins was Bobby Orr, who joined the club when only 18 and who revolutionized hockey, not only in Boston but throughout the world, by showing that defencemen could attack and score goals. He was the league's MVP on three occasions and won the Norris Trophy for outstanding defenseman eight consecutive times. Other greats have been Eddie Shore who, in the Bruin's early days, was largely responsible for giving them their reputation as a "joy-through-brawling" team, and Phil Esposito, five times NHL scoring leader.

Football has been the least successful major league sport in Boston with the Patriots' only glory being in 1986 when they reached the Super Bowl on a wild card and were then mauled by the Chicago Bears. The signs were never auspicious for professional football. The Patriots play at Foxboro, which is 25 miles south of Boston, and William H. Sullivan Jr, who purchased the franchise for just $25,000 in 1965, won few friends when he later eponymously named the stadium. Sullivan started his career as publicity manager for that other Boston baseball team – the Braves – who have long since (1953) de-camped Boston, first to Milwaukee and then to Atlanta.

Still, the Patriots have produced such superb players as John Hannah, who played with them for his entire career and who was selected by *Sports Illustrated* as "the greatest lineman of all time."

Collegiate endeavors: With few exceptions, those 50 colleges and universities situated within 30 miles of Boston make little impact at the national level on the college sports scene. In a word, they are parochial. One exception is Boston College, a name respected in both football and basketball and a

member of the Big East Conference. The College is sometimes invited to post-season football bowls. Then, on occasions, Harvard or Boston University has won the NCAA hockey championships. Four members of the United States hockey team which so dramatically overthrew the Russians to win the 1982 winter Olympics at Lake Placid were from the Boston University squad.

In crew, Harvard shine not only on the national but also on the international level. Indeed, the entire Harvard eight represented the US at the 1968 summer Olympics in Mexico City. Harvard, joined by Boston University, MIT and Northeastern, also do

well on the national level in dinghy sailing. Back on land, Harvard, more often than not, is the country's top college squash team.

Boston has always been well represented at the Olympics. At the first modern games, held in Athens in 1896, athletes from the Boston Athletic Association and the Suffolk Athletic Club provided the nucleus of the US team and the hop, step and jump – the very first event of the modern Olympics – was won by James Brendan Connolly from Boston.

Red Auerbach and not so young fan.

THE BOSTON MARATHON

"A win at Boston is the most important prize in the world of marathoning." So said Fred Lebow, director of the New York marathon. It all began in 1897 when 15 runners lined up in Ashland and, when the gun was fired, started to run to Boston. Thus began the world's oldest annual marathon, held on Patriot's Day (or the nearest Monday to that day), and drawing its inspiration from the marathon at the first modern Olympics in 1896.

Since 1907 the race has started at Hopkinton rather than Ashland and, since 1927, has been run over the official Olympic distance of 26 miles, 365 yards. The race passes through eight municipalities and is watched by about 1½ million spectators. It is mainly downhill, although those who suffer the agonies of "Heartbreak Hill" would scarcely agree.

Apart from 10 years between 1973 and 1983 when the laurel wreath crowned an American entrant seven times (on four of these occasions the winner was Bill Rodgers from Massachusetts), foreigners have dominated since World War II. First the Finns held the limelight, winning six times between 1954 and 1962. Then Boston became a happy hunting ground for the Japanese who have won seven times since 1953.

Few foreign winners, great as they may be, are long remembered by the public but two American winners have become legends. Clarence DeMar won Boston for the first time in 1911 and for the seventh time in 1930. He continued to compete until 1951 when he was 61. The legendary Mr "Boston Marathon," John A. Kelley (Johnny the Elder to distinguish him from John J. Kelley, no relation, who won in 1957) ran his 58th consecutive Boston in 1989 at the age of 81. He had won twice (1935, 1945), been second seven times and was in the top 10 a total of 19 times. "There are other good marathons," he said, "but they don't have tradition. The other marathons are all Johnnies-come-lately."

Men and women break records at Boston. In 1947 Yun Bok Suh, a Korean, broke the world marathon record for men. Liane Winter of Ger-

many broke the women's world record in 1975 and, eight years later, Joan Benoit, running for a local club, lowered it still further. In 1990 John Campbell of New Zealand lowered the Masters' world record. Also in 1990 Moussetapha Badid of France and Jean Driscoll of the US broke the men's and women's world records for wheelchair marathoners. On six occasions the American men's and on four occasions the American women's records have been broken.

The first wheel-chair competitor raced unofficially in 1970, completing the course in about seven hours. Now, official wheel-chair winners have finished and showered before the first non-disabled athlete breaks the tape. Visually impaired runners also compete.

Women first began to run in 1966 but official entries weren't accepted until 1972. Bedlam broke loose in 1967 when K. Switzer, an official entrant, turned out to be Katherine Switzer. When an official tried to bar her from running, her burly boyfriend physically intervened. Katherine ran.

In the early 1980s it appeared that the marathon, despite its tradition and worldwide appeal, might have to be abandoned. Big bucks – or rather, their absence – were at the heart of the problem. It was at this time that annual big city marathons became ten a penny and awarded prize money. Not so Boston; it remained an amateur event in which athletes ran for prestige and for fun. And the organizers, the Boston Athletic Association, could not generate large television revenues because the race is held in the middle of the day on a Monday – scarcely prime viewing time.

Once again, as he had more than 200 years before, John Hancock, this time in the shape of a financial company bearing his name, came to the rescue with a multi-million-dollar sponsorship deal. Now, prize money at Boston, the only marathon to offer equal prize money in all classes to both men and women, is equal to that awarded at other major marathons and the event is assured of sound financial backing into the 21st century.

Today, about 8,000 line up for the starter's gun. Many more would love to compete, but Boston is the only city marathon which requires pre-entry time qualifications.

The visual arts did not come easily or soon to Boston. When, about 1630, New England was born in the "howling wilderness" neither the harsh reality of survival or the narrow path of Puritan theology lent itself to the pleasures of painting, sculpture or the decorative arts. These, if not actually proscribed, were clearly a matter of suspicion in a society that found its expression as well as its aesthetic in religion and government.

In no time, however, the founding fathers were lamenting a drift in their progeny who demanded prosperity as much as salvation from the wilderness. As the old virtues of piety, moderation, and industry conflated a warm and heady desire to succeed, Boston created an ambitious mercantile society. Its members, unafraid of the little pomps and vanities their parents had abhorred, determined to have its fair share of culture and a civilized enthusiasm for the arts.

Beginnings: Eighteenth-century Boston, like any self-respecting English provincial capital, was pretty much a matter of status symbols and luxury goods – portraits and tombstone carvings, silver tea pots and coats of arms on carriage panels. There was no artistic past; even if there had been, nobody would have cared. Boston was a thoroughly modern town: everything was fashion and the latest style. The cult of the past would arrive only later.

Monumental sculpture and history painting, the touchstones of the visual arts on the continent, would not be appreciated to any real degree – and then only in a limited manner – until the early 1800s and the Federal era. Landscape painting would not thrive before the coming of the Victorians. Genre painting appeared with the Edwardians and the "Boston School" of 1900.

In artistic terms, however, great strides were made in the 18th century by Bostonians

Preceding pages: *West Church* by Maurice Prendergast. **Left**, *Mrs Fiske Warren and her daughter* by John Singer Sargent. **Right**, students at the Museum of Fine Arts.

as gifted as John Singleton Copley and Paul Revere, and the general level of artistic achievement was unsurpassed, and quite probably unmatched, in the American colonies. Copley's portrait of Revere, now in the Museum of Fine Arts (MFA), is the result of fortuitous meeting of artist and sitter, and worth careful study for what it tells of 18th-century Boston – practical, proud and unafraid of a dignified opulence.

The message is writ large in Copley's

great portraits of Boston's mercantile aristocracy which are also seen at their best in the MFA. Keeping these faces in mind gives added meaning to a visit to King's Chapel, where it is easiest to find the 18th century in the modern city. The air is chill and sweet with an unmistakable New England tang.

The Revolution changed many of the players, but the game remained the same as Boston entered the 19th century and the era of its greatness. Even so, the arts remained more than a little suspect in the young republic. John Adams, with a whiff of brimstone worthy of his ancestors, still pondered whether the arts, those suspicious hand-maidens of luxury and aristocracy, had any place in a democracy. "Are we not," he cautioned with fretful anxiety, "in too great a hurry in our zeal for the fine arts?"

Federal Boston, unlike earlier periods, remains very much in evidence, with Charles Bulfinch's gold dome of the State House – it was originally gray – dominating Beacon Hill. Aesthetically, the city today is its own greatest asset, with the carefully preserved Federal townscape of the Hill blending seamlessly with the Victorian sweep of the Back Bay.

Nineteenth-century Boston took pride in

much of this Brahmin culture, where the unpredictable tendency of artists to comment and to criticize was curbed with the flattery of dinner invitations and with kind words. In a few notable cases – Copley and Hunt, for example – a handsomely dowered daughter tempered the force of artistic fury.

The Athenaeum: No cultural institution was as central to the arts in Federal Boston as the Boston Athenaeum. In a series of increasingly grand homes, it mounted Boston's first public exhibitions of painting and sculpture and assembled the city's first generally accessible public collection of art. By 1850, it had taken up residence in the Italianate

its transformation of the "howling wilderness" into the "American Athens" – no mean feat in a scant 200 years when the odds are against you. Educational, charitable, and cultural institutions (with "fair" Harvard generally given pride of place) were carefully nurtured as the proper sphere for a "Brahmin" aristocracy, rich beyond the wildest dreams of their immigrant ancestors and heavy with intellectual pretension.

Artists were admired and assimilated as the ornaments of that society. This high regard is sometimes said to account for the decorative rather than incisive character of

palazzo on Beacon Street where it remains. Some of its collection also remains, and some has gone to enrich the holdings of the MFA, whose parent the Athenaeum became in 1870 when it divided its responsibilities between literature and the visual arts. The Athenaeum was a potent force in the flowering of American painting and sculpture in the 19th century and its grand home is redolent with that penetrating taste that marked Federal America's neoclassicism.

By the time the Athenaeum had transferred its mandate in the visual arts to the new MFA, taste itself was changing and there were new gods for the new museum age. Ruskin, the Renaissance and Florence had superseded Rome and the neoclassic ideal, and in Boston the robust graces of the ancient world had been replaced with the languid artfulness which became so much a part of the late 19th-century culture in the city. Ruskin disciples and Harvard professors succeeded in turning the American Athens into a kind of Florence on the Charles. Genteel enthusiasts, weak and well-bred as water, returned to Europe to a nostalgic reality peopled with Bostonians whose literary equivalents are familiar from the novels of Henry James and Edith Wharton.

and who married so well that Bostonians paid more attention to his taste than they might otherwise have done. They patronized his French friends, and acquired fine collections of French pictures into the bargain.

Hunt introduced the Barbizon painters (placing so many Millets locally that those which found their way to the MFA make that museum's holdings unrivaled anywhere in the world). He created an enthusiasm that outlived him, reaching what is surely its ultimate expression in the dozens of Monets that poured into Boston. Forty of them happily also found their way to the MFA.

Most private collections formed in 19th-

The terrible social and political catharsis of the civil war brought forth a rich artistic flowering in New England. Culturally, Boston tended to define itself in terms of education and morality, but this would always he challenged, after the 1850s, by a bold and unexpected interest in modern French art. Its earliest champion was the painter William Morris Hunt, a New Englander who had studied in France with Couture and Millet,

century Boston were smaller and generally less showy than their counterparts in New York. They were, however, often more discerning, and ranged through the entire history of taste with a remarkable lack of prejudice. The MFA has been heir to quite a few of these collections, and its galleries in Huntington Avenue are unsurpassed in areas as diverse as Asian and classical art and 19th-century French painting.

In the realm of plastic arts, the MFA's Egyptian Old Kingdom collection, unrivaled except at the Cairo Museum, is the result of joint Harvard-MFA expeditions

Left, Ken Beck, Boston artist in South End. **Above left**, Boston Athenaeum. **Right**, Courtyard of Isabella Stewart Gardner Museum.

which began in 1905 under the direction of Dr George A. Reisner. The glorious sculpture and the architectural pieces in the Indian Art Section owe much to joint MFA-University of Pennsylvania expeditions. Incidentally, the MFA is entirely supported by private gifts, bequests and annual subscriptions: it receives no assistance from public funds.

A number of other institutions, mainly educational, have also assumed the role of the private collector, and well repay the trouble of a visit. The Fogg Art Museum at Harvard is close enough to the city to qualify as a local museum. Further away are the Rose Art Museum at Brandeis University in

Waltham with its remarkable contemporary American pictures, and the Wellesley College Museum in Wellesley with its distinguished historical collection (the superb ancient marble known as the "Wellesley youth" is alone worth the trip).

Collecting as a cultural pursuit began rather later than it did elsewhere in America, and the few early local collections of importance have long since been dispersed, as have those of early institutions such as the Athenaeum. Several important collections from the second half of the 19th century were embedded more or less intact in various local

museums, but one – the finest of them all – has been preserved as it was created, a few hundred yards from the MFA. For many, the Boston Museum with all its masterpieces takes emotional second place to the Isabella Stewart Gardner Museum, for where it is great, the Gardner is unique.

Idiosyncratic museum: Isabella Stewart, born in New York in 1840, became a Bostonian when she married the financier Jack Lowell Gardner. The Brahmin and his daring, vivacious wife, whose actions were often frowned upon by proper Bostonians, became enthusiastic art collectors and filled their Commonwealth Avenue home with treasures from frequent trips to Europe.

Gardner died in 1889 and Mrs Jack set about building the Venetian palazzo of her dreams and embellishing it with her collection of spectacular paintings, sculpture, furniture and textiles. Fenway Court opened with a private party on New Year's Day 1903 when Mrs Gardner received her guests at the head of the double staircase while 50 members of the Boston Symphony Orchestra entertained. Logs burned in each room as guests indulged in two of her delights: doughnuts and champagne.

Mrs Gardner lived on the top floor of Fenway Court until her death in 1924 and she still presides there in the shape of her controversial portrait painted by Sargent in 1888. It caused a Boston scandal because Mrs Gardner appeared in what was then considered to be a revealing low-cut gown.

Fenway Court's surfeit of masterpieces has less to do with its glory than one might expect, for although masterpieces are certainly not in short supply, most museums would consign a good part of the collection to the storeroom. Nobody would dream of doing that to her Giotto or Piero della Francesca, her Degas or her Sargent, much less her Titian, easily the most beautiful in America, but even Titian gracefully gives price of place to the ensemble she lovingly created and legally preserved.

In an age when museums have almost totally decontextualized the works of art in their galleries, it is a pleasure to add that Mrs Gardner's context makes her Titian sing with an added resonance. There is really nothing more wonderful, or more of a piece with Boston, than the Gardner.

Fenway Court is often said to have inspired a revival of interest in local artists and revived a long tradition of local patronage, but in truth Boston, like most American cities, was (and, alas, is) conspicuously unenthusiastic about the home-grown product. A flurry of chauvinistic interest in the painters Gilbert Stuart and Washington Allston in Federal Boston was not followed by a like interest in their successors (the best, like Winslow Homer, simply left town as a result), and was soon entirely supplanted by a taste for foreign old masters. Boston pa-

the Boston Public Library, MFA and Harvard's Widener Library, the work of William Paxton and Edmund Tarbell clearly also grew out of the aesthetic shock administered by Mrs Gardner's superb Vermeer at Fenway Court. (This Vermeer and several other treasures were stolen in 1990.)

The Boston School summarized everything that Boston had come to admire in the arts: technical skill, languid sentiment, and an often maddening refinement brought to the study of a narrow, genteel world, Looks can be deceiving, because the style took root with the rude health of a roadside weed and its practitioners are still numerous and popu-

tronage of American sculptors followed the same downward curve, from brisk interest to benign neglect, although a taste for public monuments made Boston a marvelous place in which to stroll and to look at statues.

Painting would flourish once again around 1900 with the emergence of the "Boston School." Encouraged by the vital example of John Singer Sargent, who indulged a perhaps misguided taste for mural painting in

Left, viewing sculpture at Wellesley College Museum. **Above**, *Boston Common at twilight* by Frederick Childe Hassam.

lar. Their work, in fact, fuels the success of today's Newbury Street art market.

Newbury Street, long the center of the art market and the luxury trades in Boston, has always suffered because of its proximity to New York. Madison Avenue is too close for comfort and collectors, no less than artists, regularly fall subject to its variety and charm. Nonetheless, artists both serious and admirable remain, and the graduates of the art schools and universities continually swell the ranks. The arts in Boston still flourish with a determination worthy of the rocky soil that gave them birth.

By American standards, Boston is old. Cobbled streets lit by gas-lamps can be found, and the city has dozens of National Historic Landmarks as well as 7,000 individual buildings designated as historic landmarks by the city fathers. Yet, because of the hundreds of thousands of students who flock here (and the many who remain after graduation), Boston is a young city well endowed with comedy clubs and restaurants and a vibrant musical and theatrical life. It also boasts superb museums and outstanding modern architecture.

Boston is also a small city. Its population is 580,000 and its area 46 sq. miles. Greater or Metropolitan Boston, with nearly 100 towns, encompasses 3 million people and covers 1,100 sq. miles.

Lacking a "main drag," Boston consists of 14 tight little neighborhoods, each of which believes in territorial imperative. Thus, those who reside in Dorchester, Charlestown or South Boston (all part of the city) scarcely ever admit to being from Boston: rather, they belong to Dorchester, Charlestown or South Boston. On the other hand, those who live in Newton or Quincy, both within the metropolitan area, are perfectly content to be called Bostonians.

The city's two major attractions are the Freedom Trail and Faneuil Hall Marketplace. The former consists of 16 sites, many of which played a seminal part in the history of the nation and all of which played a major role in the development of Boston. The Marketplace, revived in the 1970s, is the prototype for all such enterprises in and beyond the United States and is said to attract even more visitors than Disneyland.

The harbor – which has always been Boston's and Massachu-setts' greatest natural asset – has been resurrected and the waterfront is now a joy. Then there is the river. Paris may have the Seine and Cairo the Nile, but locals exalt the glorious Charles River which separates Boston and Cambridge. The latter, home of both Harvard University and the Massachusetts Institute of Technology, is not part of Boston but is a city in its own right with a population of about 100,000 and more than a dozen National Historic Landmarks.

Boston is also an excellent base for half- and full-day excursions, either to the coast or inland. To the south, Cape Cod and its magnificent sand dunes beckon; to the north, Cape Ann is much more rugged yet still boasts delightful beaches. History is never far away. Concord and Lexington, Plymouth and Provincetown, Salem and Gloucester, all of which played their part in the birth of the nation, await the traveler.

Preceding pages: Christian Science Complex; Swan boats on the public garden lagoon; Faneuil Hall marketplace. **Left**, no fear of getting lost.

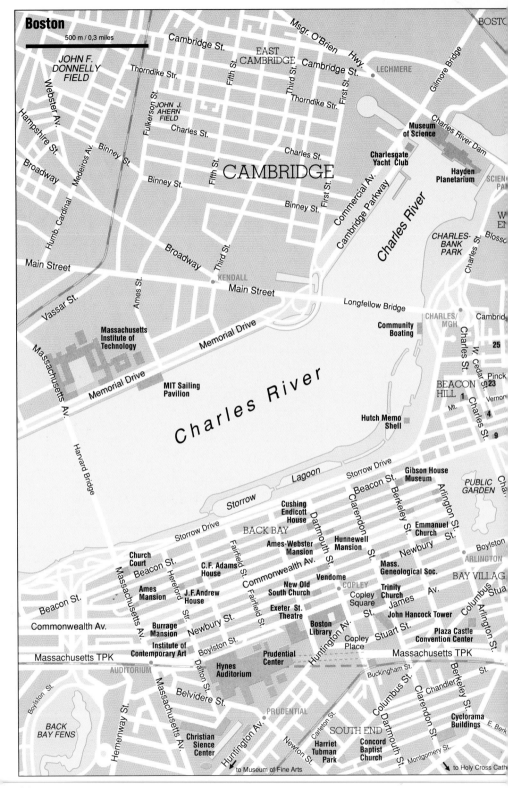

Boston

500 m / 0,3 miles

BOSTO

JOHN F. DONNELLY FIELD

Cambridge St.

Msgr. O'Brien Hwy.

EAST CAMBRIDGE

Cambridge St.

LECHMERE

Thorndike Str.

Fifth St.

Third St.

First St.

Gilmore Bridge

Webster Av.

Hampshire St.

JOHN J. AHERN FIELD

Fulkerson St.

Thorndike Str.

Charles St.

Museum of Science

Charles River Dam

Broadway

Medeiros Av.

Binney St.

Fifth St.

CAMBRIDGE

Charles St.

Charlesgate Yacht Club

Hayden Planetarium

SCIEN PA

Humb. Cardinal

Binney St.

Charles St.

First St.

Commercial Av.

Cambridge Parkway

Charles River

CHARLES-BANK PARK

W EN

Blosso

Binney St.

Main Street

Broadway

Third St.

KENDALL

Main Street

Longfellow Bridge

Community Boating

CHARLES/ MGH

Cambrid

Charles St.

25

Vassar St.

Ames St.

Massachusetts Institute of Technology

Memorial Drive

W. Cedar St.

Pinck

Massachusetts Av.

Memorial Drive

MIT Sailing Pavilion

Charles River

Hutch Memo Shell

BEACON HILL 1

Mt.

23

Vernon

Charles St.

4

9

Harvard Bridge

Lagoon

Storrow Drive

Storrow

Storrow Drive

Gibson House Museum

Beacon St.

Clarendon St.

Berkeley St.

Arlington St.

PUBLIC GARDEN

Cha

Cushing Endicott House

BACK BAY

Dartmouth St.

Emmanuel Church

Ames-Webster Mansion

Hunnewell Mansion

Newbury

Boylston

Church Court

Beacon St.

C.F. Adams House

Commonwealth Av.

Vendome

Mass. Geneological Soc.

ARLINGTON

BAY VILLAG

Fairfield St.

Hereford

Massachusetts Av.

Ames Mansion

J.F.Andrew House

New Old South Church

COPLEY

Copley Square

Trinity Church

James St.

John Hancock Tower

Av.

Columbus

Stua

Arlington St.

Beacon St.

Exeter St. Theatre

Fairfield St.

Boston Library

Copley Place

Stuart St.

Plaza Castle Convention Center

Commonwealth Av.

Burrage Mansion

Newbury St.

Huntington Av.

Massachusetts TPK

Institute of Contemporary Art

Boylston St.

Prudential Center

Massachusetts TPK

Berkeley St.

St.

Massachusetts TPK

AUDITORIUM

Dalton St.

Hynes Auditorium

Buckingham St.

Columbus St.

Chandler St.

Boylston St.

Belvidere St.

Hemenway St.

Massachusetts Av.

PRUDENTIAL

Carleton St.

Clarendon St.

Dartmouth St.

Cyclorama Buildings

E. Berk

BACK BAY FENS

Christian Sience Center

Huntington Av.

SOUTH END

Harriet Tubman Park

Concord Baptist Church

Montgomery St.

Newton St.

to Museum of Fine Arts

to Holy Cross Cath

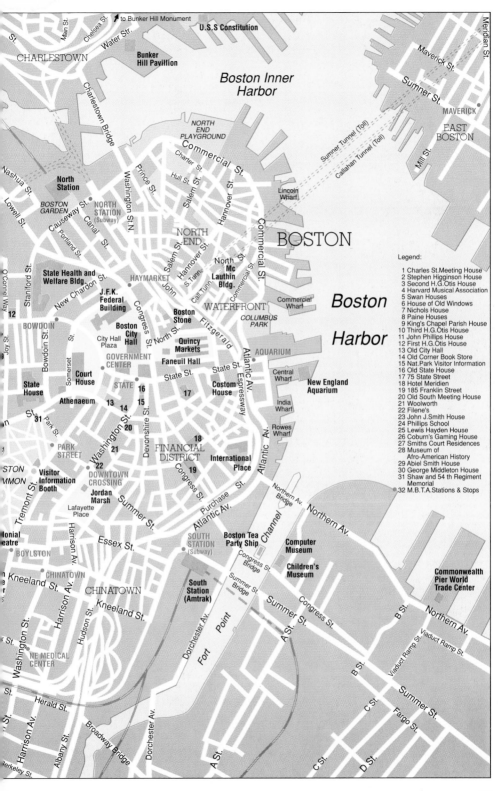

Legend:

1 Charles St.Meeting House
2 Stephen Higginson House
3 Second H.G.Otis House
4 Harvard Musical Association
5 Swan Houses
6 House of Old Windows
7 Nichols House
8 Paine Houses
9 King's Chapel Parish House
10 Third H.G.Otis House
11 John Phillips House
12 First H.G.Otis House
13 Old City Hall
14 Old Corner Book Store
15 Nat.Park Visitor Information
16 Old State House
17 75 State Street
18 Hotel Meridien
19 185 Franklin Street
20 Old South Meeting House
21 Woolworth
22 Filene's
23 John J.Smith House
24 Phillps School
25 Lewis Hayden House
26 Coburn's Gaming House
27 Smiths Court Residences
28 Museum of
   Afro-American History
29 Abiel Smith House
30 George Middleton House
31 Shaw and 54 th Regiment
   Memorial
32 M.B.T.A.Stations & Stops

BEACON HILL AND BOSTON COMMON

In many ways, Beacon Hill and the Boston Common make an unlikely pair. Beacon Hill is an essentially residential neighborhood. It's reserved, quiet, and as dignified as the old Boston families who have traditionally chosen to live there. The Common, on the other hand, is loud and lively, with all kinds of characters passing through. It's the nation's first public park and the democratic heart of Boston, a place where anyone with a soapbox is welcome to state their mind. Together, the two areas have a dynamic but balanced relationship, and it's safe to say that neither would be the same without the other.

Hub of the Solar System: Beacon Hill rises from the northern border of the Common at Beacon Street, peaks at the crest of old Mt Vernon, and then slopes down to the Charles River and the West End. Located within this small, protected enclave is one of the city's loveliest quarters. The streets are relatively long and narrow, the sidewalks are lit by gaslamps, and the tidy rows of Federalist houses still reflect the air of gentility so valued by their 19th-century inhabitants.

By accidents of history and geography, Beacon Hill is divided into three distinct sections. The South Slope, generally recognized as classical Beacon Hill, is bordered by Beacon, Pinckney, Bowdoin and Charles Streets. The less exclusive North Slope runs down the opposite side of the Hill from Pinckney to Cambridge Streets. And the Flat Side, which is built entirely on landfill, occupies the broad area of level ground west of Charles Street and bordering the Charles River.

Beacon Hill isn't the oldest neighborhood in Boston, nor is it the wealthiest or necessarily the most interesting. Its importance to the city is based on the class of people who lived there. From 1800 to about 1870, Beacon Hill was the home of Boston's oldest, wealthiest and most distinguished families, the so-called Brahmins. Appleton, Cabot, Lodge, Lowell – the list includes several hundred – all of them related to early Boston settlers, many of whom made their fortunes in the China trade.

The relatively modest homes of Beacon Hill were perfectly suited to the Brahmins' peculiar blend of wealth and self-restraint. As a member of one of its most important families put it, Beacon Hill was the kingdom of the "cold roast" Bostonians, wealthy enough to buy good meat but too frugal to warm it up. Which is not to say that there was a lack of *noblesse oblige*. What Brahmin families withheld for personal fastidiousness they often gave away in the name of civic responsibility. Many of Boston's finest institutions (including the Common) have benefited from the Brahmins' "wholesale charity."

Beacon Hill was a fitting home for the Brahmins in another respect: the new neighborhood fulfilled an old Puritan

myth. It really was John Winthrop's "city upon a hill," and in a new country dedicated to individual achievement, it was the perfect place for the Elect to survey the world around them.

By about 1870, many of the old families began leaving Beacon Hill for more spacious homes in the Back Bay, which was then being developed. The Hill fell on relatively hard times for some years until its charms were rediscovered by a new generation of residents in the mid-1900s. Today, most single-family homes have been made into apartments or condominiums, but externally it still represents a remarkably complete picture of 19th-century architecture and urban planning.

It seems ironic, but the history of Beacon Hill isn't nearly as exciting as other Boston neighborhoods that figured more prominently in the colonial and revolutionary periods. You'll undoubtedly hear about the Hill's illustrious residents (Henry James, Louisa May Alcott, Charles Sumner and Oliver Wendell Holmes, just to name a few), and there are plenty of stories about Charles Dickens hanging around with Henry Wadsworth Longfellow and "Jamie" Fields, and about Edgar Allen Poe getting kicked out of parties for drunkenness.

Yet, for a neighborhood so rich in historic associations, the history of Beacon Hill is most distinguished by its lack of weighty events. There were no battles here, no catastrophes and no world-shaking discoveries. In fact, considering the number of scholars who have populated the neighborhood over the years, more history was probably written in Beacon Hill parlors than ever transpired on the hill itself.

There are a few exceptions, of course. A murder, for example. In 1849, an upper level Brahmin, George Parkman, was killed and dismembered by Dr John Webster, a Harvard Medical School professor, and then stashed in the basement of his laboratory. The event caused quite a sensation, and Brahmin

Snow on Beacon Hill's Mt Vernon Street.

society, always mortified by excessive attention, was doubly mortified by the sordid nature of the crime.

A community of free blacks gathered on the North Slope of Beacon Hill in the early 1800s and many of its members were leaders in the anti-slavery movement preceding the Civil War. The National Park Service has recently organized a Black Heritage Trail that includes several important sites in the history of Beacon Hill's early black population (*see panel, page 104*).

But if digging up old facts isn't your cup of tea, don't worry. The real magic of Beacon Hill isn't in the history, it's in the experience. Of all the neighborhoods in Boston, this is the most insulated and self-contained. It's as if the architects designed it as an answer to the old Puritan dilemma – how to be in the world but not of it – because Beacon Hill is both a part of, and apart from, the surrounding city.

The first thing you notice on entering Beacon Hill is exactly this sense of

separation. It feels as if you've left modern Boston behind and stepped into a19th-century village. Traffic thins out, the streets narrow and city noises begin to fade. This is the Boston of another age. It's a town of red brick and cobblestone, of hidden gardens and graceful bay windows. Flower boxes brim with color. Elm trees shade the sidewalk. Aside from a few other tourists, there's almost no one on the street.

The effect is created by a number of factors, but the most important element is stylistic homogeneity. Aside from the cars parked along the street, there are very few intrusions from the modern world, and thanks to an aggressive program of historic preservation, an abundance of original details still exist. But above all, Beacon Hill owes its special ambience to its original developers and to the native talents of the untrained housewrights who designed and built most of the homes.

State House and South Slope: The first European resident of Beacon Hill was

Window boxes abound on Beacon Hill.

BLACK HERITAGE TRAIL

When Massachusetts declared slavery illegal in 1783, the migration of runaway slaves to Boston increased enormously. Free blacks settled in the North End but later moved to the North slope of **Beacon Hill**. This trail on the Hill explores the history of that community.

Begin in tiny **Smith Court** where, at one time, all the houses were occupied by blacks. Facing these is the **African Meeting House**, the oldest black church in the nation still standing. Dedicated in 1806, it was called "the haven from the loft" because of the practise in Old North Church of relegating black worshippers to the loft. It was also known as "Black Faneuil Hall" because of fiery anti-slave meetings held here. These culminated in 1832 when William Lloyd Garrison founded the New England Anti-Slavery Society. In his words: "Faneuil Hall shall ere long echo with the principles we have set forth. We shall shake the nation by their mighty power."

Next door, at the corner of **Joy Street**, stood the Abiel Smith School, dedicated in 1834 to the education of the city's black children. Yet voices of integration were already being heard, for, although the black community had fought hard for this school, some were opposed arguing that it would crystallize segregation. Led by William C. Neill, who lived in Smith Court and who was the first published black historian, they formed the Equal Schools Association (separates are not equals) which called for the school to be boycotted.

In 1850 the State's highest court ruled that the school provided an education equal to that of other public schools in the city and so blacks did not require to be admitted to the public system. However, in 1855 the State Legislature outlawed segregation and the Smith School was closed.

Near here, at the corner of **Phillips** and **Irving Streets** was the **Coburn Gaming House** which was a "private palace... the resort of the upper ten who had acquired a taste for gambling." Also on Phillips Street (No. 66) is the **Lewis and Harriet Hayden House**. This was one of the most im-

portant of the many "underground railway" stops on the Hill which sheltered fugitive slaves on their way to freedom in Canada. In 1853 the Haydens were visited by Harriet Beecher Stowe who was researching for her book *Keys to Uncle Tom's Cabin*. She was astonished that the house was a haven for 13 slaves. It is said that Hayden kept two kegs of gunpowder in the basement so that the house could be blown up if searched.

And so to **Charles Street** where the **Meeting House** of that name was built in 1807 for the Third Baptist Church. In the mid-1830s the Church's segregationist traditions were challenged by Timothy Gilbert who invited black friends to his pew. He was expelled and, with other white abolitionist baptists, founded the First Baptist Free Church. It became Tremont Temple, "the first integrated church in America." In 1876 the Meeting House was bought by the African Methodist Episcopalian Church and, in 1939, was the last black institution to leave the Hill.

Further up the Hill, at **68 Pinckney**, is the handsome home which belonged to John J. Smith, a distinguished black statesman who migrated to Boston from Virginia in 1848. Stationed in Washington during the Civil War, he was a recruiting officer for the all-black Fifth Cavalry. Subsequently, he was thrice appointed to the Massachusetts House of Representatives, then to the Boston Common Council.

The large red-brick building at the corner of Pinckney and **Anderson Streets** is the **Phillips School** which, when opened to blacks in 1855, became the city's first inter-racial school. The clapboard house at **Nos. 5–7 Pinckney** is the oldest (1791) existing home on the hill to be built by a black person. The lot was purchased by G. Middleton, a black equestrian, and Lewis Glapion, a mulatto barber. Middleton, a colonel in the Revolutionary War, led the all-black company "Bucks of America."

End the tour across from the State House at the handsome bronze plaque which honors **Robert Gould Shaw and the 54th Regiment**. This, the first black regiment in the north, was recruited in Massachusetts. Shaw, a young white officer from Boston, volunteered for the command. He and many members of the company were killed.

the Rev. William Blackstone, an English hermit who settled on the Shawmut Peninsula several years before the Puritans. After selling most of his land to John Winthrop, Blackstone retired to a small, 6-acre estate at the foot of the South Slope. At the time, the area was called Trimount after the three distinct peaks (Sentry Hill, Mt Vernon and Cotton Hill) that rose above the Common. Over the years that followed, all three summits were gradually flattened by as much as 60 feet and the excess soil and rock were used to fill in the tidal flats where Charles Street is today.

In 1737 Beacon Hill got its first building of any true substance and Boston got the finest "mansion-house" on which it ever laid eyes. The house was built by Thomas Hancock, a wealthy merchant and the uncle of John Hancock, who inherited both house and fortune after his uncle's death. The landmark stood on Beacon Street overlooking the northeast corner of the Common until 1863. Today, the site is marked by a plaque.

In 1803, the Hancock mansion was joined by a building that continues to dominate Beacon Hill: the **Massachusetts State House**. The State House is the masterpiece of Charles Bulfinch, the most important architect of his day in Boston, and possibly in the entire United States.

Today, the State House's appearance is the result of several significant changes. The original red brick structure is now backed by an ungainly rear extension and flanked on either side by marble wings. Although clumsy, the new additions haven't detracted from Bulfinch's dignified facade, which features a grand two-story portico surmounted by the famous gold dome.

Actually, in Bulfinch's original design the dome was covered with white shingles; then, in 1802, Paul Revere sheathed it in copper and later, in 1861, it was gilded with gold leaf. The only other time the dome changed was during World War II, when it was painted black in case of an air attack.

A stately pair of doorways.

Inside the State House, the most impressive rooms are the few that survived the building's alterations. Especially notable are the **Senate Chamber**, the **Reception Room**, the **House of Representatives** (home of the beloved Sacred Cod) and **Doric Hall**, a vaulted, columned, marble chamber that rises beneath the dome. Across from the State House the unobtrusive entrance to the **Athenaeum**, at 10½ Beacon Street, leads to a superb interior based on an Italian palazzo and permits the hoi polloi to glimpse the interior of a Brahmin stronghold. Founded in 1807, the Athenaeum, whose barrel-vaulted fifth floor is nirvana for the book lover, contains the library of George Washington and also houses a notable collection of American portrait paintings.

At about the same time that the State House was being completed, Bulfinch became involved in another large-scale project on Beacon Hill. Together with several other enterprising townsmen (including Harrison Gray Otis, Joseph Woodward, Jonathan Mason and William Scollay), Bulfinch became a member of the Mt Vernon Proprietors which bought about 19 acres of pasture on the South Slope. Plans were drawn to level the summit of the hill, lay out streets and subdivide house lots.

The Proprietors' originally intended to build free-standing homes surrounded by gardens, but the economics of development soon dictated a more efficient plan – joining homes at a common wall. At first, two or three houses were built together, and then, as the pace of development quickened, entire streets were lined with single unbroken rows. Although Bulfinch designed several of Beacon Hill's grandest estates, most of the buildings were erected by untrained builders. Their instincts for proportion, sturdiness and modest ornamentation still define the neighborhood's essential character.

A tour of the old Mt Vernon properties is limited entirely to the **South Slope**. The best place to start is on the

Ranger gives directions on the Common.

northeast corner of the Common, directly in front of the State House. From here, proceed straight down Beacon Street until you reach the corner of Charles Street.

Fronting the Common along its northern border, **Beacon Street** is the Hill's public face. This is Oliver Wendell Holmes's "sunny street that holds the sifted few." The buildings here are among the oldest on Beacon Hill, and they boast a level of grandeur and ornamentation that is largely unmatched by the rest of the neighborhood.

As you stroll down the hill, be sure to take note of the **John Phillips House** (1 Walnut St.) and the **Third Harrison Gray Otis House** (45 Beacon St.), both designed by Bulfinch between 1804 and 1808. "Purple panes" still hang in the window frames of **King's Chapel Parish House** (63–64 Beacon St.) and of **39** and **40 Beacon Street**. The unusual color is caused by a chemical defect, but since the glass was installed in the early 1800s the purple panes have become a part of Beacon Hill folklore.

Take a right at the corner of **Charles Street** and then turn right again at one of the narrow cross streets that lead up the slope. The first and most intimate one is **Chestnut Street**. The combination of simple structures, modest scale and artful detailing make this one of the most pleasing streets on the Hill. The buildings are especially notable for the delicate use of ornamentation, including wrought-iron balconies, bootscrapers, Greek Revival porticos and fan lights, all of which tend to vary and lighten the plain brick facades.

Again, there are far too many distinguished homes to list, but a few highlights include the **Charles Paine Houses** (6–8 Chestnut St.), the **Swan Houses** (13, 15 and 17) and **No. 29**A, all attributed to Bulfinch. The home of historian Francis Parkman is located at **No. 50**, and the **Harvard Musical Association**, the country's oldest music library, is at No. 57A.

Take time to explore the narrow lanes

that intersect Chestnut Street. Many of the smaller houses on **Willow**, **West Cedar** and **Acorn Streets** were originally servants' quarters and kitchens that serviced the wealthier households. Today, these slender byways are among the most private locations on the Hill. Acorn Street, the steep cobbled alley lined with gas lamps and flower boxes, is not to be missed.

Following Willow Street uphill, you immediately come to **Mt Vernon Street**. Here the houses are larger, the street wider, and the families more distinguished. In one of his more snobbish moments, Henry James called it "the only respectable street in America."

The highlight of Mt Vernon Street, and the crown of Beacon Hill, is **Louisburg Square**, a small rectangle of grass and trees surrounded by a cobblestone plaza and stately homes. The gently rippling bowfront houses on the west side of the square (**numbers 8 to 22**) have been called the finest rowhouses in Boston, and possibly the

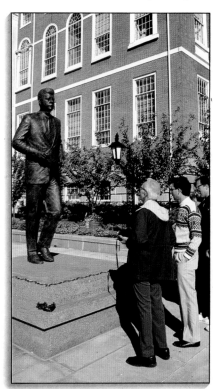

US. Louisa May Alcott lived at **No. 10** and, at **No. 20**, Jenny Lind married her accompanist Otto Goldschmidt.

Just beyond Louisburg Square, in the direction of the State House (to the southeast), is an impressive series of freestanding mansions. The **Stephen Higginson House** at No. 87 and its much-altered neighbor at **No. 89** were both built by Charles Bulfinch between 1804 and 1809. The **Second Harrison Gray Otis House**, next door at No. 85, was built by Bulfinch several years earlier. The brownstone mansions across the street were constructed in 1850; their Gothic touches are a striking counterpoint to the other buildings on the street. The **Nichols House Museum** (55 Mt Vernon St) is also a Bulfinch creation, and, until a recent theft, was open to the public.

At the opposite end of Louisburg Square, **Pinckney Street** runs along the crest of Beacon Hill, separating the South Slope from the less affluent North Slope. Several noteworthy homes here include **No. 24**, the **House of Odd Windows**, which boasts the most eccentric design on the Hill.

"The Rim of Decency": Beyond Pinckney, the **North Slope** pitches toward Cambridge Street and the West End. Nowadays, this is the bohemian half of Beacon Hill, one of the few places where artists, writers and students can still find tiny yet affordable apartments. Socially, the North Slope was never the equal of the South. From the very beginning, it was considered the "bad side" of the Hill, and according to some of the South Slope's high-minded residents, the label still applies. It is only since the most recent wave of gentrification that the social gap has really begun to narrow.

Although the North Slope doesn't share the same architectural pedigree as the South, it tends to be somewhat friendlier and more relaxed. Unlike its southern neighbor, the North Slope's social life is fairly visible and neighborhood business often spills over into the **Fun on the Common.**

streets. On **Myrtle Street**, for example, there's a pizzeria, a café, a corner grocer and an old-fashioned, two-chair barber shop where people meet and have the sort of casual conversations that make the place feel like a living neighborhood rather than just a collection of interesting buildings.

The students bustling up and down **Temple Street** near **Suffolk University** animate the neighborhood even further, and every now and then music can be heard blasting from an apartment window or car horns can be heard honking on Cambridge Street.

The North Slope was the site of Beacon Hill's earliest development, a small huddle of buildings along the Charles River established about 1725. Almost immediately, the North Slope Village began to take on an unsavory character. Its proximity to the river and its detachment from town made it a perfect spot for sailors who were more interested in taverns and bordellos than the rigors of Puritan life. North Slope entrepreneurs were only too glad to oblige them, and within a few years Boston had its first red-light district. Among sailors, the village became known as Mt Whoredom, and for nearly 100 years it rankled the morals of god-fearing citizens everywhere in Boston.

In the early 1820s a crackdown forced the last of Mt Whoredom's "bawdy houses" to shut down, and the area started to change. By then, the city's substantial black population had already begun to move in, and in a few short years the North Slope became a black community center and a hotbed of abolitionist activity.

Elsewhere on the North Slope, be sure to stroll past the four, quiet, charming cul-de-sacs that run off Revere Street. **Rollins Place** is especially interesting because the classical two-story portico at the end is a mere facade. There's nothing behind it but a 20-foot cliff dropping down to **Phillips Street**. The other alleyways – **Goodwin Place**, **Sentry Hill Place** and **Bellingham**

The Frog Pond on the Common.

Place – are equally enchanting, each paved with red brick and lined by compact rowhouses. Branching off from opposite sides of Phillips Street (near the corner of West Cedar), are **Primus Avenue** and a very narrow passage known as **Flower Lane**, two other alleyways well worth investigating.

The North side of the Hill ends in wide, busy **Cambridge Street** on whose far side are several interesting buildings. At the west end of this street is the **Old West Church**, a handsome red-brick federal building from 1806. The original church was razed in 1775 when the British thought that the Americans were using it as a steeple from which to signal to their compatriots in Cambridge.

The current building, a Methodist church, is an oblong meeting house fronted by a rectangular block rising in several stages to a square cupola beneath which are swag-ornamented clocks. The large, empty interior has a balcony, supported by delicate columns with attenuated acanthus-leaf capitals, running around three sides.

Next door is the first **Harrison Gray Otis house**, designed by Bulfinch in 1795 and now owned by the Society for the Preservation of New England Antiquities. This, the most distinguished old mansion still standing in Boston, is a completely symmetrical three-story rectangular block of red bricks, with each story being defined by a brownstone string course. Enter and observe the last years of 18th-century Boston. The interior has been meticulously restored with furniture and portraits, canary-yellow wallpaper and mirror-panelled doors which would reflect candlelight. The basement contains an architectural museum.

Further to the east on Cambridge Street is the sprawling **Massachusetts General Hospital**, possibly America's greatest hospital. Its very first building, the Bulfinch Pavilion and Ether Dome, was designed by Bulfinch just before he departed for Washington to work on the United States capitol. Enquire at the hospital's main entrance for directions to this building which is an historic landmark twice over: once because of its architecture and once because here ether was used as an anaesthetic for the first time. The Federal-style building stands on a high podium and the main entrance is approached by two stairways that lead to the sides of a portico formed by 10 unfluted Ionic columns.

The Flat Side and Charles Street: The remaining part of Beacon Hill, a broad area of level ground built entirely on landfill, is known as the **Flat Side**. Its outstanding feature is **Charles Street**, Beacon Hill's only commercial street, while its most distinguished building is the **Charles Street Meeting House**, located on the corner of Mt Vernon Street (*see panel, page 104*). In 1982 its interior was gutted and converted into shops and offices.

Relative to the other two sections of Beacon Hill, the Flat Side occupies a neutral position. It has few of the grand

Shopping on Charles Street.

110

associations boasted by the South Slope and almost none of the negative ones tagged on the North. As a result, people tend to overlook the residential areas, although here, as elsewhere on the Hill, the overall effect is of a quaint 19th-century town located in the middle of a modern city.

Most people come to the Flat Side to shop on Charles Street, which tends to be less hectic than downtown and more casual than the boutiques on Newbury Street. Antiques are a local specialty and there are several good bookstores, restaurants and cafés. Il Dolce Momento, on the corner of Charles and Chestnut streets, is a good place for Italian pastries, *gelato* and a stiff cup of espresso, although nearby Romano's Bakery tends to be less crowded and more reasonably priced. It's especially pleasant in the winter when they stoke up the fireplace.

Probably the most popular attraction on the Flat Side is the **Bull & Finch**, a neighborhood bar located on the corner

of Beacon and Brimmer streets that's said to be the inspiration for the popular television series *Cheers*. The success of the show has transformed the place into a major tourist attraction, and people wait at the door both day and night. If it's a couple of cold ones you're after, walk right by and head over to the **Sevens Pub** on Charles Street, where you can still belly up to the bar without being crushed by curiosity-seekers.

Although the architecture of the Flat Side isn't as old or interesting as the rest of the Hill, there is an exceptionally handsome row of granite houses on Beacon Street directly across from the **Public Garden**. When they were built in 1828, most of the Flat Side was still underwater. The houses actually stood on the Mill Dam, which started at the edge of the Common and arched across the Back Bay.

Elsewhere on the Flat Side, the finest homes tend to be gathered on **Brimmer**, **Lime** and **Mt Vernon Streets**. There are also two very interesting courtyards

Charles Street Restaurant.

tucked into the block immediately off Embankment Road. **Charles River Square** is a hidden enclave of tidy rowhouses surrounding a rectangular plaza. About a half-block away, the rowhouses at **West Hill Place** use concave facades to define a circular courtyard; there's a tunnel in back that opens to Charles Street. Unfortunately, with the intersection of three major highways only a few hundred feet away, the sound of traffic often penetrates the superb isolation these lovely courtyards must have enjoyed in the past.

No Common thing: The **Boston Common** is such an integral part of Beacon Hill that it's impossible to talk about one without mentioning the other. Although the two areas represent different aspects of Boston, they are linked by history and should be thought of as elements of a larger whole.

The Common, a pentagon covering about 50 acres, is bounded by Beacon, Boylston, Charles, Park and Tremont Streets. It is both a geographical and social crossroads and for those unfamiliar with the city is probably the best place to start a visit. Those one is most likely to bump into represent a cross section of the city: Chinese women practising *tai-chai* in the shade of an ancient elm tree, Italian men taking a walk with their grandchildren, blacks rapping, and office workers soaking up the sun while enjoying their lunch.

Buskers entertain and, during the summer, children cool off under the fountain in the **Frog Pond**. In colonial times sheep and cows slaked their thirst at the pond. Later, proper Bostonians fished in it for minnows in the summer and ice-skated on it in the winter.

Most people don't realize that the Common is probably the oldest and least changed section of Boston. It was established more than 350 years ago, when John Winthrop and his neighbors bought the original 50 acres from the Rev. William Blackstone. In 1640, the townsmen agreed to preserve the land as a "Comon Field" (*sic*) on which **Winter sports on the Common.**

112

sheep and cattle were to be grazed, and it soon became a popular spot for sermons, promenades, and, in the years before the Revolution, political protest. Militias used the land as a mustering ground, and public hangings were conducted at the Great Elm, which stood on the Common until 1876. Among the heretics who met a cruel end here was Mary Dyer, the heroic Quaker who insisted on the right to worship freely.

Although it's now surrounded by modern buildings, the **Old Granary Burial Ground**, located near the corner of Park and Tremont streets, was originally a part of the Common. The first body was committed in 1660, making it one of the oldest cemeteries in Boston. Among the historic figures buried here are Samuel Adams, Peter Faneuil, Paul Revere, John Hancock, Elizabeth "Mother" Goose and the victims of the Boston Massacre. Unfortunately, the headstones have been moved so many times, they no longer correspond to the actual graves, some of

which are four bodies deep. Believe it or not, the neat rows we see today are an accommodation to the lawnmower. Still, the icons and inscriptions carved into the stones are absolutely fascinating, and, considering the nature of the place, more than a little chilling.

The sturdy Georgian steeple next door to the Burial Ground belongs to the **Park Street Church**, which occupies the site of the old granary building after which the cemetery is named. The church was designed by Peter Banner and completed in 1810. Henry James described it as "the most interesting mass of brick and mortar in America," and renowned abolitionist William Lloyd Garrison launched his public crusade against slavery from the pulpit in 1829. The church is responsible for giving this part of the Common its nickname – "Brimstone Corner" – after the fiery sermons delivered by its Congregationalist ministers and the barrels of gunpowder stored in the basement during the War of 1812.

Left, Paul Revere's tomb in Old Granary Burying Ground. **Right**, trolley tours start from Tremont Street.

During the American Revolution, the Common was transformed into a British military center. As many as 2,000 Redcoats were quartered here during the occupation of Boston, and several dozen British soldiers killed at the Battle of Bunker Hill were interred at the **Central Burying Ground** in the southeast corner. It is the fourth oldest cemetery in Boston, but few of note are buried here.

Most activity occurs on the fringe of the Common, near the **Park Street underground station** – the first subway station in the nation and now a Historic Landmark – at the northern end of Tremont Street. Here, vendors sell ice-cream, hot-dogs, T-shirts and other souvenirs and, on occasions, religious fanatics vent their wrath.

Here also is the **Visitors Information Booth**, where one can pick up free maps and other literature and where the Freedom Trail starts. Several privately operated sightseeing "trolleys" (in reality, conventional wheeled vehicles with trolley-like bodywork) that run every 10 or 15 minutes set off on their city tours from here.

Although some guides seem to be more interested in auditioning for comedy clubs than giving useful information, the trolleys are a good way to become acquainted with the city, especially if time is limited. Best of all, one can hop off the trolley wherever one likes, explore on foot for a while and then re-board a later trolley. There's hot competition between look-alike trolley companies; it can be a problem to ensure that you re-board the right vehicle.

The west part of the common is devoted to athletic endeavor – baseball, tennis, volley ball and frisbee are all popular – and to large public meetings.

Elsewhere on the Common are several works of public art. Outstanding is the 70-ft **Soldiers and Sailors Monument** which is located atop Telegraph Hill on the western side of the park. It is dedicated to the Union forces who were killed during the American Civil War.

Revivalist meeting on the Common.

MUSIC MAKING

Boston is positively awash with music. That's not surprising, given that the very first orchestra in the nation was formed here in 1810 or 1811 (records are hazy) under the baton of Johann Christian Gottlieb Braubner who also helped to establish the Handel and Haydn Society. This, America's first organization dedicated exclusively to music, sang Haydn's *Creation*, the first oratorio to be sung in the land, in King's Chapel in 1815.

Boston's most renowned ensemble is the Boston Symphony Orchestra (BSO) or simply Symphony; it was founded by Major Henry Lee Higginson in 1881 and tickets for its concerts are handed down from generation to generation. The BSO gave its first performance in 1881 in the Music Hall under the baton of George Henschel. This was an enormous success and in its first year almost 85,000 attended the orchestra's 20 concerts and the same number of rehearsals. The halcyon days of the much loved orchestra begin at the start of this century when they moved into today's Symphony Hall which, although not the most handsome of buildings, boasts superb acoustics.

Now, about 250 concerts, attended by an audience of 1½ million, are performed annually. Millions more listen to recordings and broadcasts of the orchestra which, in 1918, under the baton of Karl Much, cut the world's orchestral recordings and then, in 1926, under the direction of Serge Koussevitsky, made the first orchestral broadcast in the nation.

Come magnolia time, the conductor and leading performers of the BSO disappear and, with the big cats away, the mice begin to play popular music. The auditorium is filled with tables, and champagne corks pop. These are the Pops; they began in 1885 as the Promenade Concerts and most proper Bostonians find them just a little *déclassé*. Yet tickets are hard to come by during the two-month season. Some say that the word Pops is not derived from popular music nor from popping champagne corks but rather owes its origins to the fact that a march called *The Pops*

was played in very first week of these concerts.

In July the orchestra transfers to the Hatch Shell, an outdoor music stand on the banks of the Charles River and there delights enormous audiences (35,000 have been known) with a series of outdoor performances – the Boston Pops Esplanade Concerts – lasting for four weeks. Arthur Fiedler, who conducted from 1919 to 1979, and his successor, John Williams (the present conductor), are invariably linked with Pops which has introduced the joys of classical music to untold thousands.

The recently formed Boston Philharmonic, which plays in Jordan Hall, immediately across the road from Symphony Hall, has many devotees. Music is also made by the Pro Arte Chamber Orchestra, founded and conducted by a Harvard University minister, Larry Hall. It specializes in works by Boston composers and during its first 10 years offered 24 world premiers of these musicians. The Boston Camerata Chamber, Banchetto Musicale and the Cantata Singers and the John Oliver Choral and many other groups come into their own at the biannual Boston Early Music Festival which has a worldwide reputation.

And, all the time, the city's two major music schools (New England Conservatory and the Berklee School of Music) make music with innumerable groups and orchestras. So, to a lesser extent, do the half-hundred colleges and universities in Greater Boston.

Try as it will, Boston has never been a major force in opera – although when Jenny Lind, the Swedish nightingale, came to Boston in 1850 she conquered and was conquered and, after her marriage, returned to live at Louisburg Square on Beacon Hill. The first Boston opera company opened in 1909 with a performance of *La Gioconda* but by 1915 was bankrupt. Sara Caldwell resurrected the company as The Opera Company of Boston in 1958 and, with many vicissitudes, has kept it going, filling the repertoire mainly with less popular works.

Even though the charismatic Caldwell attracts the best singers and mounts brilliant productions, Boston has never taken opera to its heart. Nevertheless, 1990 saw the opening of a second company, the Boston Opera Company.

THE NORTH END

An angel flies over the **North End**. It happens every year during the Feast of the Assumption. She is the messenger of the Madonna del Soccorso, protector of the fishing fleet and patron saint of Sicilian immigrants. She floats above the street, her arms outstretched to the crowd below, and then releases a basket of white doves. The birds fly into the night, and the angel disappears.

This year, the little girl who played the role of the angel looked somewhat hesitant as she dangled from a pulley three stories above the street. Yet, although not more than nine years old, she played the part flawlessly. Her satin robe shimmered against the night sky as she was lowered to a statue of the Madonna. When the crowd began to cheer, a smile lit up her face.

Earlier that day, the men of the Fishermen's Club carried the Madonna through the streets in a day-long procession of brass bands and traditional Sicilian music. As they passed from one block to another, people threw money from the windows or pinned it to the Madonna's gown. At every stop the men lowered the platform and then hoisted it back onto their shoulders with a great show of effort. A cry went out: "*Viva la Madonna!*" And the crowd answered back: "*Viva !*"

The Island of North Boston: Three hundred years ago, the North End was known as the "island of North Boston." On colonial maps it looks like an irregular thumb jutting into the Atlantic Ocean with a canal, called the Mill Stream, cutting it off from the larger Shawmut Peninsula. Today, the **John F. Fitzgerald Expressway** runs the same course as the old canal, and cuts off the neighborhood even more abruptly. Water no longer surrounds the North End, but it's still set apart from the rest of the city – a cultural island, Boston's Little Italy.

Sociologists describe the North End as an "urban village." Old-world attitudes are still very much a part of life here. They are enacted in public rituals like the Feast of the Assumption as well as in day-to-day life. Italian is spoken in the streets, family is the center of social activity, and in general, community is valued over privacy.

The neighborhood also looks and sounds like an Italian *quartiere*. Many streets are narrow and crooked, laundry flaps on outdoor clotheslines, and produce is sold at open-air stands. The sense of community is so thick you can almost feel it in the air, and it's not unusual to find three or even four generations sharing the same small space – children playing in the street, young couples talking in cafés, and old folks watching from the stoops. If there is a prevailing sound in the neighborhood, it's the buzz of conversation. Talk is like glue here: it holds everything together, making this one of the few Boston neighborhoods where people are still

Preceding pages: the North End. Left, what's a parade without a band? Right, the saints are honored at parade.

actively involved in each other's lives.

In fact, the community is so tightly knit that it is often difficult for outsiders to gain anything but a superficial impression. The best that most visitors can hope for is a fragmented view – a collection of tiny insights into the way North Enders think and feel. Inevitably, the most compelling images are drawn from the neighborhood's social life. It might be a Saturday at Haymarket when vendors turn Blackstone Street into a raucous open-air market, or an early morning mass at St Leonard's Church when old women dressed in black come to light candles and say the rosary. It might be a group of slick young immigrants "just off the boat" arguing about soccer in the middle of Hanover Street, or old men playing cards at a social club tucked away in a quiet alley.

Whatever you find, the scenes are likely to be strange, affecting and oddly varied. Put them all together, and you'll begin to understand what makes life in the North End so special.

Ups and downs: Historically, the North End has had its ups and downs. When the Puritans arrived in 1630, it was a marshy finger of land with few apparent virtues, although, as one member of the party wrote, it was well-protected from the "Woolves, Rattle-snakes and Musketos *[sic]*" that they found so troublesome at their Charlestown camp. By the late colonial period, the small cluster of timber houses had become one of Boston's most fashionable quarters, with several fine homes and some of the richest families in town.

Unfortunately, most of the prominent residents were Tories who, when the British evacuated in 1776, hightailed it to Canada and took their money with them. Rich Yankees pulled out too, preferring the more genteel atmosphere of Beacon Hill, which was just then being developed. Artisans, sailors and tradesmen filled the empty houses, and for the remainder of the 19th century the North End was a workingman's quarter dominated by the shipping industry.

Restaurants abound...

In the mid-1800s, the North End was overrun by European immigrants, and the neighborhood became a slum notorious for its bordellos, street crime and squalid conditions. The Irish were the first to settle in any great numbers, pouring into the neighborhood after the Potato Famine of 1846. Under the leadership of political bosses like John "Honey Fitz" Fitzgerald, they dominated the area for well over 35 years, muscling their way into mainstream society by way of hard work and the Democratic political machine.

East European Jews followed the Irish and by 1890 had established a thriving residential and business district along Salem Street. The Italians – most of them from the southern provinces – were the last to mount a substantial presence, but by the 1920s they had established an overwhelming majority. By then, most other groups had begun to move out, and the Italians have dominated the neighborhood ever since.

In recent years, the North End's well-earned reputation for neighborliness has made it a prime target for gentrification, especially along the waterfront. Rents are skyrocketing, condominium conversions are up, and some old-time residents are getting priced right out of their homes. With the old guard aging and the new generation moving out, some dyed-in-the-wool North Enders worry that the old neighborhood is slipping away. But, although it's true that the Italian population isn't as large as it used to be, the spirit of the community is no less persistent.

Good eats and history: Most people come to the North End for one of two reasons. During the day they visit historic sites, and at night, they come to eat. Both activities are certainly worthwhile, but there's much more here than the Freedom Trail and the customary bowl of linguine.

By and large, the North End isn't much to look at. Unlike Beacon Hill or the Back Bay, it isn't a planned community. There isn't a uniform architectural

...and the quality of food is high.

style or much interest in large-scale historical preservation: in fact, quite the opposite. The North End has an improvisational quality, as if the neighborhood was built piecemeal without the benefit of an overall plan. What evolves is a hodgepodge of buildings, some quite attractive, others downright ugly. Many were built in the late 1800s as tenement houses for European immigrants. The concern at that time wasn't how pretty a building looked but how many people could be crammed inside.

The archaic street plan makes things even more confusing. The North End is one of those places where it's easy to get lost and probably best that you do. With alleyways and sidestreets running off in every direction, all kinds of unconventional spaces can be discovered in the neighborhood's less-traveled areas. Turn a corner, and you're likely to bump into anything from a vegetable garden to a street festival.

When you tire of walking around the neighborhood, head for one of the cafés and watch the neighborhood walk around you. Chances are you'll be in good company. At any given time, in any given café, at least a handful of North Enders are doing the same thing.

The best place for people-watching is **Hanover Street**, the neighborhood's central thoroughfare and the heart of its business district. Restaurants and cafés stretch from one end to the other, and a steady stream of tourists walk the Freedom Trail. If you're looking for a place to eat, you can't really go wrong here, or for that matter, anywhere else in the neighborhood. Making a selection is more a question of style than of quality.

From Hanover Street, turn right on Parmentier Street and then left to enter **North Square** where the **Pierce-Hichborn** and **Paul Revere houses** stand side by side. The former, which belonged to Nathaniel Hichborn, Paul Revere's cousin, is an asymmetrical, three-story, brick building built between 1711 and 1715 in the new English Renaissance style. This was a radical

The home of Paul Revere.

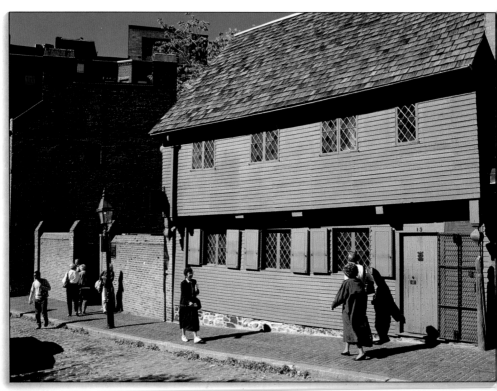

departure from the Tudor-style wooden dwellings built in the previous century. It was restored in 1949.

A polymath's home: Paul Revere's house, a two-story dwelling with an overhanging second floor, was built in 1676 and is the oldest house in downtown Boston. When Revere purchased the house in 1770, the third floor had been added, but early this century this was removed to "restore" the building to its original appearance. It is furnished today much as it was when it was home to Paul and the first Mrs Revere, who bore him eight children, and then, when she died, by the second Mrs Revere, who bore him a similar brood.

One of the upstairs rooms is covered with wallpaper which is a reproduction of paper made in Boston towards the end of the 18th century. It also contains several pieces of the furniture which belonged to the Reveres. A cabinet displays attractive silver, some made by Revere. Outside, in the courtyard, is a 931-pound bronze bell cast by Revere, generally acknowledged to have been the best bell-maker of his time.

Return to Hanover Street via Fleet Street and, after 150 yards, reach **St Stephen's Church** with its white steeple. Built in 1804 as a Congregationalist Meeting House, this simple, dignified structure is the only one of five Boston churches designed by Bulfinch which still stands. It has had a checkered history. In 1813 it became a Unitarian Church and in 1862 it was acquired by the Roman Catholic archbishopric. Eight years later, when Hanover Street had to be widened to accommodate traffic, the church was moved back 12 feet and raised 6 feet; then, in 1965, it was restored to its original level and to its Bulfinch stark simplicity.

The **Paul Revere Mall**, known locally as the **Prado**, faces St Stephen's Church. Built in 1933, this generous brick courtyard is the liveliest public space in the North End – a sort of Americanized piazza where kids run around, old folks play cards, and footsore tourists take a breather from the Freedom Trail. In addition to the traditional Italian fountain, the Prado features a magnificent equestrian statue of Paul Revere, modeled in 1885 by Cyrus Dallin and cast in 1940. On the south (left) wall, bronze panels recall the history of Boston and its people.

At the far end of the Prado a small gate opens to the rear of **Christ Church**, also known as **Old North**. To the left of the gate is the three-story (originally it was two) brick home of Ebenezer Clough, built in 1712.

The Old North, Boston's oldest church, is one of its most treasured historical monuments. Built in 1723 to house the town's second Anglican parish, the Old North is most famous for its part in Paul Revere's ride to Lexington. On April 18, 1775, Robert Newman snuck out of his home and placed two lanterns in the belfry as a signal to Revere – "one, if by land, and two, if by sea" – that the British army was advancing to Concord. Ironically, General

Angel in the Old North Church.

Gage is said to have watched the Battle of Bunker Hill from the very same belfry only a few months later.

Old North's steeple, 191 feet high, has always been Boston's tallest and a major landmark. Twice, in 1804 and again in 1854, it was blown over by hurricanes and subsequently faithfully restored to the original. America's first peal of eight bells hangs in the belfry; it was first rung in 1745 and has tolled for every departed President of the nation since George Washington died in 1799. The bells were cast in England and range in weight from 620 to 2,545 pounds, with a total mass of 7,272 pounds. They are a "maiden peal" because each bell has a perfect tone without having been filed down or machined and are said to be the sweetest in the nation. Paul Revere, at 15, came to this church and, with some other lads, signed a contract to ring the peal.

Enter the church, whose interior has been painted white since 1912. High pew boxes, designed to keep in the warmth of hot coal or bricks which were placed on the floor on wintery days, are still intact, with the names of the family owners engraved on bronze plates. The clock at the rear of the church and the four baroque Belgium cherubs which surround it date back to the opening of the church. So does the organ case, although the actual instrument dates only from 1759. The bust of George Washington, in a niche to the left of the apse, was the first public memorial to the great man. The church has 37 crypts, containing, it is claimed, 1,100 bodies.

Immediately to the north of the church is a small garden with markers recounting historic events and distinguished persons of the parish. One of these informs that "Here on 13 Sept. 1757, John Childs, who had given public notice of his intention to fly from the steeple of Dr Cutler's church, performed it to the satisfaction of a great number of spectators." Childs made three flights, once firing a pistol in mid-air: alas, nobody knows how he flew.

Mama mia – such wonderful shopping!

124

Next to the church is a gift shop, at the rear of which is a tiny museum. The museum's major treasure is the *Vinegar Bible*, sent by King George II to Christ Church in 1733. It derives its name because of a typographical error on one of its page headings in which "Parable of the Vinegar" appears instead of "Parable of the Vineyard."

A postscript must be added. Nobody is certain that the church is actually the Old North Church outside which the lanterns were hung: in 1775, several churches stood in the North End.

On exiting from the church, walk up Hull Street for about 150 yards to **Copp's Hill Burying Ground**, one of Boston's oldest cemeteries and the North End's quietest corner. In the colonial period, the base of the hill, known pejoratively as New Guinea, was occupied by Boston's first black community and about 1,000 blacks are buried in the cemetery's northwest corner.

A tall black monument remembers Prince Hall, who helped found Boston's first school for black children. However, his main claim to fame is that he was the founder, in 1784, of the African Grand Lodge of Massachusetts, the world's first black Masonic Lodge. Near here is the tombstone of "Capt. Daniel Malcolm, Merch^t." who is remembered for smuggling 60 casks of wine into port without paying the duty. He asked to be buried "in a Stone Grave 10 feet deep," safe from British bullets. His body may have been safe, but his tombstone was not: on it are scars made by the Redcoats who singled out this patriot's gravemarker for their target practice. In the southeast corner of the cemetery is the Mathers family tomb, where Increase, Cotton and Samuel are possibly buried.

Backtrack down Hull Street to **Salem Street**, on which the Old North Church stands, and turn right. A stroll of about 600 yards leads to **Cross Street**, from where you can leave the North End by the underpass. As you exit from the underpass, observe the **brass inlays** on the ground. This sculpture depicts the debris – newspapers, rotten vegetables, fish – after a Saturday in **Haymarket**.

Do not be confused by the name. There is a Haymarket Square and a Haymarket Station, but in recent years the term refers to an event rather than to an actual place. Every Friday and Saturday a crowd of fruit and vegetable sellers, fishmongers and butchers transform **Blackstone Street** into a wild open-air market. It is the closest thing to the streets of Naples or Palermo one is likely to find on this side of the Atlantic. Even for those not shopping, it is a thrill to elbow their way through the throng and to listen to the vendors haggling with customers.

If you visit in the summer, be sure to catch one of the local feasts. They are held almost every weekend in July and August, with Sundays being by far the most exciting days, and usually involve street fairs, entertainment, processions and, at least once a year, the famous flying angel.

Saturday morning at Haymarket.

CHARLESTOWN

Charlestown, which today is a northern suburb of Boston, was founded in 1629, one year before Boston, when 10 men with their families and servants were sent by the Massachusetts Bay Company to inhabit the company's New England holdings. One year later this scant band was joined by John Winthrop, who would become the colony's first governor, and his shipload of 800 Puritans.

Conditions were difficult, disease was rife, the water was foul and fear of Indians was ever-present. In 1631 Winthrop and many of his followers crossed the Charles River estuary and settled in Boston. However, the doughty few who remained prospered and by the end of the 17th century had established a democratic town meeting, founded a church and school, built a mill and even hanged Massachusetts' first witch. The town thrived and became the fourth busiest port in the country. However, in 1776 it was razed by the British and consequently none of the buildings bordering its tree-lined streets pre-dates 1800.

Charlestown is usually reached via the **Charlestown Bridge**, although a more pleasant and exciting approach is to board the ferry at **Long Wharf** for a short voyage to the *USS Constitution* National Park. Alternatively, the orange line of the "T" can be ridden to the **Community College** stop.

Charlestown's **City Square** is entered from the bridge. Immediately to the northwest is small, leafy **John Harvard Mall**, in the center of which stands a solid, granite memorial to this Charlestown man who "was sometimes minister of God's word" and who, when he died in 1638 aged 27, bequeathed his library of 300 books and half his estate to the struggling Newtone College which thereupon assumed his name. Harvard Mall is where the first settlers built their fort. Eight plaques embedded in the walls recount the subsequent early history of the settlement.

Immediately to the right of the mall is tiny **Harvard Square** where No. 27, built *circa* 1800, is one of the very few stone houses in Charlestown. It originally served as the town dispensary. Above the mall is **Harvard Street**, a dignified curving street where many notables lived in still-standing, handsome mid-19th-century houses with mansards and bow windows. Turn left and return to City Square, passing No. 16 which was occupied by Edward Everett who was governor of the state and president of Harvard.

A grand old lady: Diagonally across the square is the **Charlestown Navy Yard** which, during its heyday (1825–68 and World War II) employed thousands of men. Now, after years of desuetude it is enjoying a resurrection not only because of the *USS Constitution* and other tourist attractions but because many buildings have been recycled into hand-

some apartments and hi-tech laboratories. The towering masts of the *Constitution*, which can be seen from afar, dominate the yard and are the magnet that attract visitors to the Park.

"Old Ironsides," whose copper sheathing, bolts and fittings were made by Paul Revere, was built in Boston and first sailed from the harbor in 1778 in a shakedown cruise. Thirty years later she was de-commissioned after being involved in 40 victorious engagements including sinking the British warship *Guerrière* in 1812. During this battle the *Constitution* earned the nickname "Old Ironsides" when a rating, on seeing the enemy's cannon balls apparently bouncing off her side, exclaimed "Her sides are made of iron!" The *Constitution* had been constructed of "live oak" which is found only in the sea islands of Georgia and which is said to have five times the durability of common white oak.

The fact that the *Constitution* is moored in Boston and has not long since been scrapped is the result of several land battles. In 1830 she earned a reprieve when the young Oliver Wendell Holmes penned a poem "Ay! pull her tattered ensign down,/Long has it waved on high," which touched the nation's heartstrings. Holmes, portrayed by an actor, can be seen in stove hat wandering about the Navy Yard, often accompanied by Captain Isaac Hull who commanded the *Constitution* in her engagement with the *Guerrière*.

Then, in 1911, when she was to be used as a target ship, the Massachusetts Society of the Daughters of 1912 intervened and finally, in the 1920s, when she was in need of restoration, Boston schoolchildren contributed their pennies to a drive which spread throughout the land. In 1954, legislation was enacted making Boston the permanent home port of the *Constitution* and here she proudly sits, the oldest commissioned warship in the world and liable to be called at any time to serve in the Persian Gulf or the Mediterranean.

Oliver Wendell Holmes, Captain Isaac Hull and tourists at Navy Yard.

130

However, since 1897, apart from a 22,000-mile voyage in 1921, she leaves her berth only on July 4 when tugs pull her into the harbor where she fires her cannons in joy rather than in anger.

Further insight into the *Constitution* and life aboard her can be gained by visiting the **Constitution Museum**, about 600 yards east of the mooring. Between the two, and a couple of hundred yards to the south, the sleek, grey World War II destroyer *USS Casin Young DD-793* can also be visited. Although she was built in California 14 sister-ships were launched in the Charlestown Yard during World War II; at that time, it employed 50,000 workers who constructed 141 ships and serviced 5,000 others.

Rest those weary feet in the wardroom of the **Boston Marine Society**, just beyond the Constitution Museum. The two main purposes of this Society, formed in 1741 by Boston sea captains, was to start a "box" – it can still be seen and still functions – to provide assist-ance to members and their families in times of distress and "to make navigations more safe." Even today, the Society appoints the Pilot Commissioners who, in turn, appoint the Boston Harbor pilots. The Museum's two rooms are rich in paintings, models of ships (including those great clippers built across the harbor in East Boston at the yard of Donald McKay), and much nautical memorabilia.

Outside the Navy Yard, at its west end, stands the **Bunker Hill Pavilion**. It presents an excellent wrap-around show, *The Whites of Their Eyes*, which owes its title to the command given to the American army at the battle of Bunker Hill not to shoot "'til you see the whites of their eyes."

A "ragtag and bobtail" army: And so to Breed's Hill where, in Monument Square, a 221-foot high granite obelisk (the **Bunker Hill Monument**) soars upwards from the heart of an immaculate sward the size of three or four football fields, which is surrounded by

Gentrification is the name of the game.

iron rails and pierced by four gates. This is where, although on an area probably twice as large, was fought the Battle of Bunker Hill, which actually lies about 300 yards to the north.

The cornerstone for the Monument was laid on the 50th anniversary of the battle and the Monument was dedicated in 1843. Its construction resulted in the first commercial railroad (horse-drawn) in the nation. This was required to haul the massive granite blocks from their Quincy Quarry to the Neponset River from where they were barged to Charlestown. Alongside the Monument is a small museum with several exhibits including an excellent diorama of the battle. A climb of 294 stairs leads the visitor to the top of the Monument, but the views are somewhat disappointing.

At the south part of the park, between the obelisk and the main entrance gate, the Massachussets Gate, stands a bronze statue of Colonel William Prescott who commanded the American forces at the battle.

Leave Monument Square via **Winthrop Street** and immediately enter **Winthrop Square** which, for a century, was the **Training Field** where Charlestown boys learned the art of war. From here, soldiers were sent to fight in the Revolution, the War of 1812 and the Civil War. Monuments and plaques at the north of the Square remember those who did not return. The **Old Training Field School** from 1827 at the south border of the square is now a handsome private residence.

Descend Winthrop Street for a couple of hundred yards and turn right onto **Main Street.** At Nos. 55–61 is the post-revolutionary home of Deacon Larkin, who lent Paul Revere a horse for his famous ride to Lexington. Incidentally, the horse was not returned.

Continue along Main Street. The immaculate three-story **Warren Tavern Club** at No. 105 was one of the first buildings erected after the burning of Charlestown by the British and is the oldest tavern in continuous use in Boston. It is also probably the oldest extant building in Charlestown.

Continue further on Main Street, passing handsome three-decker clapboard houses painted in a variety of hues and be surprised by an incongruous imposing French château, formerly the Charlestown Savings Bank. Beyond this and across the road is the **Phipps Street Burying Ground** where at least 100 graves are pre-1700 burials and about 10 times that number are pre-1800 burials. This, one of the three oldest cemeteries in Boston, provides the best historical record of pre-revolutionary Charlestown. This is because of a unique layout: families were buried in rectangular plots which were arranged to correspond to the locations of their homes. Although John Harvard is not buried here, a monument to the preacher was erected by Harvard graduates in 1828.

From here, it is just a couple of hundred yards to the Community College stop of the "T".

USS Constitution. Right, Bunker Hill monument.

DOWNTOWN

To walk the streets of Downtown Boston today is to walk with the ghosts of colonial settlers upon ground now shadowed by modern skyscrapers. As the centuries have passed, many street names have changed. But the streets themselves follow much the same design as they did back in the 1630s when Anne Hutchinson, the Women's Lib leader of her day, was ousted from her home on what is now School Street, or in October 1746 when the Rev. Thomas Prince of Old South Meeting House "prayed up" a hurricane that wrecked an invading force of French warships.

There's nowhere more appropriate for beginning such a walk than at **Downtown Crossing**, where **Summer** and **Washington Streets** intersect. At this spot, you are standing at the very hub of Downtown Boston – a huge bronze disc embedded in the sidewalk assures you of the fact. What the bronze plaque doesn't tell you is that South Boston is east of Downtown Boston, that East Boston is north of where you stand, and that the North End just north of Downtown Boston is south of East Boston. Also, as you stand at the center of Downtown Boston, if you move your feet a few paces to the west, Summer Street becomes Winter Street without changing its face or its direction.

Those who love the city are generally indifferent to Downtown's directional peculiarities. They are more concerned with the unique aspects of its personality, such as the assured presence of the friendly horses of the city's mounted police during snowy Christmas holidays at Downtown Crossing.

Bargain basement: As for other things unique – well, right there at Downtown Crossing, just at your elbow, is the entrance to the internationally popular **Filene's Basement**. Its clientele has ranged from royalty to rag ladies, from Presidents to peons, all drawn by its system of bargain-slashing, each hoping to outwit, outwait or outgrab the other at the correct instant for a sensational bargain. An $800 Brooks Brothers suit goes on sale in the Basement at $400; if unsold after seven days, it's $200; after 14 days, $100; after 21 days, $50. After that, if it's still ungrabbed, it is donated to charity. Fun shopping? Sometimes it's a riot.

Sharing Summer Street with Filene's is the flagship store of the **Jordan Marsh** chain. This outfit had its beginning on a frosty morning in 1851 when young Eben Dyer Jordan made his first sale in his newly-opened shop – one yard of red silk ribbon, sold to a little girl for two cents. This was a big deal for a man who had sailed down from Maine five years earlier with just $1.25 in his pocket. It was also to become a big deal for the evolution of American department stores, many of which followed the Jordan Marsh formula to success.

By contrast with that commercial

coup, Boston's financiers today handle transactions of mega-millions. Although not nearly as important as New York in general financial transactions, Boston has carved out for itself some special niches. Mutual funds, in which it still leads the field, began here in 1925 and, nearly a century earlier, the concept of venture capital, which still thrives here, was introduced in Boston. Many families and institutions throughout the nation depend on conservative Boston firms, hidden in unobtrusive offices, to handle their trust funds.

The financial neighborhood reaches roughly from **Federal** and **High Streets** near the waterfront to **Franklin** and **State Streets** near **Post Office Square** on the north. This part of Downtown, especially State Street, is a superb architectural sampler where the visitor can observe a wide variety of styles. Step into **Exchange Place**, **Church Green Building**, **One International Place** and **75 State Street** and gawk at their glorious marble halls.

Back in the early 1900s, the architectural symbol of Boston's Financial District was the then-new 495-foot **Custom House Tower**; it rose like an obelisk in **McKinley Square** where **India Street** intersects State Street. In those days, the tower not only dominated the waterfront skyline but its presence also sparked and dominated considerable hot argument among style-conscious financiers, some of whom applauded the tower, some of whom loathed it. The original Custom House, it seems, had been a thing of true beauty, designed by the architect Ammi B. Young. When dedicated in 1847, it was a superlative example of Greek Revival architecture, featuring Doric granite columns and a graceful dome: a building of classic lines and proportion.

But then in 1913–15, along came the firm of Peabody & Stearns with a commission to reshape the structure with a fresh and more practical design. They proceeded to top the columns and the dome with an additional 30 floors of

The Central artery bisects downtown.

office space crowned by decorations that included winged beasts, scrolls and a huge clock face. The result still provokes occasional architectural disputes, but whether for good or ill, the old structure has now lost its mission and is dwarfed by towering new buildings. Meanwhile, the top of the tower has become a favorite nesting place for peregrine falcons. They do some of their best swooping over the deep canyons of the tall counting houses.

Visit, in this part of town, **185 Franklin Street** to view the re-assembled attic from nearby Court Street from where, on June 3, 1875, Alexander Graham Bell sent speech sounds over a wire electrically. The telephone was born. On display here are the world's first telephone switchboard and the world's first commercial telephone.

Elsewhere, much of Downtown Boston has changed or disappeared during the past half-century. The famed Boston Wool District, with its firm links to Australia and to New England textile mills, has dwindled to a mere shadow, nearly wiped out in the Depression of the 1930s. The same applies to the downtown Leather District, crippled by the emigration and death of the New England shoe industry.

From Downtown Crossing, walking south along Washington Street toward **Kneeland**, you soon pass on the right the site of the old **Adams House** and restaurant of the same name. This was once a terminal stop on the early Boston–Hartford–New York stage coach route. Passing **Avery Street** on the right, you arrive next at the seedy remnants of the **Combat Zone**, which until recently was one of the sleaziest and most notorious enclaves of commercial vice on the East Coast. Thanks to public outrage and the demands of civic leaders, it has been politically garroted to near extinction. Most of the topless bars and sex pockets have been wiped out. Little remains.

Alongside the Combat Zone (and gradually absorbing its streets and al-

Sunset on the Customs' House tower.

leys) is Boston's colorful **Chinatown**, guarded at its eastern gateway, diagonally across **Atlantic Avenue** from **South Station**, by a looping arch and an ornate pair of stone dragon dogs. Chinatown, whose main drag is **Beach Street**, is not very large but is packed with oriental restaurants and exotic stores that draw thousands of tourists and regulars nightly from the abutting Theater District on Tremont Street and the hotels to the west. It's great fun to visit but not much fun for the residents who throng its sidewalks and stores.

On leaving Chinatown and turning right on Kneeland, one steps immediately onto **Stuart Street**. This takes the visitor past the **New England Medical Center** on the left. But meanwhile it may not be easy to walk past **Jake Wirth's** old-time dark-and-sudsy restaurant on the right. Here generations of newsmen, theater people and artists have relished the dark brew and brauschweitz, served by white-aproned waiters. It's a place that never changes.

Stuart's next step is to intersect with **Tremont Street** in the heart of the **Theater District**. Here a turn to the right takes one almost immediately to **Allen's Alley**, honoring the wry and witty comedian Boston's Fred Allen, who left his imprint on most aspects of show business, from burlesque to musical revue, and from New York radio to Hollywood television. Allen loved his Boston. As he once remarked: "California is a great place to live – if you're an orange."

Proceeding north, with Boston Common on the left, Tremont Street passes West Street, Temple Place and St Paul's Cathedral on the right and arrives at **Winter Street**. Part way down Winter, towards Downtown Crossing, lies **Winter Place**, a narrow alley leading to the elegant and perenially popular **Lock-Ober's Restaurant**, home of delightful servings of scrod and lobster, and of many a clandestine dinner in the small dining rooms upstairs.

To continue up Tremont is to come **Chinatown.**

quickly to **School Street** on the right. At the corner of School and Tremont is the venerable **Parker House Hotel**, where Charles Dickens conducted literary seminars and where Ho Chi Minh waited on table. Awaiting us down School Street is a truly rich mix of Downtown Boston's notable past, which we shall explore in short order. But first our route calls for a visit to nearby **Government Center**.

Honky-tonk no more: Here, just one block up the street, Tremont intersects **Court Street** and comes to an end. Now we are standing at what used to be the entrance to **Scollay Square**. Over there to the left was the Old Howard burlesque theater, the stage-home of such show-stoppers as Ann Corio, Jimmy Durante and Sliding Billy Watson. Off to the right was the Crawford House, where dancer Sally Keith nightly twirled her two top tassels in opposite directions, openly defying the laws of physics. Helter-skelter, here and there across this once-grimy and magnetic

acreage, were tattoo parlors, fortune tellers, gypsy palmists, cheap gin mills, snap-photo joints, hash houses, Joe & Nemo hot dogs, and whatnot.

This is all remembered with nostalgia by generations of college students, traveling salesmen, suburban sightseers, vacationing Walter Mittys, and especially by sailors from the ships of all the world's great navies, who ganged into Scollay Square to start many a rousing conflict of their own.

But then, by 1960, along came urban renewal. In rumbled the bulldozers to level not only Scollay Square but the entire residential West End. Scollay Square suddenly became the new squeaky-clean Government Center. The planners wiped out almost every physical vestige of the past. They created an emptiness fanning out from Court Street and called it **City Hall Plaza** – a delightful place for those who like acres of dull bricks unrelieved by shrubbery or trees. They built **New City Hall**, a grotesque pile of niches, grot-

eft, Estonian native dress t Quincy market which s (right) a reat place or a snack.

toes, squares and holes, described by much of the Boston press as "the ugliest pigeon coop in the world."

Just beyond the brick-laid plaza – sadly without a fountain – rises the **John F. Kennedy Federal Office Building**, ready to provide help on income taxes, Social Security and assorted other problems. But you don't have to be a local Presidential product to get a Boston building named after you. Former Speaker of the House John McCormack of South Boston, for example, was honored in the naming of the Center's new Post Office and Custom House Building. Another former Speaker, Thomas "Tip" O'Neill of neighboring Cambridge, has his name on the new **Federal Office Building**, across the way on **Causeway Street**.

Returning to the corner of Tremont and School streets, we arrive at **King's Chapel**, an early stop on Boston's Freedom Trail. The Chapel had its origins in the 1680s when Britain's King James II made a colossal political blun-der by sending to Boston a clergyman whose job was to install in the town the very thing the Puritans had hated and fled: a branch of the Church of England.

The Rev. Robert Ratcliffe's welcome upon arrival in Boston was a loud roar of protest. This bothered him not one whit, and since he had no church in which to hold services he teamed with the royal colonial governor, Sir Edmund Andros, to usurp the church the Puritan-Congregationalists were using, the Old South Meeting House.

Finally in 1688, Andros seized a piece of land belonging to a Sir Isaac Johnson, and there the original King's Chapel, a wooden structure, was built in 1689. This was replaced in 1754 by the present structure, built of granite blocks ferried from Quincy 8 miles to the south. The dedication was attended by hundreds of crown-hating locals who hurled garbage, manure and dead animals at the presiding Anglicans.

Next to the Chapel, on Tremont Street, is Boston's first cemetery,

Financial district with eclectic architecture.

THE FREEDOM TRAIL

The Freedom Trail was born in 1951 and, in 1974, part of it became Boston's National Historical Park. Although its individual attractions are several centuries older it was only in 1951 that William Greenough Schofield (a contributor to this book) suggested that the sites that make up the trail be linked in a numbered sequence. Until then, according to Schofield, "tourists were going berserk, bumbling around and frothing at the mouth because they couldn't find what they were looking for. Nobody knew where anything was nor how to get there."

Now the route, officially a National Recreational Trail, consists of 16 sites which are linked by red bricks or a painted red line: all played a part in the Colonial and Revolutionary history of Boston. The trail begins at the Visitor Information Booth at the Common. It climbs to the State House and next goes downhill to the Park Street Church and the Granary Burial Ground and then crosses the road to King's Chapel and its burial ground. Next, it goes through the heart of downtown passing the Benjamin Franklin Statue, the Old Corner Book Store, the Old South Meeting House, the Old State House, the Boston Massacre site and Faneuil Hall.

Something of a hiatus then occurs until the North End is reached with Paul Revere's House, the Old North Church, and Copp's Hill Burying Ground. From here it is about 1 mile across the mouth of the Charles River to the *USS Constitution* and the Bunker Hill Monument. (There is no red line between the last two sites.)

Free guided tours (allow 45 minutes) are available at the State House and at the *Constitution* where long, long lines are often the order of the day. Park Rangers are on hand at the Old State House, Faneuil Hall and the Bunker Hill Monument. Admission is charged at Paul Revere's House and at the Old South Meeting House.

The trail, about 3 miles long, takes visitors through varied neighborhoods: the "Old Boston" of Beacon Hill; the Italian community in the North End and the Irish community in Charlestown. The average visitor spends at least half-a-day walking the trail but distractions are many and it is possible to spend two or three days strolling along the red line and making occasional and intriguing detours.

Ranger-led tours, lasting 90 minutes, leave frequently from the National Park Visitors Center at 15 State Street. These cover six of the 16 sites: Old South Meeting House, Old State House, Boston Massacre site, Faneuil Hall, Paul Revere's House and Old North Church.

The commentaries are informative and accurate and the remarks of tourists often amusing. One elderly lady asked why the settlers had to follow the red line to get where they were going. "I suppose the British made them do it," suggested a friend. "No wonder they had a revolution," said the old lady. Another tourist enquired if the Charles River was extremely shallow. "Not at all," replied the Ranger at which point the visitor wondered how Paul Revere "rode" across it. Yet another tourist was disappointed at failing to see Lincoln's Tomb.

Those too indolent to walk or who fear that, in spite of the red line, they will get lost, can board one of the trolleys operated by three companies for a 90-minute, 6-mile swing through Beacon Hill, Back Bay, Chinatown, Charlestown and Downtown. The companies, although in hot competition, do not attempt to sell these excursions as Freedom Trail Tours but they do pass close to most of the sites and passengers may alight as often as they wish and then re-board a later trolley.

On these pseudo-trolley tours the aim of the commentary is to entertain rather than to instruct and inaccuracies are not uncommon. Passengers are invited to believe that Duke Ellington was a student at Berklee College of Music; that Harvard College was originally called Emmanuel College; that General Hooker, whose statue stands outside the State House, gave his name to the oldest profession. None of these statements is true. One guide informed his audience that a movement was afoot to have Charles Street designated as a National Historical Monument; the fact is that all Beacon Hill (of which Charles Street is part) was so designated many years ago.

King's Chapel Burying Ground, in use from 1630 to 1796. The Bay Colony's first Governor, John Winthrop, was buried here in 1649. The monument at the corner of the burying ground honors a French naval adjutant, Chevalier de St Sauveur, chamberlain to the French king's brother, Count d'Artois. St Sauveur was killed by a Boston mob in September 1778 while ashore buying food for his shipmates.

Moving a few yards down School Street, on the left we come to the site of the first school in America. This was the original Boston Latin School, which opened its doors to pupils in 1635, and accounts for the naming of School Street when it was laid out in 1640.

Old City Hall rises in the immediate background here, a massive pile of granite columns, balconies and window ledges. Built for politics, it now features a restaurant and office space; in its forecourt is a bronze statue of Benjamin Franklin, with pedestal tablets chronicling the important events of his life.

A few more yards down the slope and we come to the intersection of School and Washington Streets. And here on the left is one of Downtown Boston's most loved and best preserved colonial structures, the **Old Corner Book Store**. Originally on this site stood the home of the celebrated and courageous Anne Hutchinson. She lived here from 1634 to 1638 when she was banished from town by colonials who objected to her principles of free speech. In exile, she was killed by Mohawk Indians.

The big Boston fire of October 3, 1711, destroyed Anne's cottage. It was replaced by the present structure in 1712, and through the years has served as an apothecary shop, a dry goods store, a private residence, and in 1828 became the home of a book store and publishing house – with printing press driven by teams of Canadian horses. In the Golden Age of American Literature this was a popular browsing place for the likes of Whittier, Emerson, Stowe, Alcott and other distinguished writers.

Entertainmen which can be exhausting, abounds at Quincy marke

By the 1960s it had become a pizza parlor, from which level it was rescued and restored by its present owners, the Boston Globe company.

At this point we cross Washington Street to the juncture of Spring Lane and turn right. A walk of only a few yards brings us to one of the most important forum locations in the growth of American independence, **Old South Meeting House**. The land on which Old South was built was originally a sloping cornfield and potato patch owned and tilled by Governor Winthrop. When he died, it was taken over by a preacher, John Norton, whose widow Mary offered it to her neighbors in 1663 as a church site. The grateful parishioners quickly built themselves a Meeting House of oak and cedar-board which served them for over 60 years.

One of the more important events that took place at Old South occurred on a bitterly cold, blizzardy, midwinter morning. This was the baptism of a squawking baby named Benjamin Franklin, born just around the corner on Milk Street. As a parish pastor later described it: "This little quivering mass of flesh, hardly a day old, was carried across the wintry street to be baptized on January 6, 1706, the parents evidently thinking that the midwinter climate here was less to be dreaded than the climate in the other world."

In March of 1727, the old wooden structure was pulled down and replaced by a beautiful new church of brick and mortar, styled after the graceful London churches of Sir Christopher Wren. New Old South, dedicated on April 26, 1730, was destined for a place in American annals as the most important Meeting House in American colonial history. Here was the scene of scores of protest meetings denouncing British taxation, the Stamp Act, the presence of British troops, the Townshend Acts.

Ultimately, on the night of December 16, 1773, it was the launching pad for the crowd of enraged Bostonians who stormed out to overrun Griffin's Wharf

ity Hall
Плаza
oncert.

and stage the Boston Tea Party. Early in the Revolution, the Redcoats turned Old South into a stable and riding school for the horses of the Queen's Light Dragoons. George Washington corrected that situation in March 1776.

Turning back now on Washington Street, we pass Spring Lane and Water Street on the right and arrive next at the intersection with State Street, and there stands the **Old State House**, which was the seat of colonial government.

Since 1632, in the Pudding Lane–King Street–Crooked Lane area (now **Congress Street**) there had been stocks and pillory, a whipping post and a thatched-roof church of sorts. And here in 1658, the Bostonians built their first official Town House, headquarters for royal rulings and for demonstrations for and against hanging Captain Kidd for piracy. The great fire of 1711 burned the place flat, but within two years the colonists rebuilt with a larger brick structure. On December 9, 1747, another great fire gutted the building and de-stroyed valuable town records (plus thousands of bottles of wine) but left the brick walls standing, as they are today. The walls even survived the horrendous conflagration of 1872, which leveled most of Downtown Boston's center.

It was in this building on December 16, 1761, that James Otis delivered his impassioned outburst against the Writs of Assistance. And it was here on the night of March 5, 1770, that a group of citizens got into a hostile shouting match with British soldiers, on King Street just outside the east wall. Belligerent colonists swelled the crowd on one side, Redcoat reinforcements rushed in on the other. Rocks and snowballs filled the air, bayonets clanged, somebody fired a shot, and thus was born the **Boston Massacre**. Five colonists including one black, Crispus Attucks, were killed. Today, alongside the Old State House wall, a ring of cobblestones marks the site where they fell, in the very shadow of the courtyard.

Bostonians hold a warm affection for this storied old building. It still displays the Lion and Unicorn symbols of British dominion. It still features the white balcony where the Declaration of Independence was first read to the citizens of Boston. Across the road at 15 State Street is the **National Park Visitor Center** from where guided walking tours of the Freedom Trail begin.

From the rear of the Old State House, going north on Congress Street to the rear of **New City Hall**, an open turn to the right leads to the Faneuil Hall–Quincy Market complex. Here, fronted by a statue of Sam Adams, stands **Faneuil Hall**, designated by James Otis as "The Cradle of Liberty."

Faneuil Hall, built for the commercial benefit of Boston's merchants, was personally financed by young Peter Faneuil, whom John Hancock labeled "the topmost merchant in all the town." It was dedicated on September 10, 1742, in the hurly-burly action of **Dock Square**, which had market stalls on all four sides – waterfront, fish market, hay

Old State House.

market and sheep market. From the day of its opening, it became a forum for the raw opinions of rebels and patriots from Sam Adams to Paul Revere. In 1806, the hall was expanded by the architect Charles Bulfinch. It is still in demand as a forum for oratory and opinion.

Main attraction: Adjacent to Faneuil Hall is the marketplace of that name, a vibrant, contemporary, urban spot redolent with history. **Quincy Market**, as it is often called, was constructed in 1826 and served for almost 150 years as a retail and wholesale distributive center for meat and produce. By the mid-1950s the entire area had become extremely seedy and plans were afoot for its demolition. Fortunately, re-cycling came to be the word and the market was renovated to its former glory – leading, it is claimed, to the resurgence of urban marketplaces throughout the nation.

The market consists of three long buildings. The center one is of granite with a Doric colonnade at either end and a dome and rotunda in the center. Tree-lined malls separate this building from two longitudinal side buildings which are built mainly of brick. The ground floor of the main building bulges with more than 40 foodstalls while the upper floor has several somewhat more formal restaurants. More than 100 retail stores compete for your money in the lateral buildings, which also house a number of restaurants. These include **Durgin Park**, which has been here since the 1830s. Its waitresses are famed for harassing and insulting patrons, who appear to love the treatment.

A lively flower market adds further color, as do many charming wooden push-carts from which peddlers sell their wares, most of which please tourists. Entertainers – jugglers and clowns, musicians and magicians – perform regularly. Little wonder that **Faneuil Hall Market** is now one of the major tourist attractions, not only in Boston, but throughout the nation, and is visited during summer by more than 50,000 people a day.

Shopping carts abound at Quincy market.

Immediately to the west of the north building is a handkerchief-size park containing two bronze life-size likenesses – one seated, one standing – of James Michael Curley. The shine on the seated statue's knee suggests that many visitors like to perch there.

North from here on **Union Street** leads immediately to the **Union Oyster House**, or **Ye Olde Oyster House** – whichever you prefer to call it. This may date back to the origin of the street itself in 1636, and was specifically mentioned in a plan of 1708.

The building housed the *Massachusetts Spy* newspaper from 1771 to 1775. It then became the headquarters for Ebenezer Hancock, brother of John Hancock and paymaster for the Continental Army. It was the temporary home of Louis Philippe, later ruler of France (1830–48). He eked out his exile in Boston by teaching French to students in his second-floor bedroom. As for the oyster angle, one legend is that the place sometimes served up 35 barrels of Cape Cod oysters a day, with Daniel Webster regularly downing six oysters per glass of brandy – and he drank several of the latter.

Ebenezer Hancock lived in the neighboring house owned by his brother John; it is just a few steps along and to the right, on **Salt Lane**. The city's oldest brick house, it dates back to 1660 when it was owned by Boston's first Town Crier, William Courser.

Here, where Marsh Lane, Salt Lane and Creek Square intermingle, is the **Blackstone Block** where three centuries of architecture can be found. And here, at Salt Lane corner, sits the **Boston Stone**, a huge stone ball and a stone trough, shipped from England in 1700 to serve as a paint mill. While grinding out oil and pigment, it also was established for more lasting use as the Zero Stone – that point from which all distances from Boston were measured.

Most citizens were unimpressed; they weren't planning to leave Downtown Boston anyway.

Al fresco dining at Quincy market.

148

AN ARCHITECTURAL HODGEPODGE

Boston is a living architectural museum peopled with devoted and caring curators, not all of whom are architects. However, the city does have three schools of architecture and, in Charles Bulfinch and Henry Hobson Richardson, Boston produced two of the nation's greatest architects. Frenzied brouhahas are generated by the height of a new building, by alterations or by changing the color to an existing one, and neighborhood committees defend to the last ditch the integrity of their territory. Witness the sidewalk sit-down of Brahmin matrons when the brick sidewalks of Beacon Hill were to be replaced with asphalt. About 7,000 of the city's 120,000 buildings have been designated as historic landmarks.

Boston's buildings, as its citizens know, are as essential to the character of "the Hub" as are the legendary figures of its illustrious past. Each generation has left its mark which, as time passes and as preservationists are heard, becomes more indelible. Although show-stopping buildings are evident, the city's architecture is mainly conservative and cohesive, building on the past, often returning to English precedents and often employing that old Boston friend, the brick.

Certain parts of the city have suffered from failed attempts at urban renewal, which consisted in bulldozing and constructing inhumanly scaled developments, but much of old Boston survives. It is a walker's city, and its architectural delights require an observant eye. They lie in doorways, details, and handsome ensembles in which the whole is greater than the sum of the parts.

Little survives from the early days of the settlement but the wooden Paul Revere house has been restored to its original state and is typical of its time. Although the Puritans would have preferred to have left pomp and pretension in England, the Loyalists and their Colonial Governor could see no reason why a provincial capital should not be as comfortable as London and, as the city became prosperous, its architecture became more monumental. There appeared first Georgian and then, from the drawing board of Bulfinch and Asher Benjamin, brick Federalist buildings, some of which survive on Beacon Hill.

The Greek War of Independence fueled a "Greek mania" which swept the city. Alexander Parris, a follower of Bulfinch, designed Quincy Market and St Paul's in the form of severe Greek temples. The Custom House, designed a few years later by Ammi Young, is in the form of a Greek Doric temple. The use of granite slabs enhanced the monumentality of these buildings and was harbinger of the unique "Boston granite style" which is seen in many buildings, some recycled, along the waterfront.

Brick bowfronted houses, which Bulfinch introduced, are undoubtedly Boston's most characteristic structure. These stand on Beacon Hill, the Back Bay and the South End and, with their undulating facades, create handsome, uniform blocks. French culture was much admired in Boston in the second half of the 19th century and many of these houses, especially in the Back Bay, are topped by mansard roofs which create a vague French ambience.

Another 19th-century legacy are clapboard triple-decker houses, sometimes referred to as Irish battleships, which are especially found in the Streetcar Suburbs such as South and East Boston and Dorchester. Their survival in Boston long after they had disappeared in other parts of the nation was the result of lenient fire laws. .

Significant, and a joy to behold, is the integration of new architecture into old structures. Graham Gund, a Boston-born architect, has been especially successful in this realm – for example, his Church Court condominium units in the Back Bay. Modern apartments, echoing architectural details found in older townhouses in the immediate vicinity, have been melded with a late 19th-century puddingstone Gothic Revival church. Exchange Place, where a skyscraper tower sheathed in glass is impeccably married to a rustic pink granite facade by a five-story climate-controlled greenhouse-atrium, is an exciting downtown example of compromise between preservationists and developers. Other downtown examples abound and lead to an animated skyline rather than to one of flat-topped boxes.

THE WATERFRONT

From its earliest days Boston was a busy seaport and, indeed, until the second half of the 19th century, was the busiest port in the nation. Its apogee was reached in the middle of that century when, it was said, 15 vessels entered and left the harbor every day of the year. Then, warehouses and counting houses occupied a dozen wharves at which clippers, "the highest creation of artistic genius in the Commonwealth," unloaded and loaded their cargoes.

These included baubles for Indians on the Pacific coast who traded sea otter pelts with the Chinese in return for silk. Tea was despatched all over the world. Sugar and molasses from the Barbados and Jamaica were made into rum, then bartered for slaves in Africa.

In the second half of the 19th century the port went into decline, a process hastened when, in 1878, the construction of Atlantic Avenue severed the finger-like piers from the rest of the city. With the building in the 1950s of the Expressway, which, mile for mile, was then the most expensive stretch of road ever built in the country, Boston finally turned its back on its patrimony.

Waterfront revival: Then, in the 1960s, with the restoration of Quincy Market and Faneuil Hall and the building of City Hall Plaza, the resurrection began. Abandoned warehouses on dilapidated, rickety wharves were transformed into condominiums. Berths once occupied by barques and brigantines became home to elegant cabin cruisers and sleek sloops, many belonging to those living in the condominiums. Offices and hotels, restaurants and museums were also built and the population of longshoremen, truckmen, and Irish laborers was replaced with realtors, lawyers and tourists. The waterfront has regained its excitement.

Leave the Quincy-Faneuil carnival, cross under the Expressway and imme-

diately enter **Columbus Park**, a small grassy sward with the **Rose Kennedy Rose Garden** and a children's playground. A trellised walkway leads to the waterfront which, at this point, has been landscaped into a romantic area of cobblestones, bollards and anchor chains. On the left stretches **Commercial Wharf** with a granite warehouse in which the second set of sails for the *USS Constitution* was made. It has been recycled into condominiums with a mansard, for which Bostonians have such a predilection.

The best example of a recycled warehouse stands behind you on the far side of **Atlantic Avenue**. The **Mercantile Wharf Building,** originally twice its present length, is constructed of rough Quincy granite ashlar blocks and is the masterpiece of Boston Granite Style. Those interested in architecture will wish to continue along **Richmond Avenue**, at the north side of this building, and then immediately turn right onto **Fulton Street** to see the

McLauthlin Building, the first cast-iron building in New England. This five-story 19th-century jewel has delicate rounded arched windows separated by subtle pilasters and each level is separated by a string course. Its perfect, repetitive rhythm is marred only by the upper level.

From here, a right turn on **Lewis** leads back to **Atlantic Avenue** which very soon becomes **Commercial Street**. Proceed northwards past **Lewis** and **Union Wharves**, both of which have gentrified, granite warehouses. Enthusiastic sailors might wish to make for the **Boston Sailing Club** at the end of Lewis Wharf where an excellent fleet of boats awaits them. (Minimum membership is one month.)

When the **Pilot House**, on the north side of this wharf, was being renovated in 1972, a false floor was discovered, fuelling speculation that the building may have been used not only by pilots but also by opium smugglers. More grisly was the finding of two embracing skeletons in the basement of **Usher House**, which stood on this wharf and which was demolished in 1880. This prompted the claim that the skeletons were those of the sailor and the young wife of an elderly man about whom Edgar Alan Poe wrote in his macabre novel *The Fall of the House of Usher*.

Granite is replaced by red brick on the next wharf, **Lincoln**, where a massive red building with magnificent rounded arched windows covering five stories has been recycled into apartments. The north side of Lincoln Wharf is bounded by **Battery Street**, whose name gives the clue to the fact that here, in 1646, the **North Battery** was built in order to command the entrance to the inner harbor and the Charles River. It was from here that, in 1776, British troops were ferried to Charlestown to take up their positions in the battle of Bunker Hill. Battery Wharf is now the home of **Bay State Lobster**, the place to see the "real thing before it's red."

Immediately beyond this, on the site

Live in a condominium with your yacht at your doorstep.

now occupied by the **Coastguard**, once stood **Hartt's Naval Yard** where the *USS Constitution* was built and launched in 1797.

A free outdoor swimming pool just beyond this, the northern extremity of wharfland, awaits those who are hot and tired. Others might wish to proceed on an immaculate waterfront esplanade to the **Charlestown Bridge** which, after about a mile, leads to Charlestown. To continue an exploration of the waterfront, return to Columbus Park.

Immediately to the south of the Park is **Long Wharf**. When built in 1710, it was, if not one of the wonders of the world, at least the wonder of the region. The wharf, which had roots near the Customs House, stretched out into the harbor for almost 2,000 feet. It was here, in 1790, that the *Columbia Rediviva*, the first American ship to sail around the world and the first to participate in the China trade, berthed after her 35-month, almost 50,000-mile voyage. And from here, in 1819, the first missionaries for Hawaii departed and in 1895, Joshua Slocum set off aboard the *Spray* on the first-ever one-man voyage around the world which lasted 38 months. Would Nathaniel Hawthorne – who, in his capacity as a customs officer, often visited the wharf – still write: "Long Wharf is devoted to ponderous, evil-smelling, inelegant necessaries of life"?

Gaze out from the beautiful esplanade at the end of the wharf to North Boston and to the planes taking off from Logan airport. These are the successors to the flying clippers which Donald McKay built on land now occupied by the airport. Mackay's clippers, epitomized by the *Flying Cloud*, were the fastest and most beautiful sailing ships ever to fly the stars and stripes. Boats for Provincetown, the Charlestown Navy Yard and the Harbor Islands depart from Long Wharf.

The Harbor Islands: Scattered about the 50 square miles of the harbor are 30 islands. Some (**Moon, Long, Castle,**

City skyline from cruise boat.

Deer, Hog) are now connected by bridges or causeways to the mainland, and three (**Governor's**, **Apple** and the aptly named **Bird**) have become one and are now Logan Airport.

Even before the arrival of the white man, the Indians fished from and raised crops on these islands. Then, during the 18th century, they were popular resorts for Bostonians who would visit to enjoy not only the sea air but also the illicit pleasures of gambling and boxing matches. Later, the strategic importance of these islands as guardians of the city was appreciated and, over the years, forts were constructed on **Peddock** (**Fort Andrews**), **Lovells** (**Fort Standish**) and **Georges** (**Fort Warren**).

Other edifices devoted to social reform – hospitals, poorhouses, reformatories and prisons – were also built. Still later, some islands were used for the disposal of sewage and other wastes while others fell into desuetude.

However, some islands still remain for the sybarite and seven of them constitute the **Boston Harbor Islands State Park**. Georges, with its massive and practically intact Fort Warren, where Confederate prisoners were housed if not in luxury at least in comfort, is the **Park Headquarters** and the kingpin of the group. (The voyage from Long Wharf to Georges Island takes 45 minutes.) From Georges, during the summer months, free water-taxis serve **Gallops**, **Lovells**, **Peddocks**, **Bumpkin** and **Grape Islands**. **Great Brewster** is a bit more difficult to reach.

These islands will scarcely satisfy the beach-bum or the swimmer (Lovells is best for these pursuits) but, with their nature trails, wild plants and birds, they should bring joy to nature lovers and will certainly appeal to the fisherman and the historian. All provide superb views of the city skyline and, as one expects of any decent archipelago, they harbor buried pirate treasure (Lovells) and ghosts (Georges).

Great Brewster, most rugged of the

four Brewsters, offers magnificent panoramas of the inner harbor, the Atlantic and the **Boston Light** which stands on **Little Brewster**. The lighthouse, built in 1716, was the first in the nation but the building which you can visit (occasional excursions) was constructed only in 1782 after the British had blown up the original before departing Boston in 1776. The lighthouse, a National Historic Landmark, is the only one in the nation still manned by keepers. The war of 1812 again found the British in the harbor and, near the light, the British ship *Shannon* engaged the American frigate *Chesapeake*. The British won the battle but not immortality: that went to Captain James Lawrence of the *Chesapeake* with his command: "Don't give up the ship!"

Fish, chips and tea: Back on the mainland, Long Wharf on its south side joins with the vestigial remains of **Central Wharf**, built according to Bulfinch's plans in order to accommodate the overflow of the China trade. The wharf is now home to the **New England Aquarium**, which is fronted by an always busy plaza. Impossible to miss the aquarium for, in the plaza, high in the air, a bright red sculpture, *Echo of the Waves*, slowly rotates. In the center of the plaza water flows through a large basin, at the bottom of which stands a bronze sculpture, *Dolphins of the Sea*. Immediately to the left of the aquarium entrance, harbor seals frolic and provide free entertainment for those too impecunious to enter the aquarium.

Nobody has told the rockhopper penguins in the enormous **Ocean Tray**, which covers most of the floor of the Aquarium, that the cold water section is their territory and that the warmer water is for the jackass penguins – and so they swim from island to island and the two groups freely intermingle.

Soaring skywards from the floor of the Ocean Tray is the giant **Ocean Tank**, the world's largest cylindrical salt-water tank, in which giant turtles, sharks, moray eels and a multitude of

snack at
oston
Harbor Hotel
t Rowes
Wharf.

other fish swim in and out of a spectacular man-made coral reef. At set times, a diver enters to feed the tank's occupants. A ramp gradually winds around the tank, ascending for four stories and providing a view of more than 70 tanks containing thousands of fish from throughout the world. A hands-on tidal pool enables small fry to become acquainted with the marine world.

The **Discovery**, a floating pavilion whose design is evocative of a Mississippi river steamer, is moored alongside the main building and contains a large theater where dolphins and sea lions show how intelligent they are. Shows are not devoted to tricks but rather, this being Boston, are educational. However, they are also entertaining. The **Voyager**, which belongs to the Aquarium, makes whale-watching cruises (see page 253: rain checks if whales not seen) with a naturalist aboard who also lectures on the harbor and its islands.

Immediately south of the Aquarium, on the stump of **India Wharf**, the horizontal has been replaced by the vertical. On the site of a four-story Bulfinch building that stretched for hundreds of feet, two rather unattractive 40-story towers now soar skyward. They were designed by I.M. Pei, the Sino-American architect educated at Harvard and MIT. It says much for Boston that the giant minimal stainless-steel sculpture which occupies the space in the angle formed by the towers has not been vandalized.

Next comes **Rowe's Wharf**, entered through a monumental, gold and russett post-modern six-story arch. The **Boston Harbor Hotel** stands where formerly stood the South Battery, built in 1666, and then warehouses. The wharf, no longer busy with clippers and barques, is now the terminal for sleek commuter craft that serve the south shore and Logan airport. Some harbor cruises also depart from here.

Continue on Atlantic Avenue for about 600 yards, then turn left onto **Congress Street Bridge**. Here, on a short wharf attached to the bridge, stands the **Tea Party Exhibit** which consists of a small museum and the **Beaver II** moored at a wharf alongside the museum. The *Beaver II*, a Danish brig built in 1908, has similar lines to the *Beaver*, the smallest of the three tea ships which moored at Griffins Wharf on that fateful December evening in 1773 when a band of patriots disguised as Mohawk Indians boarded the ships and threw all their tea – 340 chests containing 90,000 pounds of the leaf – into the harbor. This was the famous act of defiance against the British Crown for having imposed taxes without granting representation. (**Griffins Wharf** stood about 300 yards northwest from the exhibit and is remembered by a plaque set in the walls of a commercial building at the foot of **Pearl Street**.)

On leaving the Tea Party Exhibit, turn left and make for a giant, 40-foot high milk bottle, a vintage lunch stand from the 1930s. It marks the entrance to the **Children's Museum**, the third oldest **Computer Museum**.

such attraction in the world. There's nothing elegant about this museum; occupying a former warehouse, it is a place where, apart from some dolls and their houses in glass display cases, the visitor is encouraged to touch, to push, to twist and to shove the exhibits, to blow bubbles and to clamber on suspended sculpture.

The museum also attempts to instil visitors with social conscience. A major exhibit is the Kids' Bridge, which helps children learn about other cultures and racial diversity. This learning process is furthered by a complete Japanese home, a gift from Kyoto with which Boston is twinned. Youngsters are encouraged to use wheel chairs in the "What If You Couldn't" section, whose aim is a better understanding of those with disabilities. A recycling shop sells waste material from factories and shows how to make silk purses from sows' ears.

In the **Computer Museum**, above the Children's Museum, visitors can type on a 25-foot long keyboard. This is accomplished by jumping on the keys – as hard as you like. This is no ordinary keyboard and those who wander past the 4/$ key will find themselves within a two-story desktop computer with parts blown up to 50 times their normal size. The entire evolution of computers is also on display and computer-animated films are shown in this, the world's first museum devoted to telling the story of the information revolution.

On exiting from the museums, the visitor cannot but admire the view of the densely packed new soaring skyscrapers of the **Financial District**. Turn right and reach, after 200 yards, **Northern Avenue**. Across the road is the dilapidated **Fan Pier** which, if city planners had had their way, would have been the jewel in Boston's waterfront restoration. Proceed westwards along this avenue for the **World Trade Center** and for some of the city's most popular seafood restaurants. Early risers might like to be on **Pier 4** around 6.30 a.m. when a daily fish auction is held.

Feeding penguins at the Aquarium.

BACK BAY & FENWAY

The **Back Bay** has been likened to so many different places that it's difficult to know which comparison is closest to the truth. Depending on who you ask, it is Boston's Champs Elysées, Fifth Avenue or Nob Hill. All have an element of truth, but none captures the whole.

Here are grand boulevards, stately mansions and inspiring Victorian churches. But here too are glass-plated modernism, condominium conversions and the brash consumerism of the *nouveaux riches*.

Perhaps the most accurate thing you can say about the Back Bay is that it is a product of vision. Unlike Downtown or the North End, where streets and buildings grow according to their own organic logic, the Back Bay is the result of meticulous urban planning. It is a deliberate creation, literally manufactured from the ground up. And although unified in style and proportion, it doesn't feel regimented or artificial. There always was enough room for personal whimsy to give the neighborhood a human touch.

Originally the Back Bay was exactly that – a shallow estuary that reached well beyond Columbus Avenue. In 1814, a developer, Uriah Cotting, built a dam across the bay from the Boston Common to Sewall's Point, near today's Kenmore Square. His plan was to harness the bay's tidal currents in order to power some 80 mills. Unfortunately, Cotting died before his Mill Dam was finished. In the end, there was far less tidal power than he had expected, and only a handful of mills were built.

With the tides now obstructed by the dam, the estuary became stagnant and the sewage that, until then, had always been channelled into the Back Bay began to present a problem, especially when the wind shifted east. In 1849, the mayor declared the Back Bay "offensive and injurious to the large and grow-

ing population," and after eight years of political wrangling a plan was finally approved to fill it in. The first trainload of gravel was dumped into the fetid water in 1857, and for more than 30 years a new load arrived every 45 minutes, 24 hours a day. When the project was finally completed, 450 acres of new land had been created.

Fortunately, the rush of speculation that accompanied the project was tempered with respect for quality and a concern for the public good. From the very beginning, the Back Bay was looked upon as an opportunity for Boston to take its place among the world's great cities, and there was enough public interest – and private capital – to ensure that it measured up to the proper standards.

Most people accepted that the city needed more space for parks and civic institutions, and a remarkable 40 percent of the new land was reserved specifically for these purposes. Generous though it was, there were definite limits

Preceding pages: Back Bay with, in background, Charles River Basin and Cambridge. Left, John Hancock tower. Right, one of Boston's finest.

to public beneficence. With so much at stake, there was never any question about who was in control. The Back Bay would ultimately bear the stamp of society's upper crust.

By the mid-19th century, Boston's upper class was beginning to pull away from its Puritan moorings. The Brahmins' inclination for thrift was being challenged by a new spirit of self-indulgence and worldliness and by the rise of the *nouveaux riches*. The change in attitude had a clear impact on urban planning. Unlike Beacon Hill, which was styled on the old English model, the Back Bay was influenced by the more cosmopolitan French approach. Its inspiration was the sweeping boulevards and elaborate architecture of Paris. By the time construction started, the eclectic phase of American architecture was in full swing. Architects began integrating Classical, Gothic and Renaissance motifs into their designs as each stylistic revival came in and fell out of fashion.

By 1900, construction of the Back Bay was virtually complete, and apart from a few isolated structures, it remains essentially unchanged. Today, it is perhaps the finest cache of Victorian architecture in the country and it also boasts a unique historical element. Because construction was started in the east and gradually moved west, the long streets are like a timeline chronicling the progression of styles during the latter half of the 19th century.

Mapping out the territory: Geographically, the Back Bay falls into two distinct areas. North of Boylston Street, the neighborhood is criss-crossed by a perfect grid. The cross streets are even organized in alphabetical order from Arlington to Hereford. Other than Newbury and Boylston Streets, this area is almost exclusively residential.

South of Boylston, the tidy grid gives way to the logic of public spaces. This is where the Back Bay gets "lumpy", each lump defined by a large, self-contained development. Altogether there are four:

Victorian tea dance on a swan boat.

Copley Square, Copley Place, the Prudential Center and the Christian Science Headquarters. Although several large apartment buildings stand here, the area is predominantly occupied by department stores, hotels, shops and offices.

One other section of the Back Bay stands alone: the **Public Garden**. Adjacent to the Common, it was built of landfill in 1859, some 200 years after the Common was established. Its designer was George Meacham. This lush 24-acre rectangle, probably the prettiest, most relaxing park in Boston and a perfect spot to begin a Back Bay tour, features flower beds, exotic trees and several splendid works of sculpture, including the magnificent equestrian statue of George Washington facing the Arlington Street gate.

The Garden's central attraction is the **Lagoon**, surrounded by enormous willow trees and crossed by an enchanting mock-suspension bridge. The swan boats that make lazy figure eights in the water have been operated by the same

family, the Pagets, for three generations. Don't forget to bring bread: the ducks are always hungry.

The Public Garden is fronted by an impressive line of buildings, including the **Arlington Street Church**, the **Ritz-Carlton Hotel**, the **Atlantic Monthly** and **Harbridge House**. The Arlington Street Church is perhaps the most impressive. It was the first building to be constructed in the Back Bay, and its elaborate spire and brownstone facade are a clear departure from the comely meeting houses favored by the previous generation of Bostonians. The Ritz-Carlton is generally acknowledged as the city's most prestigious hotel.

The Back Bay grid is immediately west of the Public Garden and connected to it by the **Commonwealth Avenue mall**. Originally, the four main streets in this section of the Back Bay corresponded to different levels in the social hierarchy, with the wealthiest old families residing on Beacon Street, the less affluent old families on Marl-

Winter in the Public Garden.

borough, the *nouveaux riches* on Commonwealth Avenue and the social climbers on Newbury Street. Homes were originally designed for single families and their corps of servants, but after the Great Depression of the 1930s many were subdivided into apartments or rooming houses. In the 1970s and 1980s, condominium conversions gutted the interiors even further. Recently, with a new generation of wealth moving in, more care is being taken to preserve historic details.

Today, although Commonwealth Avenue is still one of the most pleasant strolls in the city, it is the smart shops on **Newbury Street** which grab most attention. Unfortunately, **Beacon Street** attracts too much traffic to carry off its traditional reserve. **Marlborough Street**, on the other hand, in spite of a lively contingent of students, is still quiet and shady. **Boylston Street**, although having some excellent stores and side-walk cafés, lacks the ambience of the rest of the Back Bay.

A long but rewarding stroll (5 miles) takes the visitor up one avenue and down the next. Start on Beacon Street at the Garden and finish at the corner of Boylston Street and Massachusetts Avenue. En route, the observant will see many great old houses and a host of architectural styles.

The **Gibson House Museum** (137 Beacon Street) is a historic Back Bay home with original Victorian furnishings. Beacon Street also boasts the **Fuller Mansion** (No. 150), an impressive Italian Renaissance house built in 1904. Several blocks away, at the corner of Massachusetts Avenue, the **Church Court** development integrates the facade of a 19th-century church into a lively condominium complex.

Turning the corner, Marlborough Street has a number of charming Queen Anne houses including numbers 276, 257 and 245, all built between 1883 and 1884. Although Marlborough is generally more modest than the rest of the neighborhood, there are a few excep-

Magnolia time in the Back Bay.

tions. The **Cushing-Endicott House** (No.165) and the **Hunnewell Mansion** (315 Dartmouth Street) represent two very different styles but are equally grand in size and bearing. Bainbridge Bunting, in his authoritative book *Houses of Back Bay*, suggests that the latter is perhaps the most handsome house in the district.

The Back Bay comes gloriously into its own on **Commonwealth Avenue**. A shady mall which contains half-a-dozen interesting statues runs down the middle of this French-inspired almost 100-yard-wide boulevard whose openness would have been impossible in the tight quarters of old Boston. Although the houses tend to be uniform in proportion and ambience, the play of styles on "ComAve" covers more architectural ground than anywhere else in the Back Bay and tends to give the street an almost whimsical quality. Exemplifying this is No. 176–178; it has a Romanesque rusticated stone porch which supports a bay window and a bowfront

tower topped by a conical roof. The mansard on the top floor with dormer pediments is Flemish.

There are too many notable examples to list, but a representative mix includes the **Hooper Mansion** (No. 25–27), the **Ames-Webster Mansion** (306 Dartmouth Street), the **Charles Francis Adams House** (20 Gloucester Street) and the **John F. Andrew house** (32 Hereford Street). (Not unexpectedly, some of the grandest houses occupy the corners of blocks.)

Also observe, in French Second Empire style, the former **Hotel Vendôme** (No. 160), once the most prestigious hotel in the Back Bay and one at which Presidents Grant, Harrison, Cleveland and McKinley stayed. Nor should the **Burrage Mansion** (No. 314) or the **Ames Mansion** (No. 355) be missed. They are perhaps the two wildest houses on Commonwealth Avenue, each bristling with turrets, towers and Gothic ornamentation. Both are public buildings, the former being the

Much-loved swan boats in the Public Garden.

Boston Evening Clinic and the latter the administrative offices of Emerson College; they may therefore be entered and some of their former glory savored. Those with initiative can enter several other Back Bay houses such as the **Massachusetts Genealogical Society** at 99 Newbury Street.

Soaring above Commonwealth Avenue (at Clarendon) is the tower of Richardson's Romanesque **First Baptist Church**. The tower's frieze was modeled by Bartholdi (sculptor of the Statue of Liberty) in Paris and was carved by Italian workmen. The faces in it are said to be likenesses of noted Bostonians, including Longfellow, Emerson, Hawthorne and Sumner. The trumpeting angels on the corners looking down on the Back Bay have earned the building the sobriquet of "Church of the Holy Bean Blowers."

Café culture: The parade of spectacular buildings continues on Newbury Street, but for most visitors, the architecture is secondary to the galleries and boutiques that make this a haven for Boston's "beautiful people." Outdoor cafés add a certain Continental élan to Newbury Street and provide the best vantage for the young and chic to see and be seen.

However, spare a moment to glance, between Arlington and Berkeley Streets, at **Emmanuel Church**, the first Gothic Revival Church in the Back Bay. Dominating the next block is the severe gray mass of **The New England**. Its plain granite face is offset by the 236-foot spire of the Church of the Covenant, a stirring Gothic structure with original Tiffany windows and a bristling crown of peaks and gables. The magisterial structure across the street now housing **Louis, Boston** was completed in 1864 as the Museum of Natural History, the forerunner of Boston's Museum of Science.

The old **Exeter Street Theater** dominates the opposite corner like a medieval fortress. The massive Romanesque structure was built in 1884 for a

Shopping, and a break from shopping, on Newbury Street.

group of psychics known as the Working Union of Progressive Spiritualists. An account of the temple's dedication informs that an astral spirit materialized for the occasion, appearing out of nowhere in the darkened auditorium "like a column of phosphorescent light." The Temple was converted into a theater in 1913 and is now occupied by Conran's home furnishings.

The modern concrete structure at the corner of Hereford Street is the **Boston Architectural Center**. The Richard Haas *trompe-l'oeil* mural on its rear wall is a cross-section of a Renaissance duomo. The two-story buildings on the rest of the block are converted stables where Back Bay families originally kept their horses and carriages. Be sure to take a look at the surrealist "Tramount" mural near the end of the block. Beyond this, **Tower Records**, in a dramatic modern recycled building, claims to be one of the world's biggest music stores.

Shooting for the moon: Boylston

Street separates the Back Bay in two and the change in personality is evident as soon as one turns the corner. Boylston is busier and more impersonal than Newbury and, with the exception of Copley Square, its 19th-century origins have been smothered by mammonites.

The architectural *coup de grâce* was recently delivered by **Number 500**, at the eastern end of the street, a massive office building completed in 1988. The designers appear to have taken an ironic approach to the problem of relating a modern skyscraper to its old neighbors. They have transformed the simple elegance of a Palladian window – a common feature in old Boston houses – into an enormous, looming black-glass facade. The building is fronted by an equally monstrous colonnade which, again, gives it a certain ironic continuity with the classical 19th-century revival. Located in this part of Boylston are such distinguished names as Bonwit Teller, FAO Schwartz, Shreve, Crump and Low and Hermès.

The north side of the western part of the street has smaller stores and a generous helping of outdoor cafés. Set somewhat back from the south side of the street is the **Prudential Center**, a mixed project built in the late 1950s and early 1960s and about which the *Boston Globe* said at that time: "All the daring and imagination in this country today is not being spent on launching space missiles. Boston and Prudential are shooting for their own moon." The Tower Skywalk has stunning views of the city but the shopping mall below offers little of special interest and is too far removed from pedestrian traffic to be convenient for most passers-by.

The shopping is better at two large department stores – Sak's Fifth Avenue and Lord & Taylor – located on the lower plaza closer to street level. Merging with the Prudential is the spacious **Hynes Convention Center**. Across the road is the **Institute of Contemporary Art** (ICA), housed in a 19th-century Romanesque former police station.

Between the east and west sections of Boylston is **Copley Square**, one of America's most celebrated public spaces. The plaza itself is not that inviting: a late 1980s rehabilitation was entirely inadequate and left the space, if anything, in poorer shape than before.

The boldest coupling around the square is **Trinity Church** and the new **John Hancock Tower**. When I.M. Pei's plan for the Hancock Tower was unveiled, there was a fear that the giant, rhombus-shaped skyscraper would overpower Trinity Church. At 790 feet, it is the tallest building in New England, but Pei's design has an intriguing twist. Because the building is sheathed with reflective glass, it acts like an enormous mirror. In a sense, it is both conspicuous and invisible. It steals Trinity's glory, but reflects it right back.

In its first few years, the building had one other design twist, albeit unintentional. Actually, it wasn't a twist so much as a torque – a wind torque – that caused the tower's glass panels to loosen and fall. The problem was eventually fixed, but for many people the tower is still known as "the building with the falling windows."

The best way to experience the Hancock Tower is from the 60th-floor observatory. The views are spectacular, and the "Boston 1775" exhibit gives an interesting look at the city before the Back Bay was landfilled.

The Hancock Tower is an eye-catcher, but by rights Copley Square belongs to Trinity Church. With Trinity, Henry Hobson Richardson's adaptation of the Romanesque style came into full blossom. The ingenious arrangement of large-scale structures, coupled with an artful use of masonry and ornamentation, make this one of the great ecclesiastical buildings in the US. Richardson continually altered the plans while the church was being constructed and said of his winning plans: "I really don't see why the Trinity people liked them, or, if they liked them, why they let me do what I afterwards

Summer concert at Prudential Center.

did." Visit the interior, resplendent with intricate woodwork, stained-glass windows and frescoes by John La Farge. A bronze statue of the Rev. Phillips Brooks standing outside the north transept of the church is inscribed with the Bostonian's concept of the cardinal virtues: "Preacher of the Word of God/ Lover of Mankind/Born in Boston/Died in Boston."

Across the Square from Trinity Church is the **Boston Public Library**, a Renaissance Revival palace designed by Charles Follen McKim, and built between 1887 and 1895. A 1971 addition by Philip Johnson, as dignified as the original building but with a decidedly modern turn in style, fronts Boylston Street.

Explore the sumptuous interior of the old library. The **John Singer Sargent Gallery** features a series of murals that some critics rank among his most powerful work. **Bates Hall** is a cavernous barrel-vaulted reading room wrapped in marble, oak and sandstone.

And the lovely Italian courtyard cloistered in the center of the building is one of the city's most peaceful retreats and a joy for anyone who enjoys thumbing through a book in the open air.

The third side of Copley Square is occupied by the **Copley Plaza Hotel**, an elegant Renaissance-style palace where society ladies enjoy afternoon tea between 3 and 5 p.m. And finally, the beautifully ornamented, polychromatic **New Old South Church** is a Gothic gem just off Copley Square on Boylston Street. Anywhere else, it would be the center of attention, but here it is something of an afterthought. The tower, dating from 1938, is not the original but retains much of its predecessor's stones. That tower turned out to be Boston's Leaning Tower of Pisa, tilting at the rate of about an inch a year and when dismantled in 1931 had already tilted almost 3 feet.

Finishing touches: Poised at the corner of Copley Square, **Copley Place** is the newest "lump" in this section of the

Public Library.

Back Bay. One of the most controversial projects in recent years, the sprawling, 9-acre development combines retail space, offices, hotels and parking facilities. Reactions to the new complex have generally been mixed. The exterior is neither especially offensive nor attractive, although as far as shopping malls go, the interior is quite plush. The gleaming glass canopies and crisscrossing superstructure are visually exciting, and there's an interesting stone waterfall in the central atrium that adds a surprisingly restful quality. The shops – including Tiffany, Gucci, Rizzoli Book Shop, Sharper Image, Nieman Marcus, Ralph Lauren, Bally and Louis Vuitton – are clearly targeted for the high-end of the market. A glass footbridge connects Copley Place with the Prudential Center.

Adjacent to the Prudential Center is Boston's most monumental space. It was created in the early 1970s by the **Christian Science Church**. The centerpiece is a 670-foot long reflecting pool (the pool is part of the center's air-conditioning and beneath it is a garage) whose south side is always ablaze with flowers which border a stately row of linden trees. Dominating the other long side of the pool is a basilica-like structure which is a mixture of Byzantine and Italian Renaissance and a long five-story colonnaded building.

Tucked in between the two and engulfed by the basilica is the original Mother Church, a Romanesque affair with a square bell-tower and a rough granite facade. A five-story elliptical Sunday school at the southwest corner of the pool and a 28-story administrative building at the southeast complete the ensemble.

The interior of the basilica – the church annex, entered through a handsome portico of 10 limestone columns – is a glorious column-free affair which can seat 5,000 persons on three levels. The organ is the largest pipe-organ in the Western hemisphere. The Christian Science media organization is

Christian Science complex.

CHRISTIAN SCIENCE'S EMPIRE ON EARTH

In 1866 Mary Baker – she was not yet Eddy – a religious, yet scarcely conforming, Calvinist slipped on an icy sidewalk in Lynn, near Boston, and suffered serious internal injuries. Three days later, while reading about the healings of Jesus (Matthew 9, 1–8), she completely recovered.

Mary Baker devoted her next nine years to a study of the scriptures so as to better understand the divine law underlying spiritual healing and became convinced that healing is not miraculous but a natural result of speaking and thinking in accord with God's law.

These studies resulted in a metaphysical system which she named Christ Science and set forth in a booklet, published in 1875, *Science and Health, with Key to the Scriptures*. She repeatedly revised this text to make it more effective as the "textbook" for the study and practise of Christian Science. Mary Baker hoped that the Christian church would accept her "discovery" but was rebuffed and in 1879 she and 15 followers founded the Church of Christ, Scientist with the aim of reinstating "primitive Christianity and its lost element for healing." Not until the church moved from Lynn to Boston in 1882 did the movement take off.

In 1889, Mary Baker Eddy suspended all operations in order to reconstruct the church completely and, in 1892, she founded the First Church of Christ, Scientist, in Boston, the "mother" church of Christian Science which now has more than 2,600 churches in 67 countries. In 1894 the first church was opened and the next year Mary Baker Eddy published the *Church Manual*, often called the "denomination's constitution," which she continued to revise until her death.

At Christian Science Sunday services a lesson-sermon, which members are expected to have studied during the previous week, is preached from the pulpit by two elected readers. These have as their theme 26 rotating subjects such as "God," "Man," "Reality," and consist of related passages from the *Bible* and from *Science and Health*. These two books constitute the imper-

sonal dual pastor of the church. At Wednesday evening services, congregants share healing and other experiences. Those engaged in full-time healing are called Christian Science practitioners and usually charge a nominal fee.

Eddy believed that numbers are not a measure of spiritual vitality and in the *Manual* states that statistics should not be made public. However, what is known is that this very wealthy Church is an aging organization which fails to attract many new members, especially among the young, and is currently running in the red.

The Christian Science Publishing Society, the media arm of the church, is not so coy and is proud that each week it reaches through print, radio and television more than 9 million people. It all began in 1908 when Mary Baker Eddy founded the newspaper, the *Christian Science Monitor*.

The paper, which does not have a religious bias is highly respected and its writers have won five Pulitzer Prizes: yet it has not posted a profit since 1961. It circulates to 174 countries. Circulation peaked in 1970 at about 150,000; by 1990, it had fallen to about half that figure. In 1988, there appeared a completely revamped paper which, it is claimed, will lead to a revival of circulation. Also launched was a glossy monthly, the *World Monitor,* which has a circulation of 275,000.

The Mother Church became involved in radio in 1920 and today its programs are carried on more than 200 public radio stations in the US. Short-wave radio, which is beamed worldwide via five transmitters, broadcasts 20 hours a day to 145 countries. Monitor Television began in 1985 and appears on cable for 18 hours a day. Programs are relentlessly international in content and viewpoint, although the audience consists mainly of Americans who have a limited appetite for foreign news.

Television and the *World Monitor* magazine generate revenue – unlike the paper and short-wave radio, which are considered to be an "outreach to mankind." In 1989 losses of the Christian Science Publishing Society amounted to $57 million with revenues being $30 million. How long, observers wonder, can a nonprofit institution with a public service philosophy ignore the unforgiving laws of the marketplace?

housed in the classically inspired **Publishing Society Building** which contains a comfortably appointed reading room and the *mapparium*, a remarkable walk-in stained-glass globe of the world with fascinating acoustic properties.

A few steps past the Sunday School, **Symphony Hall** puts the finishing touches to the Back Bay. The modest Renaissance-style exterior isn't nearly as impressive as the magnificent interior. A young professor of physics was hired to guarantee that the hall would be acoustically perfect, and it's no exaggeration to say that there isn't a bad seat in the house. You can catch the Boston Symphony from October to April and the Boston Pops play in May and June.

Islands of activity: Beyond the Christian Science Complex, the dense-packing of the Back Bay yields to the **Fenway**, a loose collection of institutions and apartment buildings joined by the meandering path of the Back Bay Fens. Together, these islands of activity form a sort of urban archipelago that

drifts out to Brookline without any real focus or organizing theme.

The Fenway first became fashionable in the early 1900s, when the Back Bay was nearing completion. The area was especially attractive to civic and to educational institutions that had outgrown downtown quarters and were looking for a place to expand. The **Massachusetts Historical Society** moved into a grand new mansion at 1154 Boylston Street in 1899 and **Harvard Medical School** soon followed its lead. Today, the Fenway is home to several important museums and theaters, a number of major hospitals and 14 colleges, including part of the sprawling campus of Northeastern University.

The geographical focus of the area is the **Back Bay Fens**, a major link in Frederick Law Olmsted's Emerald Necklace. Unfortunately, a busy road encircles the Fens and isolates it from the surrounding neighborhood. Joggers and allotment holders still make good use of the area, but it seems to suffer from a general lack of attention.

What attracts most visitors to the Fenway are the **Museum of Fine Arts** (MFA) and the **Isabella Stewart Gardner Museum**. The former's collection, one of the world's greatest, is housed in a massive classical structure completed in 1909 and in I.M. Pei's West Wing, built in 1981. Visitors pressed for time might concentrate on the Old Kingdom Egyptian treasures; the Asiatic collection, especially the Japanese items; Impressionist paintings, especially those of Monet; the Boston school of painters (Gilbert Stuart, Sargent and Copley); and the early American silver collection, including pieces by Paul Revere.

Those wishing a breath of fresh air will enjoy strolling in the Japanese Garden where an attempt has been made to recapture the spirit of the 18th-century New England coastline.

The Isabella Stewart Gardner Museum is within easy walking distance of the Museum of Fine Arts. The Venetian

Copley Square dominated by John Hancock tower.

palace in which the museum is housed was built by Gardner for the specific purpose of displaying her art collection. Gardner moved from her Commonwealth Avenue mansion in 1903 and lived here until her death in 1924.

Her will, the last eccentric act in a long life dedicated to shocking Boston society, stipulated that everything be preserved exactly as she left it – and so it was until 1990, when an audacious break-in removed some of the treasures. However, the museum still has enough eclectic European and American items to satisfy everyone. Exceptional works include paintings and drawings by Titian, Bellini, Matisse, Botticelli, Whistler and Sargent. Heaven can be found at the center of the palace in a glorious courtyard with a Roman mosaic pavement, a skylight and, throughout the year, an abundance of flowers.

Just north of the Fens is an institution much closer to the hearts of most Bostonians: **Fenway Park**. Built in 1912, this is the smallest stadium in the major leagues and one of the oldest. Baseball legends like Ted Williams and Carl Yastrzemski played their entire careers at Fenway, but Red Sox fans have been heartbroken since 1918, the last year Boston won a World Series.

Kenmore Square is two blocks away from Fenway Park. The intersection is a major link in the city's commuter lines and is usually choked with traffic and pedestrians. Most of the square is devoted to fast-food joints and convenience stores, with a couple of used book and record shops thrown in for the students. **Boston University** stretches along Commonwealth Avenue at the western end of the square and also spills into **Bay State Road**, a quiet strip of ivy-covered townhouses.

Kenmore Square's real claim to fame, however, is the giant "**Citgo**" sign that flashes from the rooftop of a nearby building. It's the unlikeliest landmark in Boston, but after a hard-fought battle, local devotees convinced the city to give the sign protected status.

THE SOUTH END

The **South End**, not to be confused with South Boston, is that area adjacent to and to the south of the Back Bay. It is delineated by the Southwest Corridor, Berkeley Street and Harrison and Massachusetts Avenues. This area, where land fill and building began in the 1830s, was originally called Shawmut Neck. By the middle of the 19th century its layout was very comparable to that seen today and by the 1870s the area was fully developed into a grid pattern with blocks of homogeneous red-brick three- and four-story stooped rowhouses. These lined short, often discontinuous, streets running perpendicular to the main thoroughfares.

The thoroughfares were, for the most part, unattractive wide swathes along which traffic passed as quickly as possible. Some houses had mansard roofs. Indeed, the first such roof – now so much part of the Boston architectural scene – appeared in the South End in the free-standing Deacon House which was claimed to be "one of the wonders of the mid-century."

The South End enjoyed a fleeting decade of prosperity. But, when its wealthier residents abandoned it for the new and fashionable Back Bay, it became home to the *nouveaux riches*, the working class and the latest immigrants. Among the first group was the eponymous hero of Dean Howells' novel *The Rise of Silas Lapham* who "bought very cheap of a terrified gentleman of good extraction who discovered too late that the South End was not the thing, and who in the eagerness of his flight to the Back Bay threw in his carpets and shades for almost nothing."

However, some, such as Walbridge A. Field, who had been Chief Justice of Massachusetts, remained loyal and still resided in the South End at the turn of the century. Many private homes were turned into lodging houses. By the end of the century only seven of the 53 houses in elegant Union Park (*see page 181*) remained private. Desuetude engulfed the district.

A polyglot hodgepodge: The rebirth of the South End began in the 1960s. Today, it boasts an ethnic mix as varied as its architecture is homogeneous. More than 40 nationalities – mainly Puerto Ricans, Greeks, Syrians and Lebanese – reside in the district, as do blacks, young white professionals and gays. What, one wonders, would be the reaction of George Apley's Brahmin father whom J.P. Marquand created and who, in the 1870s, left the South End the day after coming out of his home and saying: "Thunderation, there is a man in shirt sleeves on those steps."

Leave Copley Square and stroll south on Dartmouth Street for about 300 yards to **South Station**. Facing the Station is the **Southwest Corridor**, a landscaped 50-yard wide park under which the railway tracks run. This park, built in the 1980s, is a bridge which

links the Back Bay and the South End: formerly, the railway track was a barrier which separated the two.

Enter the **Southwest Corridor** and immediately turn left into **Yarmouth Street** and appreciate the attempts that have been made to retain the integrity of the South End. The right side of the street is lined with 19th-century red-brick rowhouses; the left side consists of modern, low-rent, red-brick apartments. The rounded bows, so much a characteristic of the older South End houses, are echoed in the new apartments by much more linear bays.

Return to the Southwest Corridor and, before turning into Braddock Place, which parallels Yarmouth Street, make a brief diversion via **Follon Street**, on the right side of the park, into **St Botolph Street**. This street is named after the sainted monk for whom England's Boston (a contraction of St Botolph's town) was named. **Braddock Place** is typical – but probably the least known – of half-a-dozen leafy residential squares which pepper the South End. All are handsome but none has the social cachet of Louisburg Square – or indeed of anywhere on the South Slope of Beacon Hill.

These areas all have a long, narrow garden, in which are one or two splashing fountains enclosed by wrought-iron railings. Each red-brick, three- or four-story rowhouse which lines the long axes of the square is entered by a steep stoop which often rises a full story to the second floor (in which case a door beneath the stairway enters directly into the lower first floor). All have a regular cornice line: some are topped by a mansard roof. Adding attraction is wrought-iron ornamentation in the form of balustrades, railings around small gardens and sometimes over windows and balconies.

Leave Braddock Park and turn right on **Columbus Avenue** to immediately reach the intersection of that street and **Warren Street**. Here stands the red-brick **Concord Baptist Church**, read- **Father and son.**

ily recognizable by its large octagonal clerestory. It was built in the 1870s, when many Baptist congregations moved to the South End, but most of its members now live in other parts of Metropolitan Boston. Tiny **Harriet Tubman Park**, which stands in the lee of the church, remembers the "Moses of the South," a runaway slave who organized the "underground railway," a network of abolitionists who helped thousands of slaves escape to freedom. They built secret passageways in their homes and held huge parties to cover the flight of their transient guests who were en route to freedom in Canada. Many slaves remained in Boston.

Continue on Warren Street for about 500 yards, turn left onto **Clarendon Street** and enter an enclave known as **Clarendon Park**. Its streets carry the names – **Appleton**, **Warren**, **Chandler**, **Lawrence** – of prominent Beacon Hill residents. These streets are lined by attractive small versions of Beacon Hill houses that were built, it has been suggested, to accommodate the servants of those whose names they bear.

A right, rather than a left, turn from Warren onto Clarendon takes the visitor to the undistinguished **Cyclorama Building**, recognizable by the kiosk, a salvaged lantern, which stands outside it. The Cyclorama was built in 1884 to house a gigantic circular painting (400 by 50 feet) of the Battle of Gettysburg. Subsequently, it was used for revivalist meetings, dare-devil bicycle stunts and sporting events, including boxing contests which featured John L. Sullivan, a favorite South End son. Here, in 1907, Albert Champion invented the spark plug. Since 1970 the building has been the somewhat unsuccessful home of the **Boston Center for the Arts** and has attracted a number of excellent restaurants to its immediate neighborhood.

Proceed north on **Tremont Street** for a couple of hundred yards and turn left into **Union Park**, since 1859 the South End's most distinguished residential area. Facing one another and separated

by a garden with two splashing fountains are rows of red-brick houses with swells (not the occupants but the bays which protrude from the facades), oriel windows and steep stoops.

Since gentrification began, the cost of homes here and in other parts of the South End has rocketed. This has resulted in some friction between the incoming yuppies and the indigenous population, many of whom had been living here for only a decade or so.

A great cathedral: Exit from Union Park, cross **Shawmut Street** and continue to **Washington Street** to be greeted by the imposing towering facade of the **Cathedral of the Holy Cross**. This, one of the world's largest Gothic cathedrals, can seat 3,500 and accommodate double that number. The puddingstone exterior with granite and sandstone trim has an assymetrical facade. (Even if the spires had been added, it would still be assymetrical.)

The exterior belies a truly Gothic interior, which has a vast clear space inter-rupted only by two rows of columns extending along the nave and supporting the central roof. Light enters through innumerable undistinguished stained-glass windows. The largest of these line the transept and tell the story of the exaltation of the cross by the Emperor Heraclitus and the miracle by which the cross was verified.

Until the 1980s the Washington Street "El," the elevated train line built at the start of this century, passed within yards of the Cathedral's entrance. The noise was deafening and it is claimed that the Yankees routed the line this way in order to disturb the Irish congregants. The Puritans' fortified gate and the town's gallows stood just a few hundred yards to the northeast where Washington Street, the original road to Boston over the neck of the peninsula, inter-sects with Dover Street.

Proceed northwards on Washington Street for three blocks and, lying side by side are **Blackstone** and **Franklin Squares**, two geometrical, flat, grassy

Sport – the great equalizer.

areas, each about the size of four football fields and each having a splashing fountain as a centerpiece. Although not built until the 1860s, the squares had already been planned by Bulfinch at the start of that century.

Each square, on its south side, is backed by a stately building. One can readily believe that the elaborate French Second Empire edifice which graces Franklin Square was once the St James', one of the city's most elegant hotels, where General Grant once lodged when he was President. The building, which might be familiar to many through the television series *St Elsewhere*, now houses the elderly.

The Blackstone building, less flamboyant and more severe, consists of brownstone rowhouses with handsome pedimented formal windows and doors enclosed by pilasters.

Continue on Washington Street for half-a-dozen blocks. Turn right into **Massachusetts Avenue** and enter **Chester Square** which, until 40 years ago, was the grandest residential square in all Boston and indeed could begin to be compared to the great London squares. Then "MassAve" was realigned and now pierces the heart of the oval park which separates the two crescents of 70 opulent rowhouses.

Chester Square debouches into Tremont Street. A left turn immediately leads to the **Pickering Piano Factory** which, when opened in 1850, was the largest building in the nation, other than the Capitol. It was saved from extinction by being converted into artists' studios and apartments. The dominating feature of this handsome six-story building is an octagonal tower, half of which projects forward from the middle of the main facade and which, above the cornice line, supports a lantern.

A right, rather than a left, turn onto Tremont leads first to **Concord** and then to **Rutland Squares**, two more handsome residential squares. Further down Tremont Street, on the right, the square campanile red-brick Roman-

esque revival tower of the **Church of the Lord Jesus Christ of the Apostolic Faith** beckons. It is now part of the very successful **Villa Victoria Housing Project**, most of whose inhabitants are Puerto Ricans and most of whose architecture is somewhat at odds with the rest of the South End.

If, at the Cyclorama, instead of continuing your explorations of the South End you had turned left onto **Berkeley Street**, proceeded for 400 yards and then turned right onto **Columbus Street** and proceeded a further 200 yards, you would have arrived at **Bay Village**, a tiny oasis which makes the South Slope of Beacon Hill look like a bustling metropolis.

(An alternative way to enter this haven is from the intersection of **Columbus**, **Arlington** and **Stuart Streets**, which is dominated by a massive, rusticated, granite, Italian Renaissance fortress whose hexagonal tower is a landmark. This building, now the **Plaza Castle Convention Center**,

was once the armory of the First Corps of Cadets.)

Village in a city: Bay Village, which has been described as Beacon Hill on mud-flats, was developed in the 1820s when the Back Bay was still a tidal basin and a quarter of a century would elapse before the first buildings appeared in the South End. Today, the neighborhood, consisting of half-a-dozen short, gas-lit streets lined by uniform red-brick rowhouses, still has a 19th-century ambience. Many of the painters, housewrights, paperhangers and cabinet makers who created the grand homes on Beacon Hill built and lived in these, their much more modest homes, in Bay Village.

Enter the Village by **Piedmont Street**, which faces the Plaza Castle's Arlington Street facade. There's nothing too attractive here, but note above one of the entrances on the right an "N" surrounded by laurel leaves. This is the "Napoleon Club," America's first gay bar. It owes its location to the fact that Bay Village is close to the city's Theater District and, during prohibiton, was filled with speakeasies. Piedmont Street is soon crossed by **Church Street** – its church is long since gone – which is the start of a tranquil idyll far from the maddening crowd.

Turn right onto Church Street and, proceeding along it, wander into **Winchester** and **Melrose Streets**, before arriving at **Fayette Street**, the oldest street in the district. It is all quite lovely, with immaculate window-boxes filled with colorful blooms. At the end of Fayette Street is **Bay Street**, Boston's shortest street; it contains just one house – the smallest house in Boston.

Incidentally, the streets you tread and the homes you admire were originally 12 to 18 feet lower. When Back Bay was filled in, the Bay Village (then called the Church Street district) flooded and, in a mammoth undertaking, about 500 buildings were raised. From Fayette Street, turn into Arlington Street and resume the hurly-burly of life in Boston.

Left, many artists live in the South End. Right, row after row of brownstone houses.

THE CHARLES RIVER

Nature, with a hefty nudge from man, has blessed Boston with the Charles River – or, more specifically, the **Charles River Basin** which stretches upstream for about 9 miles from the mouth of the river. The basin, whose width is between 200 and 2,000 feet and which covers a moderately sinuous course, has been designated as a National Historic Civil Engineering Landmark and is on the National Register of Historic Places.

This basin, especially that part in the heart of the city, provides pleasure both on the water and on the banks, especially the south bank. In fall and spring, skiffs and larger shells skim the surface, pursued by launches from which demanding coaches shout their exhortations. Boston crews, usually collegiate, invariably win medals at both national and international level; indeed the entire Harvard eight who rowed on these waters represented the US at the 1968 Olympics. (America's top crew race, Harvard versus Yale, has been rowed on the Charles only in 1946 and 1974.)

In winter, if the basin is frozen, which happens quite often, businessmen skate to work and, if snow falls upon the ice, which is much rarer, they ski to the office. For most of the year dozens of sailboats from several sailing clubs, again mostly collegiate, tack to and fro and give a joyous appearance to the scene. And then there are marinas, home to elegant white power-boats.

The scene was not always such and before the Charles River Basin came into existence in 1908 the stench from tidal mud flats filled the air.

Not only does the Charles, which was christened by the 15-year-old Prince Charles who, 10 years later, became Charles I of England, bring enormous pleasure to Bostonians and to visitors but it has also played an important role in history. Paul Revere rowed across its

waters before taking to horse, the *USS Constitution* was built at its mouth, and the first telephone conversation in the world spanned the river.

The estuary: Start a river safari at the **Charlestown Bridge** at the mouth of the river. A forerunner of this bridge was the very first bridge across the river which opened 11 years to the day after the Battle of Bunker Hill with mighty cannon salutes and shouts of:

You Charlestown pigs,
Put on your wigs,
And come over to Boston town.

The Bridge, with an enormous span of 1,053 feet and a width of 423 feet, was considered the greatest feat of engineering ever undertaken in America. Within 15 years a further three privately funded bridges had firmly linked Boston to the mainland; until then, the city had been a peninsula with something of the character of a tight little island.

Immediately upstream from the Charlestown Bridge is the **New Charles River Dam** where you can

find the **Charles River Information Center**. Push a button and activate a 12-minute audio-visual show that dramatically explains flood control and the water level in the river basin. An observation window overlooks three locks: the two for pleasure boats can be extremely busy with more than 1,000 craft passing through in a day; only a rare commercial vessel ventures into the basin via the third lock. Just beyond this, on the Cambridge (north) side, is the **Charlesgate Yacht Club**, one of four power-boat marinas on the river.

Next, twist and turn your way for about a mile past **North Station** and the **Boston Garden** (home of the Celtics and the Bruins) to **Leverett Circle** and the **Msgr O'Brien Highway** which spans the river. Here, atop an older dam, is the **Museum of Science**.

Even before entering the Museum, observe the garden bordered by rock samples, some quite beautiful, from throughout the world. These include pieces from the Giant's Causeway in

Northern Ireland, the Rock of Gibraltar and Mont Blanc. The Museum, one of the best in the world, is very much a hands-on affair and contains hundreds of exhibits in five major fields: astronomy, energy, man, industry and nature. The visitor can determine his weight on the moon, listen to a transparent talking woman, see 15-foot bolts of lightning, watch chickens hatching, and much, much more.

The **Hayden Planetarium's** projector and multi-image system offer excellent programs on astronomical discoveries while laser light shows also excite. Those who suffer from motion sickness will avoid the **Mugar Omni Theater** where wrap-around state-of-the-art movies are projected onto a 76-foot high domed screen. For a change of pace visit the **Skyline Cafeteria** which offers superb views of the river, the city and the hills of Newton, Brighton and Brookline; it's a pity the food isn't half as good as the vistas.

A further half-a-mile upstream is the **Longfellow Bridge**, completed in 1900, and the oldest and most ornate bridge across the river. Its four readily recognizable towers have led to the nickname **Salt and Pepper Bridge**. The surroundings have been enhanced by the cleaning and greening of the basin, the activity of white wings and the oft-colorful garb of oarspeople.

At the northwest corner of the bridge the **Lechmere Canal** runs for about 200 yards to end in a circular basin at whose center is a soaring fountain. Bordering this basin is **Cambridgeside Galleria**, Metropolitan Boston's newest shopping mall. River boats leave from here for short cruises on the Charles.

The river basin: Tucked into the southwest corner of the bridge is the clubhouse of **Community Boating** which is believed to organize the world's oldest and largest public sailing program. Many an Olympic and America's Cup sailor has first put to sea here on the embankment of the Charles River. However, not all the scudding white

Dinosaur in Museum of Science.

sails of traditional center-boards and psychedelic sails of wind-surfers have set off from the Community Boating quay. Some belong to the **Massachusetts Institute of Technology Sailing Club** whose clubhouse is somewhat upriver and across from the Community Boating. Others belong to the **Emerson College Sailing Club** whose headquarters is just a few yards upstream from the Community Boating quay.

Immediately beyond this is the boathouse of the **Union Boat Club**, founded in 1851 by gentlemen interested in rowing who were also admirers of Daniel Webster's *Union Forever* speeches. In order to maintain the integrity of the riparian banks they built their clubhouse, not on the river, but diagonally across **Embankment Road** at the foot of **Chestnut Street**.

Nowhere are the river banks as busy as here. Many come to sun, to laze or to feed the ducks while others, more energetic, jog, cycle or roller-skate. There are surprisingly few fishermen, al-

though the river has many fish including goldfish, mummichog, catfish and killfish. Here, too, is the **Hatch Shell** which is home to the Pops and other concerts during summer. A large bust of Arthur Fiedler, near the Shell, remembers the man who brought musical joy to millions of Bostonians. Immediately south of the river an idyllic lagoon, spanned by four small arched stone bridges, stretches for about a mile.

The most lively part of the Esplanade is demarcated at its western end by the **Harvard Bridge**, also called the **Massachusetts Avenue Bridge** but referred to, more often than not, as the **MIT Bridge** because its northern end leads directly to that Institute's campus. This is where the river is at its widest. Look back (eastwards) from here: the vista is immense – a sheer joy to behold. To the left is the MIT campus; to the right is the Back Bay and then Beacon Hill with the glistening dome of the State House and behind that the Downtown skyscrapers. And the river is vibrant with sailing

Charles River Basin, Back Bay and Salt and Pepper bridge.

boats and shells. This is Boston at its very best. Is this vista superior to that looking west from Longfellow Bridge? It's an open question.

The casual stroller practically takes his life in his hands on crossing the MIT bridge, for it invariably teems with an infinite number of joggers, each seemingly in greater pain than his neighbor. No problems about the length of the bridge – it is painted on the sidewalk: 364.4 smoots + one ear. Oliver R. Smoot, a 1958 Lambda Chi Alpha pledge at MIT, was required to measure the length of the bridge using himself as a yardstick. Every spring and fall his successors refresh the information. He must have been rather small: a *smoot* works out at about 62 inches.

Proceed upstream past the **Boston University**, sometimes called the **Cottage Farm Bridge**, then the graceful curving red-brick **John W. Weeks** pedestrian bridge. Harvard University buildings now line both grassy shores and the next bridge, the **Larz**

Anderson, links the college buildings with the playing fields and the Business School as well as joining Cambridge and Brighton, a Boston suburb. The Larz Anderson replaced an older bridge which became so congested at football games that it prompted the *Harvard Lampoon* to parody Longfellow's *The Bridge*: "I stood on the bridge at midnight/I had left the field at five."

The river now twists through a pleasant landscape, passing boathouses and marinas and, at 1175 Soldiers Field Road, the inchoate **Sports Museum of New England** where magnificent larger than life-size wooden sculptures by Armand laMontagne will even appeal to those who do not have the slightest interest in sport. After about 3 miles **Watertown** is reached.

In the suburbs: If it is April or thereabouts then, rather than turning right and entering Watertown Square, continue for 300 yards on what is now **Watertown Street** and then bear right on **California Street** for a further 300

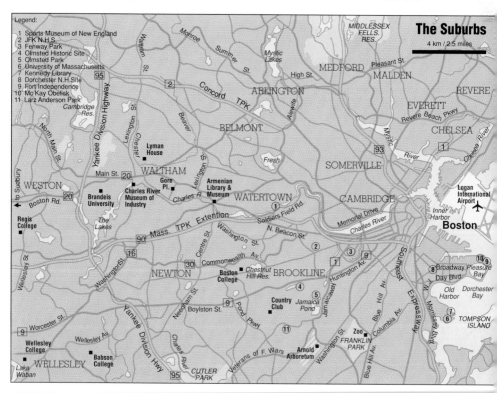

Legend:
1 Sports Museum of New England
2 JFK N.H.S.
3 Fenway Park
4 Olmsted Historic Site
5 Olmsted Park
6 University of Massachusetts
7 Kennedy Library
8 Dorchester N.H.Site
9 Fort Independence
10 Mc Kay Obelisk
11 Larz Anderson Park

The Suburbs

4 km / 2.5 miles

yards. This leads to the river and to a ladder used by herring returning from the open sea to spawn in sheltered waters. Alewife and blueback herring are the most common; rainbow smelt and American shad are not that rare.

Return to **Watertown Square** and exit to the west by Main Street (Route 20). Immediately on the right is the small but interesting **Armenian Library and Museum of America** which houses a diverse collection of Armenian textiles, ceramics, coins and religious art. Continue on Route 20 for 2 miles and then turn left on **Gore Street** to immediately reach **Gore Place**. This 22-room, red-brick mansion was designed by Rebecca Payne Gore – one of the first women to design a great home – and built in 1805 by her husband, Christopher Gore, after they had returned from London and Europe where Mrs Gore had obtained many ideas from the French architect J-G. Legrand.

Mrs Gore enjoyed her comforts and the home has some of America's first flush toilets and showers. A later innovation is the flying staircase that spirals three full flights upwards. The house, with its oval rooms and stunning wallpaper, was originally a country estate for the Gores but in later years they occupied it more frequently and were known to have 450 people for breakfast. Today, it is a treasure trove of early 19th-century European and American decorative arts; about 100 items, including paintings by Trumbull, Sargent and Singer, belonged to the Gores. The grounds, which run down to the river, cover an area of 40 acres.

On leaving Gore Place, turn right and then immediately left onto Route 20. After about 2 miles, turn right onto **Lyman Street** for a visit to the grounds of the Lyman House, **The Vale**, which was built in 1793. This long, low house (by appointment only) was greatly altered in 1882 and all that remains of the original is the oval salon and ballroom. The Vale is renowned for its landscape (open to the public) which is based on

Regatta at Cambridge boat club.

broad vistas dotted with clumps of trees and contains three venerable 19th-century greenhouses, in which grow a grapevine from London's Hampton Court and a century-old camellia tree.

Back on Route 20, pass through the center of **Waltham** and immediately turn left on **Moody Street** and continue until the river. Here is the **Charles River Museum of Industry**, an Historic Landmark. The Boston Manufacturing Company textile mill, in whose power plant the museum is located, was one of the most significant sites in the Industrial Revolution. It was the first integrated textile mill – raw material went in one end and the finished product came out the other – and was the site of the first known strike in American industry when the company announced a retroactive pay cut. The museum not only tells the story of the mill but also shows exhibits of products such as precision metal-working instruments, watches, bicycles and automobiles – aficionados will drool over the Stanley

Steamer – which were manufactured in and around Waltham.

Continue south on Moody Street which becomes **Lexington** and, after about two miles, turn right on **Commonwealth Avenue**. This route skirts the **Lakes District** where, because of it being dammed at the mill, the Charles meanders among islands and peninsulas and is beautified by lily ponds. Until the 1950s this was the site of two extremely popular recreation areas and two steamboats sailed on the river. And, in this region, one would see literally thousands of canoes. These can still be rented near the **Marriott Hotel**.

Philatelists, rather than returning to Boston, will continue from the boathouse on Route 30 West for nearly 3 miles and then turn left onto **Wellesley Street**. **Regis College** is immediately reached. Ignore the main entrance and enter at the sign **Postal Museum** to reach the **Cardinal Spellman Philatelic Museum** which is the only museum in the country custom-built for the display of stamps. The nucleus of the collection – which, with 300,000 pieces of sticky paper, is one of the world's largest – was started by Cardinal Spellman. To this have been added the Dwight D. Eisenhower collection and Papal States stamps.

On leaving the college, turn left and, after a couple of miles, regain Route 20. Here, turn left and after 10 miles (20 miles from Boston) and beyond the small town of **Sudbury** arrive at **Longfellow's Wayside Inn** which, although not on the river, stands in a bucolic setting. It claims to be the oldest operating inn in the country. Known as John How's Black Horse when built in 1661, the tavern became inexorably linked with Longfellow when *Tales of a Wayside Inn* appeared in 1863. The Inn, whose rooms can be explored, still offers "Food, Drink and Lodging for Man, Woman and Beast." In its grounds stand the **Red Schoolhouse** attended by Mary and her little lamb and a working reproduction of an **18th-century gristmill**.

Gristmill at Longfellow's Wayside Inn.

HEAD OF THE CHARLES REGATTA

An infinite number of fragile wooden craft skim the surface of the water, some occupied by a single oarsperson, others with several occupants. Tens of thousands of spectators throng the river banks while others prefer the vantage point provided by half-a-dozen bridges that span the river. The rich fall colors of the leaves on the trees bordering the river are complemented, rather than shamed, by the vivid singlets worn by some of the crews and the brilliant colors of their oar blades.

This is the scene at the annual Head of the Charles regatta – the largest one-day regatta for oarspeople in the world – which is held on the second last Sunday in October. As the oldest head of the river regatta in North America, it is known as the "daddy of 'em all" and simply referred to as "The Head."

In an era when prize money in sport has reached astronomical and obscene proportions, where every sportsperson and sporting body believes that sponsorship is a God-given right, the Head of the Charles Regatta is a breath of fresh air. There is no prize money: participants pay their own expenses and no only really cares – and many specators do not even know – who wins. That insistent American maxim that winning is all that counts is abandoned, at least for one day, in Boston.

"The Head" was conceived at a meeting in 1964 and the first regatta was held in 1965. Since then the event has grown and grown until now more than 4,000 oarsmen and women and almost 1,000 boats appear. Invariably, the majority of participants are from New England but Canada is always well represented and each year sees many crews from California and Texas and foreign crews from Peru and Puerto Rico, Australia and the Soviet Union, and England, France and Switzerland and other parts of Europe.

But exactly what is a head of the river race? It works like this: competing boats set off one after the other, at brief intervals – rather than together – and are timed over the length of the course. In other words, a head of the river race is a procession of boats. On the Charles, boats start at intervals of 15–20 seconds and all timing is electronic. It is difficult for spectators to determine which boat is in the lead but there are moments of intense excitement when a crew, faster than that ahead of it, attempts – and sometimes succeeds – in passing another shell.

The river is narrow and tortuous over part of the 3-mile course and crews that hog the center of the channel can prevent a faster boat from overtaking them. At all but the last of the six bridges the rules compel crews to use the center span of the bridge: at the last bridge, however, crews may take either the center or starboard arch. But the starboard channel is narrow and, unless a sharp turn to port is made under the arch, the crew will find themselves aground. Or perhaps an inexperienced or fatigued crew fails to negotiate the central span and it too runs aground. No one is too upset and the spectators love it.

Accidental contact between shells occurs, often if a lead boat refuses to give way. Unlike in yachting, where the slightest contact between competitors immediately results in the raising of protest flags, such incidents are accepted in good humor.

All are catered for at "The Head." Octagenarians and Olympians compete, as do men and women, grandparents and grandchildren. An unusual twist is men coxing all-women crews. Eighteen events are held, catering for singles, doubles, fours and eights and for youths, masters, grand-masters and veterans. Between 40 and 80 shells compete in each race.

The racing day is long, starting at 9.30 a.m. and finishing about seven hours later, thus giving the opportunity for many on the river banks to participate in the quintessential American custom of tailgating. Barbecues abound and liquor, although now banned at "The Head," flows.

The regatta is a great occasion for reunions of schools, colleges and clubs – of groups who have not met, perhaps, for half a century. All along the river banks, and especially at the northern end of the course, banners announce "Kirkland House, 1955," "Belmont Hill School, 1936," and so on. As one Olympic coxswain remarked: "This is not a regatta: it's a convocation."

THE EMERALD NECKLACE

The Emerald Necklace is not an heirloom but rather a 6-mile series of parks and boulevards which begins at the Public Garden (see *page 165*) and ends in Franklin Park in West Roxbury.

Frederick Law Olmsted, arguably the first landscape architect in America, and renowned as the designer of New York's Central Park, was responsible for the final master plan. Olmsted was a visionary and an idealist who found many kindred spirits who agreed with his theory that city parks should be rustic and informal and thus provide the greatest possible contrast to a brick and stone, man-made urban environment. His designs reflect a deeply thought-out approach to life and a concern for the well-being of his fellow man.

Olmsted had travelled in Europe and as a young man had walked with his brother from Liverpool to London. He found the quiet English countryside with its hedgerows, pastures and splendid trees preferable to the geometric, formal gardens favored by Con–tinental aristocracies. Unpretentious, pastoral landscapes seemed most conducive to soothing the troubled urban spirit and would return a sense of the poetry of nature to urban life. They would be the visual equivalents of democracy, whereas fountains, *grandes allées* and monumental sculpture would only reinforce the idea of an elite and would breed resentment and envy.

The landscapes of the Emerald Necklace are man-made and contrived but the intention was to make them appear as if they had stood for centuries. Trees, including copper beeches, stately elms, great stands of oaks and groves of pine, all of which are indigenous to the area, were planted among native undergrowth and flowering shrubs. Land was graded and sculpted to enhance views and to increase beauty in the same way that "natural" parks were created by Capability Brown, the 18th-century English landscape architect.

The best place to begin an exploration of the Emerald Necklace is at the beginning of **Commonwealth Avenue**, Boston's grandest street (see *page 165*) across from the **Public Garden**. Follow this to **Massachusetts Avenue**, beyond which is a confluence of over-hanging expressways. Olmsted intended this area to be a dramatic transition from city to country, and at one time it was. To the right the **Charles River** would be visible and to the left the beginning of the marshlands of the Fenway, extending beyond H.H. Richardson's pudding-stone Boylston Street Bridge. Sadly, these views are no longer possible but the imagination can put them in place.

At **Boylston Street Bridge** one looks out over the **Fenway** through which flows the **Muddy River** and here begins the Olmsted-designed portions of the Necklace that exist today. The name "Fenway" evokes images of East Anglia in England (a fen is land reclaimed

from salt-water marshes for farming) and announces Olmsted's intentions of imitating the English countryside. This area was originally intended to be a salt-water inlet and to provide a nesting ground and habitat for shore birds. However, when the Charles Basin was dammed in 1910, fresh-water reeds took over. Although not part of the original plan, they provide a picturesque rural effect.

The **Fenway Victory Gardens**, dating from World War II, are colorful throughout spring and summer and benefit from friendly competition among their green-thumbed owners. Further along is the glorious, in summer, **City Rose Garden**. Although the area is not the untamed wilderness for which Olmsted aimed, it does offer visual relief after a day of sightseeing.

Continue along **Riverway**, which soon becomes **Jamaicaway**, passing on the right **Olmsted Park**. Observe on the left the shamrock shutters at **350 Riverway**, that was once the home of "Hizhonner" James Michael Curley. This section of the Emerald Necklace retains much of its original character. After a couple of miles **Jamaica Pond**, a small jewel ringed by tree-lined paths is reached. Sailboats and rowboats can be rented at a half-timbered boathouse.

On the far side of the Pond is the village of **Brookline** which was, in the 19th century, Boston's wealthiest suburban enclave. Several interesting sites may be visited here. The **Larz Anderson Museum of Transportation** at 15 Newton Street (turn left at the northeast corner of the Pond and continue for about half-a-mile past the **Hellenic College**) has a superb collection of early automobiles housed in the carriage house of the former estate of the diplomat Larz Andersen. An excellent view of the Boston skyline is offered from the hilltop behind the museum. Across the road is *the* **Country Club**, founded in 1881 and the father of hundreds of such establishments throughout the nation.

Lilac time at the Arborietum.

Back at 43 Warren Street is the **Olmsted Historic Site** where Frederick Law Olmsted had his office and home during and after the construction of the Emerald Necklace. Drawings, plans and papers can all be seen here.

About 3 miles to the north, but still in Brookline at **83 Beals Street** (near **Coolidge Corner**), is the **John F. Kennedy National Historic Site**, birthplace of the president. His parents lived in this modest, two-story house from 1914 to 1921, but a growing family resulted in a move to larger quarters.

Return to Jamaicaway, turn right and after a short distance stop at the **Arnold Arboretum**, designed by Olmsted and a Brookline neighbor, Charles Sprague Sargent. Harvard University maintains the 265 acres, open throughout the year. The Arboretum is home to many rare trees and shrubs, including 300-year-old bonsai trees and the world's largest collection of lilacs which, every June, in Lilac Week, parade their colors.

The Arboretum, built for the study of plants, has always been splendidly maintained. Not so **Franklin Park**, a couple of miles further along the Arborway. Olmsted intended this to be the culmination of his chain of parks, a bucolic escape for the city dweller, accessible by streetcar or by foot. (The orange line terminus of the "T" is within a mile of the Park's entrance.)

Originally, flocks of sheep kept the grasses down and Bostonians played lawn tennis and croquet on Franklin Park's large pastures. Urban buildings, other than inconspicuous puddingstone structures for utilitarian purposes, did not exist. Trees were planted in the manner of an English country house park and early photographs show the realization of Olmsted's ideal. He placed Franklin alongside Central and Prospect Parks in Brooklyn as his favorite and most important designs.

Years of neglect left Franklin Park a hostile wilderness but recent efforts have returned it to something of its intended beauty. The **Zoo** has been re-

Enthusiasts at Donald McKay obelisk at Castle Island. **Far right**, studying in lee of Fort Independence at Castle Island.

vived and a handsome addition is the American Tropical Forest, a 3-acre environmental exhibit where more than a 100 free-flying birds dart among thousands of plants. Other attractions are the aviary, known as Birds' World, and the Children's Zoo. The 18-hole public **golf course** has also been refurbished.

Olmsted did not intend his necklace to stop here. Rather it would now cut a broad swathe to the northeast and to Castle Island in Boston Harbor. Trace this intended path by traveling for about 3 miles on urban rather than rural **Columbia Avenue** to **Columbia Circle.** Here, abandon Olmsted temporarily and travel south on **Morrisey Boulevard** for slightly less than a mile.

A left turn past the fortress-like modern **University of Massachusetts Boston Campus**, occupying a splendid piece of land jutting into Boston harbor, leads to the striking **Kennedy Library**, designed by I. M. Pei. This contains the president's papers and, of more interest, exhibits covering JFK's life. Personal

items on display include the president's desk and the coconut shell on which he carved a cry for help after his PT boat was sunk during World War II. A 30-minute film is part of the tour. The *Ventura*, the president's sailboat, sits behind the library.

Back at Columbia Circle, skirt the waterfront on the **William J. Day Boulevard**, Olmsted's intended Strandway, passing three turn-of-the-century yacht clubs and the **"L" Street Bathhouse** from where Brownies swim naked year-round. After 3 miles, you reach **Castle Island**, which since 1891 has been linked to the mainland.

Here stands **Fort Independence**, whose only military involvement was during the last days of the siege of Boston in 1776 when British artillery unsuccessfully bombarded the Americans on Dorchester Heights. A promenade encircles the massive fort whose antecedents date back to 1634. The park surrounding the fort offers splendid views of the outer harbor and islands, has a fishing pier jutting into the water and is a popular summer picnic spot.

An obelisk commemorates Donald McKay, the East Boston shipbuilder who was renowned for his China Trade clippers. The most famous of these, the *Flying Cloud*, held the record for sailing from New York to San Francisco around the Cape of Good Hope.

Return for about 1 mile to the intersection of **East Sixth Avenue** and the boulevard. Drive uphill through "Southie" for slightly more than a mile to **South Boston High School**, passing on the way immaculate triple-decker clapboard houses which will sometimes be flying the Irish tricolor.

Behind the school is the **Dorchester Heights National Historical site** which marks where, "out of Aladdin's lamp," American engineers built the fortifications that forced the British to depart from Boston in 1776. A 215-foot high white marble Georgian Revival style monument (irregular hours of opening) commemorates the victory.

Dorchester Heights memorial. Right, fall at the Arboretum.

CAMBRIDGE

Cambridge, separated from Boston by the River Charles and linked to it by half-a-dozen bridges which span the river, was founded in the same year as Boston. Originally called New Towne, it was the Bay Colony's first capital. It is still a city in its own right whose population of more than 100,000 makes it the second largest city in Massachusetts. Each fall this number is swollen by about 25 percent by students attending Harvard University or Massachusetts Institute of Technology (MIT), with the former being the lure that attracts tourists to the city.

Harvard Square, the focal point of Cambridge for the visitor, can be reached readily from Boston on the Red line of the "T". The square and its immediate surroundings have many restaurants and stores, and bibliophiles will be thrilled to find the greatest concentration of bookshops in the nation. Papers from throughout the world can be purchased at the large kiosk on the island in the middle of the square.

A tall, abstract, granite sculpture entitled *Omphalos* stands next to the kiosk. If the sculpture had been commissioned by Harvard rather than by the Metropolitan Transport Authority, one would have cried hubris, knowing that it was the intent of the sculptor's patron to indicate that Cambridge and not Delphi was the navel of the world. In the square the last of the world's hippies mingle with undergraduates and tourists and music fills the air as buskers play at every corner. (There are more than four because the square is amorphous.)

Colonial memories: Cambridge has a long and proud colonial history which is well worth exploring before entering Harvard. Head north from the Square on **Massachusetts Avenue**, leaving Harvard College to the right and immediately pass on the left the **First Unitarian Church** where *Fair Harvard*

was sung for the first time on the occasion of the College's 200th anniversary.

Bear left onto **Garden Street** where, on the left, is **Christ Church**, Cambridge's oldest house of worship (1761) which fulfilled the congregants' request to Peter Harrison, America's first architect (Harrison also designed Boston's King's Chapel), for "no steeple, only a tower with a belfry." When most of the Tory congregation fled in 1774 the church was used as a barracks and the organ pipes were melted down for bullets. A bullet hole in the vestibule is said to be from the rifle of a Redcoat as he marched towards Lexington. The church was re-opened on New Year's Eve, 1775, when George and Martha Washington attended worship.

Between the two churches is the **Old Burying Ground**, known as "God's Acre" in which Harvard's first eight presidents are interred. Several veterans of the Revolution, including two black soldiers, also lie here. Immediately across the road from Christ

Church is a traffic island with a granite lectern topped by a bronze plaque honoring **William Dawes**, the other messenger sent to warn the patriots of the coming of the British. Footprints of his galloping horse are simulated in brass on the pavement.

North of this is **Cambridge Common**, a veritable treasure trove of markers, memorials and monuments and a place inexorably associated with George Washington, for it was here on July 4, 1775, that he assumed command of the Continental Army. Make for the flagpole and cluster of three cannons, abandoned when the British left Boston on March 17, 1776, placed about cobblestones on the west side of the Common. A bronze relief shows Washington on horseback under an elm tree, assuming command. On the reverse side is the text of Washington's orders given here on July 4, 1775, the Congressional document that officially melded the colonial militias into a unified Continental Army. A smaller stone,

adjacent to an elm which is enclosed by an iron fence, commemorates Washington's famous elm, cut down in 1923 because it impeded traffic.

Education for women: Cross Garden Street and enter **Radcliffe Yard** where this renowned women's college (now fully integrated with Harvard) began life in 1879. To the right and left respectively are **Byerly Hall** and **Fay House**. The latter, a Federal-style building from 1806, is the oldest structure in the Yard and once housed the entire College apart from student accommodation. Byerly, with its innumerable chimneys, originally was a warren of science laboratories and was described as having "the most modern equipment for the study of chemistry, physics and astronomy." Both buildings are now used for administrative purposes with the Radcliffe President having her office in Fay House.

Across the Yard is striking **Aggasiz House** with its Ionic portico. Named after the founder of Radcliffe, it con-

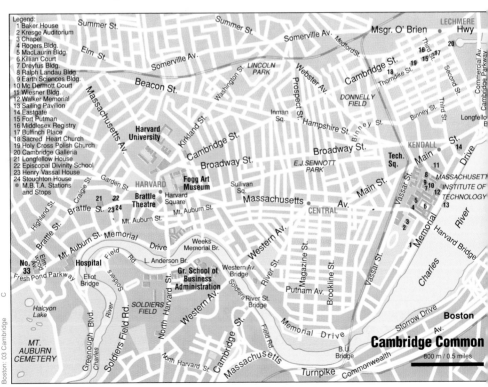

Legend:
1 Baker House
2 Kresge Auditorium
3 Chapel
4 Rogers Bldg.
5 MacLaurin Bldg.
6 Killian Court
7 Dreyfus Bldg.
8 Ralph Landau Bldg.
9 Earth Sciences Bldg.
10 Mc Dermott Court
11 Wiesner Bldg.
12 Walker Memorial
13 Sailing Pavilion
14 Eastgate
15 Fort Putman
16 Middlesex Registry
17 Bulfinch Place
18 Sacred Heart Church
19 Holy Cross Polish Church
20 Cambridge Galleria
21 Longfellow House
22 Episcopal Divinity School
23 Henry Vassal House
24 Stoughton House
● M.B.T.A. Stations and Stops

Cambridge Common

800 m / 0.5 miles

Boston: 03 Cambridge

tains a 350-seat theater where Eugene O'Neill's first play opened and failed and where Jack Lemmon got his start. To the right is the **Radcliffe Gymnasium** and to the left the **Schlesinger Library**. On the extreme left is **Longfellow House**, a long red-brick neo-Georgian affair with paired entrances framed by pilasters. It houses the **Graduate School of Education**.

The **Murray Research Center**, which studies the impact of social changes on lives, especially those of women, now occupies the ground floor of the Gymnasium. Upstairs is the **Radcliffe Dance Center**. The Schlesinger Library has an outstanding collection of literature on the history of women in America and is the country's top research center devoted to women's studies. The library, open to the public, includes a **Culinary Collection** with more than 2,300 cookbooks.

Putnam House and **Buckingham House**, the two intrusive, low, grey, clapboard buildings in the Yard – or is it the brick buildings which are intrusive? – are respectively a **Child Care Center** and a **Career Services Office**.

Rather than immediately continuing your exploration of Old Cambridge, return to Garden Street and stroll northwards for about 600 yards to the **Radcliffe Residential Quadrangle** (it is now co-educational), a pleasant affair of neo-Georgian buildings, some with cupolas. The handsome, modern **Hilles Library** which stands in the southwest corner of the quadrangle is much more than a library and is the site of the quadrennial Music-Listening Orgy during which hundreds of classical tapes are played from beginning to end without interruption.

Exit from the north of the quadrangle onto **Linnaean Street**. Turn right and, after 600 yards, you will reach No. 21, a simple, white, two-story structure which dates back to the second half of the 17th century; it is the oldest entire dwelling place in Cambridge.

Linnaean Street now enters Massa-

chusetts Avenue, from where it is a stroll of about three-quarters of a mile down the Avenue with the Harvard Law School (see *page 221*) on the left and cross the Common to regain Radcliffe Yard. Spare a glance on the north side of the Common for the two-story, gray, clapboard house at No. 7. It was here that Dr Benjamin Waterhouse lived and "cut the claws and wings of smallpox" by introducing into the US, in 1800, vaccination with "vaccine threads" that he had received from Dr Edward Jenner. Waterhouse first vaccinated his own children and then sent threads to President Jefferson who similarly treated his own children.

Tory Row: Exit from Radcliffe Yard onto **Brattle Street**, once known as Tory Row because in the 18th century most of its houses were owned by loyalists. It was also called Church Row because its residents both built and worshipped at Christ's Church.

A left turn and a 300-yard stroll through the madding crowd and the hustle and bustle of commerce to Brattle Square might cast some doubt that this is the most prestigious street in Cambridge, famous for both history and architecture, but a right turn and a walk of about three-quarters of a mile fully justifies these claims. Here, all the kerfuffle is gone and the leafy, tranquil street is lined by splendid large clapboard houses fronted by elegant porticoes, most from the 19th century but some from the 18th, each the same yet different and each standing in its own spacious grounds. Many bear blue plaques commemorating the greats who have lived in them.

Stroll first to **Brattle Square**. En route, on the right stands Harvard's handsome, modern **Loeb Drama Center**. Next door, an outdoor café fronts No. 56, a simple two-story, hip-roofed, Federal-style building, home to Longfellow's "village blacksmith." But don't search for the chestnut tree under which Longfellow met Dexter Pratt: it suffered the fate of Washington's elm **Harvard Square.**

and was chopped down in 1870 when Brattle Street was widened.

Further along, at No. 42, stands the first of the famous mansions which line the length of the street. Aside from the projecting entrance this three-story, gambrel-roofed, clapboard house is true to its 1727 origins. It was built by the future Major General William Brattle, doctor, lawyer and minister; commander of all the militia of the province and one of the wealthiest men in Cambridge. He fled to England in 1774. The mansion is now the **Cambridge Center for Adult Education**.

Next door is the **Brattle Theatre** where, likely as not, Bogie and Ingrid Bergman are playing in *Casablanca*, the great Cambridge evergreen. Paul Robeson and T.S. Eliot trod the theater's boards as did Jessica Tandy and Hume Cronyn, Hermione Gingold and Zero Mostel. In 1953 it began showing foreign film classics.

Return along Brattle Street past Radcliffe Yard. **Stoughton House**, the dark building on the left at No. 90, was designed by H.H. Richardson of Boston's Trinity Church fame, and is renowned as one of the first and best examples of domestic American shingle style. Next door at No. 94 stands the 20-room **Henry Vassal House**, originally built in the 17th century and whose eponymous owner gambled away his fortune. It was medical headquarters for the first American Army during the Revolution.

Across the road is the red pudding-stone **Episcopal Divinity School** whose faculty house (No. 101) with its curved central bay has all the graces of an English Regency villa. And so to the **Longfellow House** (No. 105), a yellow clapboard building which is the most historic house on Tory Row. The mansion, started in 1759, originally stood in 116 acres; it was one of seven Tory estates occupying the area between Brattle Square and Elmwood Avenue whose lands stretched down to the river. The house was abandoned by its owner,

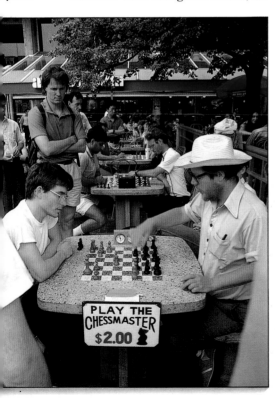

PLAY THE CHESSMASTER $2.00

John Vassal Jr, in 1774, when patriots made life difficult for loyalists in Cambridge, and it was George Washington's headquarters for nine months during the siege of Boston.

Longfellow first arrived here as a lodger in 1837 and then received the house as a wedding gift from his father-in-law and remained until 1882. Tragically, his young wife Fanny was fatally burned here in 1861. The gardens, old carriage house and the house – virtually as it was in Longfellow's time, with myriad memorabilia including a chair made from the "spreading chestnut tree" – can be visited.

Across the street is **Longfellow Park**, through which the poet would walk on his way to bathe in the river. The **Mormon Center** occupies the northeast corner of the park; the **Friends Meeting House** stands on the west side. Continue on Brattle Street, passing the large white-brick **Holy Trinity Armenian Church** with its strong eastern influence, and many distinguished homes. These include the houses (Nos. 113, 115) which Longfellow built for his two daughters, and the **Lee-Nichols House** (No. 159), built in the 1680s and now owned by the **Cambridge Historical Society** (open to the public on occasions). Then, across **Kennedy Road** (named after a Cambridge cookie manufacturer and not the President), there is No. 163, former home of Edwin Land, inventor of the Polaroid camera, and No. 165, built in 1870 by the Cambridge bookseller with whose "Quotations" the reader is undoubtedly familiar.

Turn left onto short **Elmwood Avenue** and proceed to the end where stands No. 33, a splendid three-story Georgian affair from 1767. It was used as a hospital for Americans during the Revolutionary War and has since been occupied by an illustrious line of owners. Today, it is owned by Harvard and occupied by its President.

Continue straight, cross a major intersection, and arrive on **Mount Auburn**

Longfellow's house on Brattle Street

Street where a plaque announces: "Here at the river's edge the settlers of Watertown led by Sir Richard Saltonstall landed in June 1630. Later the spot became known as Gerry's Landing for Elbridge Gerry, signatory of the Declaration of Independence and Governor of Massachusetts who lived in Elmwood nearby." (It was he who gave his name to the word "gerrymandering.")

Continue west along Mount Auburn Street for about 600 yards to the main entrance to the **Mount Auburn Cemetery**. This bucolic Westminster, whose grounds are planted with a glorious collection of foreign and native trees and shrubs, is America's oldest (consecrated 1831) and most beautiful Garden Cemetery. Interred here are Charles Bulfinch, Winslow Homer, Oliver Wendell Holmes, Henry Longfellow and Mary Baker Eddy (whose tomb is rumored to contain a telephone with an unlisted number). Although most tombs in this non-sectarian cemetery are small and modest, others are grand and the cemetery has been a showpiece of American funerary art for the past 150 years. Return to Brattle and Harvard Squares by walking or taking the trolley along Mount Auburn Street.

From Harvard Square, walk south on **John F. Kennedy Street** for 600 yards to the river. The first half of this street is occupied by stores and restaurants while the right side of the lower half is occupied by the **John F. Kennedy School of Government** which, like most of Harvard, just grows and grows.

An attractive small, public park lies between this school and the river. On the left side of John F. Kennedy Street are **Kirkland** and then **Eliot Houses**, two of Harvard's original seven handsome, neo-Georgian residential houses, distinguished by their graceful cupolas, enclosed courtyards and mellow red-brick walls. The houses, together with newer more modern fellows, stretch to the left along the river, ending in the contemporary **Peabody Terrace**, a 21-floor three-towered complex for mar-

Mary Baker Eddy's mausoleum at Mt Auburn Cemetery.

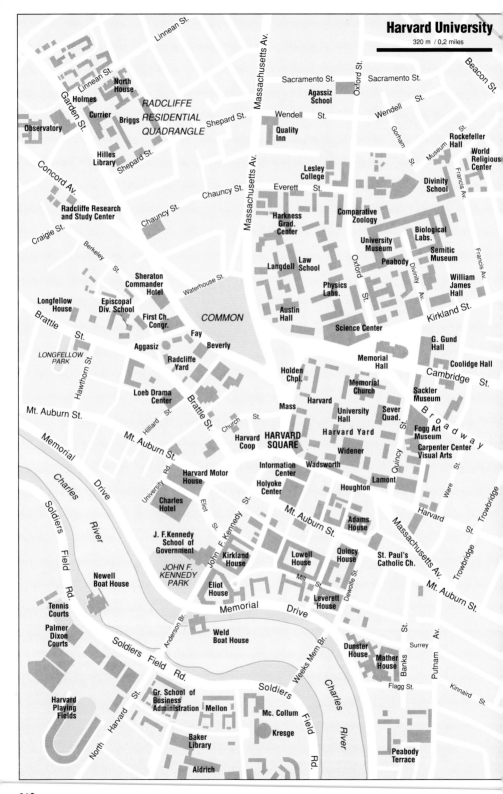

Harvard University

320 m / 0,2 miles

Linnean St.

Massachusetts Av.

Beacon St.

Linnean St.

Oxford St.

North House

Sacramento St.

Sacramento St.

Garden St.

Linnean St.

Agassiz School

St.

Holmes

Wendell

St.

Wendell

Currier

Briggs

Shepard St.

Gorham

Rockefeller Hall

Observatory

Hilles Library

Shepard St.

St.

Quality Inn

St.

Museum

World Religious Center

RADCLIFFE RESIDENTIAL QUADRANGLE

Lesley College

Francis Av.

Divinity School

Concord Av.

Chauncy St.

Everett

St.

Radcliffe Research and Study Center

Chauncy St.

Massachusetts Av.

Harkness Grad. Center

Comparative Zoology

Biological Labs.

Craigie St.

Berkeley St.

University Museum

Semitic Museum

Langdell

Law School

Oxford

Peabody

Divinity Av.

Francis Av.

Sheraton Commander Hotel

Waterhouse St.

Physics Labs.

St.

William James Hall

Longfellow House

Episcopal Div. School

COMMON

Austin Hall

Science Center

Kirkland St.

Brattle St.

First Ch. Congr.

Fay

G. Gund Hall

LONGFELLOW PARK

Hawthorn St.

Aggasiz

Beverly

Memorial Hall

Coolidge Hall

Radcliffe Yard

Holden Chpl.

Cambridge St.

Loeb Drama Center

Brattle St.

Mass

Memorial Church

Sackler Museum

Broadway

Mt. Auburn St.

Hilliard St.

Church St.

Harvard

University Hall

Sever Quad.

Fogg Art Museum

Memorial Drive

Mt. Auburn St.

Harvard Coop

HARVARD SQUARE

Harvard Yard

Carpenter Center Visual Arts

Charles River

University Rd.

Harvard Motor House

Information Center

Wadsworth

Widener

Quincy St.

Harvard

Ware St.

Trowbridge St.

Soldiers Field Rd.

Charles Hotel

Eliot St.

Holyoke Center

Houghton

Lamont

J. F. Kennedy School of Government

John F. Kennedy St.

Kirkland House

Lowell House

Adams House

Quincy House

St. Paul's Catholic Ch.

Massachusetts Av.

Trowbridge St.

Newell Boat House

JOHN F. KENNEDY PARK

Eliot House

Mill St.

Dewolfe St.

Leverett House

Mt. Auburn St.

Tennis Courts

Memorial

Drive

Palmer Dixon Courts

Soldiers Field Rd.

Anderson Br.

Weld Boat House

Weeks Mem Br.

Dunster House

Surrey

St.

Putnam Av.

Harvard Playing Fields

North Harvard St.

Gr. School of Business Administration

Mellon

Soldiers

Charles

Mather House

Banks St.

Flagg St.

Kinnaird St.

Field

River

Mc. Collum

Rd.

Baker Library

Kresge

Peabody Terrace

Aldrich

ried students which came from the drawing board of Josef Luis Sert.

Devotees of Mercury will cross the river by the **Larz Anderson Bridge** and visit, on the left, the Business School campus and, on the right, Harvard's vast Elysian **playing fields**, which are both in **Brighton**, a suburb of Boston. (The boathouse on the left of the bridge is used by women's crews while that on the right is used by Harvard men.) The **Business School** is a modest village of relatively modest neo-Georgian buildings that display a consistent rhythm of green doors, white window frames and red-brick walls.

On returning to the Square via John F. Kennedy Street, turn right onto Mount Auburn Street for further views of the Houses and, on the right, next to **Lowell House**, a red-brick building with a six-pillared entry. This is the **Fly Club**, one of eight snooty Harvard social clubs which have lost much of their exclusivity in recent years. Theodore and Franklin Roosevelt were members here, as were two other presidents, Lowell and Eliot.

The whimsical building with a gaudy door and topped by an Ibis at the rear of a wide triangular area on Mount Auburn Street is the headquarters of the *Lampoon*, Harvard's famous humor magazine. To the left of this once stretched Harvard's **Gold Coast**, so-called because of the opulent life-style of the students who lived in these buildings which were, at the start of this century, luxurious private apartments.

Harvard Yard: Continue your exploration of Harvard by crossing to the north side of the east-west arm of Massachusetts Avenue and entering **Harvard Yard**. **Wadsworth Hall**, the yellow clapboard building to the right of this entrance, was built in 1726 and was the home of Harvard presidents until 1849. It was also George Washington's headquarters for a few nights when he arrived in Cambridge. The Yard is a delightful shady oasis rather than the "unkempt sheep-commons" which

John Kirkland saw when he became president of the College in 1810. Then it was cluttered with a brewery and sundry privies. Kirkland is responsible for the trees, the footpaths and that tradition of care which still prevails.

In the center of the Yard and separating the Old from the New Yard, is **University Hall**, an 1816 granite building designed by Bulfinch. It now houses university offices but originally had dining rooms, classrooms, a chapel and the president's office. Fortunately, the architect anticipated the future for, when constructed, the rear of this building was almost as handsome as the front. And it is this rear which is now western side of the New Yard or Tercentenary Quadrangle.

The larger than life-sized bronze statue of **John Harvard** which sits below the American flag in front of University Hall is often referred to as *The Statue of Three Lies*. The statue is not of John Harvard but of an undergraduate in 1884, the year that the figure was

John Harvard and future Harvard student.

sculpted by Daniel Chester French. The inscription on the base refers to John Harvard as the founder of Harvard College. He was not: he was the first major benefactor. The inscription says that the College was founded in 1638, the year of the John Harvard bequest: it was founded in 1636.

To the west of University Hall, and facing one another, are **Massachusetts** and **Harvard Halls**. The former, erected in 1720, is the oldest Harvard building still standing and the College Clock, part of the original structure on the western gable, has been painted to resemble its 18th-century appearance. During the Revolutionary War, Continental Army soldiers were billeted here.

Harvard Hall (1766) is the third college building to stand on this site. Its predecessor was razed by a fire in 1764 which was called "the greatest disaster in the history of the College," destroying as it did the largest library in the colonies including John Harvard's books. One of the latter was saved be-cause, on the night of the fire, an undergraduate had removed it from the library. Next day, realizing the treasure he possessed, he took the book to President Holyoke who thanked him graciously, accepted the volume and expelled the student for removing it without permission.

The north of the **Old Yard** is occupied by four freshmen dormitories. To the west are the twin dormitories of **Hollis** and **Stoughton**. The former, Harvard's fourth oldest building (1763), was home, at different times, to President John Quincy Adams, Ralph Waldo Emerson, Henry Thoreau and Charles Bulfinch. During the war 600 Colonial troops were quartered here. The wooden pump outside Hollis is a replica of the pump at which students would perform their ablutions. To the east is **Thayer Hall**, a stripling which first housed students in 1870. Closing off the north end of the Yard is the granite **Holworthy Hall** (1812).

Standing between and slightly back **Episcopal Divinity School.**

from Hollis and Stoughton is **Holden Chapel** (1742), Harvard's third oldest building. The chapel, built in glorious high Georgian style and with its pediments decorated with the elaborate crest of the Holdens, was called "a solitary English daisy in a field of Yankee dandelions." Even though Harvard was founded as a ministerial school, Holden was its first chapel – more than a century after the College was founded. Later, it was the home of the Medical School and now houses offices of choral groups.

Grander by far than the Old Yard is **Tercentenary Quadrangle** or **New Yard** which, on the first Monday of each June, is the scene of Commencement. This Yard is dominated on the south by the Widener Library's massive Corinthian colonnade standing atop a monumental flight of stairs and on the north by the soaring, delicate, white spire of **Memorial Church** which honors the Harvard dead in both world wars. The rear of University Hall is on the west side and, facing this, is

Richardson's **Sever Hall**, its entrance flanked by turreted towers and the entire building rich in decorative brickwork. Built in 1880, it has been called "a turning point in the course of American architecture."

Widener, the third largest library in the US and the largest university library in the world, contains more than 3 million volumes stacked on 50 miles of shelves. It is the administrative center of the University network of nearly 100 libraries which house 11 million books. The Library is a memorial to Harry Elkins Widener, a young bibliophile who drowned in the sinking of the *Titanic*. As he had already indicated that he would donate his library to Harvard, his mother gave the University his books and the money to build space for millions more. Mrs Widener believed that if Harry had been able to swim he would have survived the sinking and so, as part of her bequest, she stipulated that all Harvard students pass a swimming test before they could graduate.

Snow does not deter students reaching Harvard's Widener Library.

Three interesting Cambridge dioramas (1677, 1755 and 1936) can be seen in the Library, whose **Widener Memorial Room**, a glorious affair of wood paneling and stained-glass windows, contains Harry's original private library which includes a copy of the Gutenberg Bible and a first folio of Shakespeare. Some claim that John Singer Sargent's murals in the anteroom to the Memorial Room "are the worst works of public art ever done by a major American painter." The adjacent **Houghton Library** has a brilliant collection of incunabula and the libraries of, among others, Cotton Mather and John Masefield. The John Harvard collection has the one book which survived the 1764 fire and "sisters" of many other works which were destroyed.

The rear of Sever Hall, just as handsome as the front, is flanked on the south by Emerson Hall and on the north by Robinson Hall. These three buildings form a unifying structure pulled together by the common use of brick and simple rectangular shapes and sometimes called **Sever Quadrangle**. If it appears uncertain whether **Emerson** should be of stone or brick, as evidenced by the massive engaged columns of brick with Ionic stone capitals, it is because stone, which was originally to be used, was found to be too expensive.

Philosophy is taught at Emerson Hall and legend has it that, when Gertrude Stein took her final examination here in a course given by William James, she left the building after writing in her examination book, "I don't want to take this exam: it's too nice out." Professor James returned her book with "Miss Stein, you truly understand the meaning of philosophy, 'A'." The first school of architecture and the first school of city planning in the nation were originally located in **Robinson Hall** which has classical bas reliefs flanking the entrance and the names of celebrated architects, sculptors and philosophers embossed below the upper windows.

An architectural hodgepodge: On exit-

Commencement at Harvard University.

HARVARD'S MUSEUMS

Harvard University boasts a number of museums whose collections any provincial city in the world would love to own. These nine museums, whose purpose is not to entertain the casual visitor but rather to educate students, are open to the public.

Administratively under one umbrella, the **Arts Museums** hold three collections, each with its own curator. Both the **Fogg** and the **Sackler** are housed in their own buildings; since early 1991, the **Busch-Reisinger** collection has been displayed in the **Werner Otto Hall**, a large extension of the Fogg. Collectively these three museums boast nearly 150,000 objects; the great majority are bequests, some on long-term loan although occasional items have been purchased.

The annual budget for the Arts Museums, which include North America's largest fine arts library, is about $7 million, of which just $500,000 is spent on acquisitions. Not infrequently Harvard alumni approach the Arts Museums for assistance in making purchases which will, when they die, go to the Museums.

Outstanding in the Fogg are the Ingres canvasses, the best collection outside France; a splendid assembly of pre-Raphaelite works and French impressionists; 27 Rodins; a Fra Angelico crucifixion; 54 Blake watercolors and a print room with 300 Durers and 200 Rembrandts. The Fogg also has an excellent collection of western sculpture featuring Romanesque works from the late 11th and 12th centuries and a dazzling display of silver.

The Sackler is devoted to works of Ancient, Oriental and Islamic art. Here is what many agree is the most magnificent collection in the world of Chinese jades. Also on show are Japanese prints and woodblocks, Persian miniatures and Greek and Roman statues and vases.

The Busch-Reisinger collection is devoted to the art of Germany with some works from other North European countries. Outstanding is 20th-century Expressionism with canvasses of Klee and Kandinsky and Max Beckman's *Self Portrait in Tuxedo*. Here too is the largest collection outside Germany of Bauhaus material including the archives of Gropius and Feininger. Among older paintings the collection is especially strong in 15th- and 16th-century items from the German, Dutch and Flemish schools. Romanesque and Gothic ecclesiastical sculpture, 18th-century Rococo porcelain, jewelry, textiles, furniture and metalcraft are also on display.

Giant totem poles, Navaho blankets, Hopi ceramics and African masks are just a few of the items on display at the **Peabody Museum of Archaeology and Ethnology**, the oldest such museum in the Americas and the most important of the four museums which constitute Harvard's **University Museums of Natural History**. Outstanding is the **Hall of the North American Indian** which focuses on the interaction between native Americans and newcomers. Other, less exciting, galleries cover the Indians of Central and South America, especially the Maya.

The greatest attraction in the Museums of Natural History is the glass flower collection in the **Botanical Museum**. These 847 remarkably accurate models are a unique collection made near Dresden, Germany by the Blaschkas between 1877 and 1936. The **Museum of Comparative Zoology** contains such treasures as Kronosaurus, a 42-foot long fossil sea-serpent from Australia, the Harvard mastodon, a 25,000-year-old elephant, a 65-million-year-old dinosaur egg, extinct birds such as the great auk and the passenger pigeon and hundreds of stuffed birds and animals. Rounding off this quartet of Museums is the **Geological and Mineralogical Museum** which exhibits a large collection of gems, minerals, ores and more than 500 meteorites.

Facing the Peabody is the **Semitic Museum**, which has little mass appeal. Its main attraction is a collection, changed from time to time, of old photographs of the Middle East.

A mini-museum in the **Science Center** houses a permanent exhibition of fascinating early scientific instruments dating back to around 1550. The collection illustrates the history of instrumentation in a broad range of subjects, from astronomy to navigation, and includes telescopes and early computing devices.

ing onto **Quincy Street** from Sever Quadrangle, the visitor is immediately faced by the striking modern **Carpenter Center for the Visual Arts**. The only Le Corbusier building in North America, it is just one of a variety of modern buildings on the Harvard campus. This led James Stirling, the English architect, whose Arthur M. Sackler Museum was severely criticized, to exclaim: "Doesn't fit in! I've simply created another animal for the Harvard architectural zoo!" And, indeed, the Carpenter is incongruous among the conventional buildings to its north and south and facing it from across the road – the **Fogg Museum**, the **Faculty Club** and the **President's House** respectively. (The President no longer lives in the house which bears his name: it is now used by the governing body.)

The most striking features of the Carpenter Center, which proper Bostonians have compared to two rhinos wrestling, is the sweeping ramp which leads from the street to the heart of the building on the upper level, the Corbusier trademarks of tall pillars, upon which the building appears to float, and concrete sun breakers which admit natural light while blocking out the sun's direct rays. Ascend the ramp and look down into the studios with artists at work.

Head north across **Broadway** to be immediately faced by Stirling's zebra, the **Sackler Museum**, a somewhat geometrical building with orange and gray striations. The two plastic-covered windows were to be the entrance to a bridge linking the Sackler and the Fogg. Further north, across **Cambridge Street**, is the slender-pillared **Gund Hall**, home of the **Graduate School of Design**. The vast studio area, which is four levels high and devoid of interior walls, is quite stunning.

Continue northwards, crossing **Kirkland Street** and enter **Divinity Avenue**. At the corner stands the 15-story **William James Hall** skyscraper which houses the University's behavioral sciences department and

Charles River and Harvard houses.

which was designed by Minoru Yamasaki. On the other side of Divinity Avenue is the **Busch-Reisinger** building; until recently, it housed the University's collection of German art.

Homogeneity is the keynote to the other buildings on 300-yard long **Divinity Avenue** even although they were built over a span of 150 years and serve a wide variety of purposes. To the right is the **Harvard-Yenching Library**, the **Semitic Museum** and the vast **Biological Laboratories**. Enter the courtyard of the last and observe Bessie and Victoria, two monster rhinos who guard the main entrance whose red and green doors are covered with intricate grille work which represents the flora and fauna of sea, air and earth.

Divinity Hall, the last building on the east of Divinity Avenue, is the oldest Harvard building (1816) devoted to its original purpose: a dormitory for divinity students. It was built because President Kirkland believed that divinity students should be isolated from the rest of the University in case they adopted "more of the spirit of the University than of their profession." One wonders how successful his ploy was, for, a quarter of a century later, Ralph Waldo Emerson in his famous "Divinity School address" claimed that the atmosphere of the school was so literary that theological students were apt to regard the ministry "as an occasion of intellectual exercise and display rather than as a means of doing good to all classes in the community."

On the left of Divinity Avenue are the **Sherman Fairchild Biochemical Laboratories** and the **University Museums**. The **Tozzer Library**, part of the latter, is said to contain America's best anthropological collection. Closing the avenue at its northern end is the **Farlow Herbarium** which contains the world's largest orchid collection.

Return to Gund Hall and cross the road to **Memorial Hall**, a huge Gothic-Ruskinian pile which, like nearly all great Harvard buildings, has its admir-

ers and detractors. Among the latter is G.E. Kidder Smith, the architectural historian: "Though not lively (it) is loved, a mammoth ugly duckling, an almost fantastic statement of the taste of its time." Memorial Hall was built in the last quarter of the 19th century to honor those Harvard dead who fell in the Civil War. Its steep, streaky bacon, polychromatic roofs were at one time topped by a soaring clock-tower whose bells called and dismissed classes. Unfortunately, the tower was destroyed in 1956 in a spectacular conflagration.

Although from the outside Memorial Hall looks like a cathedral and although its interior is tripartite, one only has to enter to be immediately informed that this is a secular building. The vast, oblong nave was used for commencement exercises and as an undergraduate dining hall. (It seems likely that it will soon be used again for the latter purpose.) The transept, in ecclesiastical terms, is the memorial part of the hall and its 17 stained-glass windows are a veritable museum of American stained glass: note especially the "Battle Window" by John la Farge. The apse, again in ecclesiastical terms, is Sanders Theater which, with seating for 1,200, is still the largest auditorium in the University. It has superb acoustics and sightlines.

West of Memorial Hall and fronted by the **Tanner Rock Fountain** is the airy, light and white, glass and concrete **Science Center**, the largest of all Harvard buildings; it won an American Institute of Architecture award for its architect, Josef Louis Sert, once dean of the Graduate School of Design. At the western end of the building five massive setbacks form a giant stairway to the stars. Despite rumors, it is not true that when trunk and tusks are put in place the Science Center will become the world's largest white elephant and will be honored with the Harvard White Elephant award which has been held for 50 years by the Widener Library!

Walk down **Oxford Street** on the eastern flank of the Science Center and

Science Center, Harvard's largest building.

turn left immediately after passing the all glass **Gordon McKay Building of Engineering and Applied Physics**. Pass between two entirely disparate buildings. To the right is the **Jefferson Physical Laboratory**, a large red-brick Victorian monster. Here, in the 1920s, a laboratory was made available to Edwin Land, a bright, young undergraduate who subsequently invented the Polaroid camera. To the left is the discrete, almost genteel, **Music Building**. Inscribed above its entrance are the words: "To Charm, To Strengthen and To Teach, These are the Three Great Chords of Might."

The Law School: Walk westwards and immediately enter an irregular yard part of which, deplorably, is a parking lot. It is flanked by a variety of buildings. Most prominent is the polychromatic **Austin Hall**, part of the **Law School**, which is somewhat evocative of Sever Hall and which bears the characteristic Richardson imprint. The portico of this Romanesque building, completed in 1881, has three glorious round arches supported by groups of intricate colonettes and a conical-capped asymmetrical turret. Facing this is the back of **Littauer Center** which is now occupied by the University's government and economic departments.

The front of this granite building with its imposing six-column Ionic portico – this is the last Harvard building in Imperial tradition – faces the **Cambridge Street Underpass.** To the west, and unsuccessfully attempting to close this pseudo-yard from Massachusetts Avenue, is the somewhat incongruous **Gannet House**, a small, white, Greek-revival building from 1838, home of the renowned *Harvard Law Review.*

At right angles and to the north of Austin Hall is the white limestone **Langdell Hall**, which is the heart of the Law School and delineates the west side of **Law School Yard**, parts of which are used as a parking lot. Because of the great length of Langdell Hall and the lack of depth of the yard, it is impossible

to fully appreciate the glory of the grand ivy-covered portico of this building with its Ionic columns and pilasters which houses part of the largest (1.4 million volumes) law library of any university in the world. The Law School, established in 1817 with six students, is now attended by 1,800 students: it is America's oldest law school. Opposite Langdell Hall and defining the southeast of the Law School Yard is the Jefferson Physical Laboratory and other red-brick buildings used by applied sciences and allied fields.

The back of Langdell Hall, almost as handsome as the front, forms the east side of a small, leafy quadrangle around which, and spreading out from, are the 17 other buildings which constitute the Law School. Much appreciated in winter are the tunnels that connect some of these to Langdell Hall.

The north side of the Law School Yard is enclosed by modern buildings of the **Harkness Graduate Center**, opened in 1949 and designed by Architects Collaborative under the leadership of Walter Gropius. All the buildings are dormitories except the **Harkness Commons**; it contains dining areas and public rooms and some unusual works of art. The Commons faces a sunken quadrangle which is frozen in winter and used for ice-skating: during the rest of the year it is the scene of football and softball games.

The central work of art and the focal point of the entire complex is the 27-foot high stainless steel *World Tree* by the sculptor Richard Lippold. Nicknamed "Jungle Gym," "Clothes Rack" and "Plumbing," it represents a primitive religious symbol common among such people as the Australian aborigines who believed that their sacred World Tree is the hub of the universe. To welcome the spring, law students have been known to indulge in strange fertility rites around this tree.

Back in Harvard Square, exit to the southeast on Massachusetts Avenue. On the first 600 yards to **Sullivan**

MIT's Great Court and McLaruin building.

Square, and even immediately beyond, there are more stores, restaurants and bookshops similar to those found around the square. A further 900 yards and, immediately before Central Square, stands the imposing Romanesque **Cambridge Town Hall** with its campanile. The large rusticated building with cupolated tower facing the Town Hall is an office building. **Central Square** is tawdry: in and around it are several inexpensive ethnic (especially Indian) restaurants.

Hi-tech: Half-a-mile beyond Central Square, you reach the first MIT buildings. A thoroughly unprepossessing building on the left houses the MIT **Museum** which contains treasures that have made MIT a leader in computer, electronic and nuclear technologies and in the atomic and space age.

Two other MIT museums are open to the public. In the **Hart Nautical Museum** in the main building are model craft ranging from Donald McKay's great Yankee clipper *Flying Cloud* to

modern guided missile warships by way of America Cup defenders. Temporary exhibits of outstanding contemporary art can be savored in the **List Visual Arts Center** in the Wiesner Building at the eastern end of the campus.

Continue from the MIT Museum along Massachusetts Avenue, cross the railroad tracks and reach the main campus. That part to the right, the west campus, is devoted to the students' social life while the larger part to the left, the east campus, is the workplace of MIT.

Kresge Auditorium and the **Chapel** are two outstanding buildings designed by the Finnish architect, Eero Saarinen. The former is an enormous tent-like structure rising out of a circular brick terrace; its roof appears to be supported at only three points by delicate metal rods and it is enclosed by thin-mullioned curtains of glass. It is very much an outward-looking building.

The much smaller chapel, a windowless, brick cylinder set in a moat and with a sculptural bell tower, is inward-

MIT's eastern campus and (right) circular chapel.

looking. Light reflected from the moat illuminates the interior in which a delicate bronze-toned screen hangs behind the white marble altar block. Slightly further west is **Baker House**, an undulating dormitory designed by the Finnish architect Lavar Aalto so that all rooms have a view of the river.

Back on Massachusetts Avenue, the imposing, domed, neoclassical facade of the **Rogers Building** (he founded MIT) with its steep stairway and four pairs of Ionic columns is the main entrance to the teaching buildings and leads to an extensive system of tunnels claimed to be the third largest in the world. These link many of the east campus buildings.

Rather than entering here, continue on Massachusetts Avenue for a further couple of hundred yards until the **River Charles**. Turn left onto **Memorial Drive** and immediately on the left is the aptly named **Great Court** (also called **Killian Court**) in front of the monumental **MacLaruin Building** with its

Pantheon-like dome and broad Ionic portico. (Richard C. MacLaruin, a Scot, was the president of MIT who took the Institute from Boston to Cambridge.) Inscribed on the buildings which enclose the court are the names of great scientists, including Darwin and da Vinci, Faraday and Franklin and two MIT benefactors, DuPont and Lowell.

A large Henry Moore sculpture adorns the courtyard. Until the 1950s MIT did not acquire works of art but now has an active Council for the Arts and major pieces of sculpture by, among others, Picasso, Nevelsohn, Lipchitz and Calder dot the campus.

Further to the east is **McDermott Court**, dominated by the **Earth Sciences Building**, the tallest structure on campus and readily recognized by the large white sphere on its roof. In front of it stands Calder's *Big Sail*, a giant free-form metal sculpture. The Earth Sciences Building is just one of four on campus designed by I.M. Pei, a Harvard graduate who also studied at MIT. Others

East Cambridge's Bulfinch Place cupola and (right) mall.

224

are the **Dreyfus Building** and the **Ralph Landau Building** which flank Earth Sciences and, somewhat further east, the **Wiesner Building**.

Further along Memorial Drive it is back to neo-classicism with the **Walker Memorial Building** which is used for a variety of purposes. Facing this is the MIT **Sailing Pavilion**. And then, still on Memorial Drive, is the austere, limestone, ivy-covered **President's House**.

Main Street and **Kendall Square**, to the east of Wiesner, are today tree-bordered areas lined by handsome, soaring buildings, most of which are of red brick. A few years ago they were a desolation. Visit the landscaped garden atop the parking lot in the heart of the **Cambridge Center**, a modern hotel, laboratory and office complex. Further west, across the rail tracks, is more of the same in **Technology Square**, an urban redevelopment project in which MIT joined with the city to clear away old factories and tenements.

The name Polaroid on some of these buildings reflects the birth of the instant camera in Cambridge. Polaroid's rival, Eastman Kodak, is well represented on the MIT campus with the **Eastman Laboratory Building** and **Eastman Court**. George Eastman, a great MIT benefactor, believed that "the progress of the world depends almost entirely upon education" and left much of his not inconsiderable estate to MIT – "the greatest institution of its kind."

East Cambridge: Proceed north from Technology Square on **Fulkerson Street** for about half-a-mile. Turn right onto **Otis Street** where, on the right, stands the **Sacred Heart Church**, a Victorian Gothic edifice in blue trimmed with granite which was built between 1874 and 1883 to serve East Cambridge's ever-increasing number of Irish immigrants. A large, terracotta and brick building 300 yards further along Otis Street now houses the elderly and stands on the site of **Fort Putnam**. It was from here that, in March 1776, the Patriots bombarded the British during

echmere
anal.

the final days of the siege of Boston.

Continue along Otis Street, lined with trim, wooden Greek revival houses representative of decorous vernacular architecture of 1820–70, until the corner with **Third Street**. Here stands the simple, Federal-style **Holy Cross Polish Church** *sans* cupola. Originally built for a Unitarian congregation in 1827, this is the oldest church in East Cambridge. It testifies to the many Polish who, together with Portuguese, Italian and Lithuanians, arrived in East Cambridge following the Civil War. They joined, in the city's factories, the Irish and Germans who had begun to arrive half a century earlier. The handsome 19th-century red-brick apartments on the same side of Third Street led to the sobriquet Quality Street.

The red-brick building across the road with Georgian cupola and modest Italianate campanile is **Bulfinch Place**, the former courthouse which has been brilliantly rehabilitated by Graham Gund into offices and the **Cambridge**

Center for the Performing Arts. The original structure, built to the plans of Bulfinch in 1812, was poorly constructed and in 1848 was re-designed as a courthouse by Amni Young. The proud eagle which stands in the central courtyard formerly crowned the main Boston Post Office. A stele at the northeast corner of this block marks where 800 British Redcoats landed on April 19, 1775, to begin their march on Lexington and Concord.

North of Bulfinch Court is the monumental red-brick 19th-century **Middlesex Registry** with four brick porticoes, two of which stand at the head of impressive stairways. The heady aroma which fills the air comes from the **Deran Confectionery Company**, immediately east of the Registry Office. This occupies what was once part of the Davenport Furniture Company, the firm that gave its name to the davenport and whose last major commission was for the furnishings of the United Nations building in New York.

Chocolate odors are preferable to those which would have emanated from the nearby J.P. Squire meat-packing plant, one of the first to use ice in processing meat. It has long since gone, as has the New England Glass Company whose 235-foot stack was taller than the Bunker Hill Monument and which, for much of the 19th century, was the largest glass factory in the world. All this activity meant that, between the world wars, Cambridge was the third most important manufacturing city in New England.

Industry has been replaced by commerce. Walk down **First Street** for 600 yards to reach the **Cambridgeside Galleria**, Metropolitan Boston's newest shopping mall. It stands alongside a circular basin in the center of which is a soaring fountain and whose waters join the 200-yard long **Lechmere Canal** which enters the Charles River. Riverboat excursions leave from the basin. East Cambridge (Lechmere) can be reached on the green line of the "T".

East Cambridge attracted immigrants from throughout the world. **Right**, sunset on the Charles River.

DAY TRIPS WEST

Lovers of history and those smitten with nostalgia will wish to "Go West" and to visit, among other places, Lexington and Concord, Harvard Village and Sturbridge.

To reach Lexington, site of the first battle of the Revolution, leave Boston on Route 2 and, after 10 miles, turn right onto Route 4–225. Immediately, on the left, is a contemporary building which houses the **Museum of Our National Heritage** where the work of American craftspeople is exhibited. Soon after, still on the left, is the russet-colored **Munroe Tavern** from 1635 which served as headquarters for the Redcoats and as a hospital on their retreat from Concord. Another mile and **Battle Green**, a triangular affair in the heart of **Lexington**, is reached. Here, on April 19, 1775, Captain Parker told his men: "Stand your ground, don't fire unless fired upon, but if they mean to have a war, let it begin here!" And it did.

The guns go bang: Atop a heap of boulders, taken from the wall behind which the minutemen shot at the British, is the **Minuteman statue**. To the right (east) is **Buckman's Tavern**, a yellow clapboard building which dates from 1690, where 77 minutemen gathered to await the British. Following the battle, the minutemen who had been wounded were carried into this tavern where they were given medical attention. It has been restored to its original appearance. Visitors, on guided tours through seven rooms, are shown a bullet hole in the door, muskets, cooking equipment and furniture.

A quarter-of-a-mile to the north of the Green is the mocha-colored **Hancock-Clarke House** which dates from 1698; it has been moved hither and thither but has now been returned to its original site. Here, on the evening of April 18, John Hancock and Samuel Adams were roused from their sleep by Paul Revere and warned of the coming of the British.

Leave Lexington on Route 2A from the northwest corner of Battle Green – the **Battle Road** – to travel alongside the **Minuteman National Historical Park**. Stop at the **Battle Road Visitor Center** (*the* best place for those interested in the Revolution to start their Lexington-Concord exploration) to watch a film showing the events which led to that fateful April 19, 1775, and an animated map of British and American troop movements. Visit also the partly uncovered Ebenezer Fiske farmhouse where, after refreshing himself with a drink from a well a minuteman found himself facing a Redcoat period "You are a dead man," announced the minuteman. "And so are you," was the reply. Both leveled their muskets; both fired; both were killed. Concord is 8 miles away, after several stops.

Concord, a handsome small town, is twice blessed, for here is where the second engagement of the Revolution took place and here, during the first half

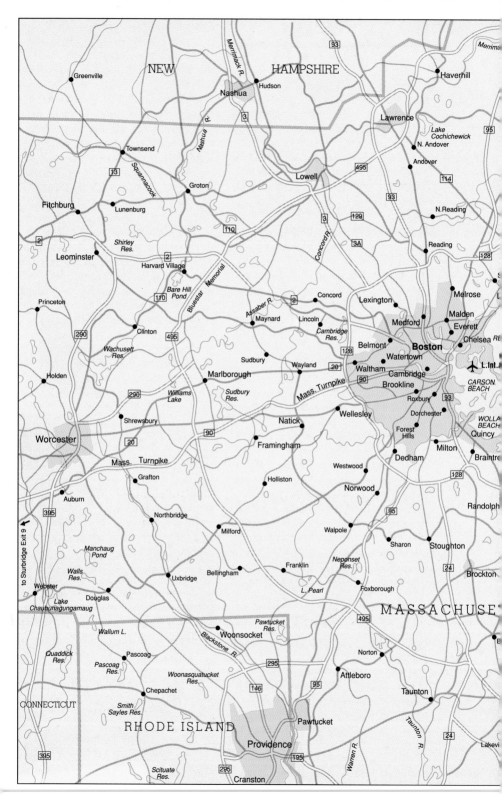

NEW HAMPSHIRE

Greenville

Nashua
Hudson

Lawrence

Haverhill

Townsend

Lowell

Lake Cochichewick
N. Andover

Andover

Groton

Fitchburg
Lunenburg

Shirley Res.

Leominster

Harvard Village

Bare Hill Pond

Concord

Lexington

Melrose

Malden
Everett

Medford

Chelsea

Belmont

Boston

Watertown

Cambridge Res.

Waltham

Cambridge

Brookline

Roxbury

Dorchester

CARSON BEACH

WOLLA BEACH

Quincy

Forest Hills

Milton

Braintre

Randolph

Stoughton

Brockton

Lakevi

Taunton R.

MASSACHUSE

RHODE ISLAND

Providence

Cranston

Pawtucket

Scituate Res.

CONNECTICUT

232

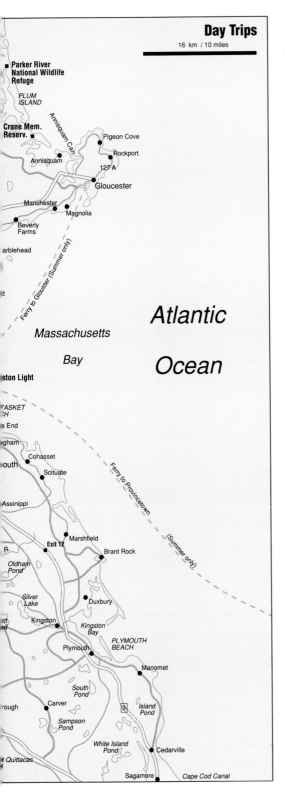

■ **Parker River National Wildlife Refuge**

PLUM ISLAND

Crane Mem. Reserv. ■

Annisquam Can.

Pigeon Cove

Rockport

Annisquam

127 A

Gloucester

Manchester

Magnolia

Beverly Farms

arblehead

Ferry to Glouster (Summer only)

Massachusetts

Bay

Atlantic

Ocean

ston Light

'ASKET 'H

s End

gham

Cohasset

outh

Scituate

Assinippi

Ferry to Provincetown

(Summer only)

Marshfield

Exit 12

R.

Brant Rock

Oldham Pond

Silver Lake

Duxbury

Kingston

Kingston Bay

PLYMOUTH BEACH

Plymouth

Manomet

South Pond

Carver

3 *Island Pond*

rough

Sampson Pond

White Island Pond

Cedarville

t Quittacas

Sagamore

Cape Cod Canal

of the 19th century, lived a handful of renowned literati. **Monument Square**, the center of the town, is where, on April 19, 1775, a British sergeant burning a cache of captured supplies inadvertently set fire to a building. The Americans massing on the opposite side of the river saw the smoke and, assuming that the British were burning the town, decided to march to its defense "or die in the attempt." Their advance was blocked by a British detachment guarding the bridge. Several roads radiate from Monument Square: all should be explored.

Begin by driving north on **Monument Road** for a little over 1 mile and then turning left to reach immediately the **National Historical Park North Bridge Visitor Center**. Here, dioramas and a somewhat disappointing 12-minute audio-visual presentation inform about the affairs which led to the battle. Visitors who choose to don colonial costume in one of the rooms are apt to disturb the peace of the Center. The gardens overlooking the Concord River and from where the **Old North Bridge** can be seen are quite beautiful.

Those who are indolent or infirm might wish to backtrack to the Bridge parking lot, but in so doing they deny themselves a walk through history. Better to stroll the half-mile downhill past the **Muster Field** (to the right), along roughly the route of the militia until you reach the bronze statue of the **Minuteman**, rifle in one hand and the other dragging a plowshare. On the plinth are Ralph Waldo Emerson's immortal words "the shot heard round the world." And so to "the rude bridge that spanned the flood." Today's bridge, with its "genuine antique look," was built in 1956.

The idyllic setting belies the bloody skirmish. To enjoy a couple of hours of sheer bliss, paddle a canoe along the winding river and under the bridge. (Canoes can be rented at **South Bridge** on **Main Street**: the river at this point is the **Sudbury** rather than the **Concord**.)

The simple, clapboard **Old Manse**, 200 yards south of North Bridge, was built in 1770 and was first occupied by the Rev. William Emerson, who watched the battle for the bridge from here. Subsequently, his grandson, Ralph Waldo Emerson, lived here for two short periods. Then, after their marriage, the Hawthornes moved in and remained for three years. It was during this period that Nathaniel wrote *Mosses from an Old Manse*, a collection of stories that secured a literary place for both house and writer.

Meanwhile, Sophia was painting and scratching the study and dining room windows with her wedding ring. The longest and most charming of her inscriptions states: "Una Hawthorne stood on this window-sill January 22, 1845, while the trees were all glass chandeliers – a goodly show which she liked much though only 10 months old."

Literary giants: Back in Monument Square, drive northeast on **Bedford Street** (Route 62) for 200 yards to **Sleepy Hollow Cemetery**. **Author's Ridge**, in the northeast corner, is the final resting place of Hawthorne, the Alcotts, Margaret Sidney, Emerson and Thoreau. An uncarved boulder devoid of any religious symbolism marks Emerson's grave.

Backtrack from the square for less than 1 mile on the Lexington Road to the junction with the **Cambridge Turnpike**. Here stands the **home of Ralph Waldo Emerson** and the **Concord Museum**. In the former, Emerson wrote his celebrated essays ("A foolish consistency is the hobgoblin of little minds, adored by little statesmen, philosophers and divines") while in the latter, a brick building, is Emerson's study which, apart from one round table, was transferred in its entirety from the wooden Emerson home because of fear of fire. The excellent museum consists mainly of a series of beautifully furnished reconstructed rooms from the 18th and 19th centuries. Its Thoreau Gallery boasts the largest collection of artifacts

Young Redcoat displays his medals.

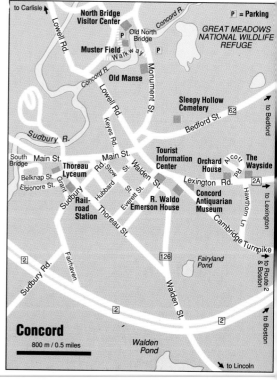

Concord

associated with Thoreau, including furnishings from his Walden Pond abode; pride of place in the Revolutionary Room belongs to a lantern, one of the two hung from the Old North Church as a signal to Paul Revere which informed him that the British were proceeding to Concord by sea rather than by land.

One mile further along Lexington Road stands the shaded, brown, clapboard **Orchard House** where the Alcott family lived from 1858 to 1877. Here Louisa wrote *Little Women* and *Little Men* and her father, Bronson, founded his school of philosophy whose students met in a large building at the rear of the house. Both may be visited. Much memorabilia is on display.

Just beyond this is **The Wayside** (not to be confused with Longfellow's Inn of that name), the home of the Concord Muster Man on the day of the battle. In the next century the Alcotts resided here before moving to Orchard House. Observe the Alcotts' piano and explore a tower study where Hawthorne, who bought the house in 1851, lived and attempted to write, eventually turning in desperation to travel writing and saying he would be happy if the house just burned down. It did not and was occupied by Margaret Sidney, author of the *Five Little Pepper* books.

For a change of pace some might wish to drive west from Concord for 12 miles on Route 62. The attraction here is the **Nashoba Valley Winery** which makes wines, not from Concord's famous grapes, but from such fruits as peaches and pears, cranberries and blueberries.

And so to **Walden Pond**, reached by returning towards Concord and then traveling south on **Walden Street**, which crosses Route 2, for 1½ miles. The pond is relatively small and one can take a gentle stroll around it in about an hour. Best time to visit is the fall. During summer, when the Pond becomes a giant swimming hole, Thoreau would have been unable to separate himself from "the mass of men (who) lead quiet lives of desperation."

On a lazy river at Concord.

RELICS OF THE INDUSTRIAL REVOLUTION

Eleven miles north of Route 3 is **Lowell**, site of another revolution. (Lowell can also be reached directly from Boston by driving 23 miles on Route 93 and then 8 miles on Interstate 495 South.) "Spindle City" was the setting for the American industrial revolution early in the 19th century and became the world's leading textile producer. Canals were constructed and the **Merrimack River** was harnessed to power eight major red-brick textile mills. These were staffed with mill girls from the area who boarded in model dormitories and had to attend the city's handsome **St Annes Church** each Sunday.

The local girls were replaced by successive waves of immigrants: Irish, French-Canadians, Afro-Americans, Portuguese, Poles, European Jews and, in the 20th century, Armenians, Asians (Lowell has been called the "Cambodian capital of America") and Hispanics. Before long the Utopian philosophy of Francis Cabot Lowell and his co-investors was abandoned and Lowell's sweat-shops were no better than those in Europe and Asia.

Today, textiles (mainly synthetics) are produced in only two mills and Lowell has fallen on hard times. Recycling of the magnificent mills and boarding houses was introduced just in time and

wholesale destruction prevented.

All this and more is recounted – and at times interpreted – by National Park rangers for much of Lowell is now a **National Historic Park**. The longest and most fascinating tour (it lasts just over two hours) involves genuine trolley rides, traveling on a barge through canals and locks and some walking. The **Visitors Center** offers a variety of exhibits and a multi-image slide show; the **Lowell Heritage State Park** shows how canals, water-wheels and turbines worked. Also visit the **New England Quilt Museum** where antique and contemporary quilts are on display.

Close to the Visitors Center is the home of Whistler's father where **Whistler's etchings** are displayed. The commemorative **sculpture of Jack Kerouac**, a Lowell man who in his novels captures the Lowell of the second quarter of the 20th century, stands in **Eastern Park Plaza**.

Lawrence, "Queen of the Mill Towns," 8 miles north of Lowell on Interstate 495 and then 5 miles north on Route 3, developed after and is smaller than Lowell. At sunset, views along the Merrimack River, with its red-brick mills and more than a dozen soaring smoke stacks, are positively stygian. Lawrence, unlike Lowell, had no Utopian pretensions and 30,000 mill workers went on strike for two months in 1912. The "Bread and Roses" strike was marked by murders and mass arrests but finally won wage increases for textile workers throughout New England. The story of Lawrence is recounted in its **Heritage State Park**, located in a mill boarding house.

From Lawrence, travel 4 miles east on Interstate 495 and turn south at exit 47. **North Andover** is reached after 7 miles. Exhibits in the **Museum of American Textile History** explain the history of woolen textile manufacturing, with emphasis on the transition from hand to machine production during the industrial revolution. Carding, spinning and weaving are demonstrated.

For a change of pace, travel south for 2 miles on Route 28 to peaceful, colonial **Andover**, home of **Phillips Academy**, one of the most prestigious preparatory schools in the nation. Its **Addison Gallery of American Art** houses a superb collection of American paintings and sculpture.

Those in search of further industrial history should continue south from Andover towards Boston. The **Saugus Iron Works National Historic Site**, the country's first iron works (1646), is located just east of Route 1 about 10 miles north of Boston. Rangers lead visitors through the impeccable reconstructed plant and explain, step by step, how iron was manufactured in the mid-1600s. The **Iron Works House**, the only surviving structure of the original complex, is a splendid example of 17th-century American Elizabethan architecture.

Near here, on Route 1, is the **Hill Top Restaurant** which boasts the largest turnover of any restaurant in the country. Seating 1,500 in five dining rooms, Hill Top, readily recognized by a herd of life-size plastic cattle bordering the highway, specializes in inexpensive steaks.

A cairn of stones stands alongside the site where Thoreau lived between 1845 and 1847. "I went to the woods, because I wished to live deliberately, to front only the essential facts of life, and see if I could not learn what it had to teach, and not, when I came to die, discover that I had not lived." The cairn stands about 600 yards counter-clockwise from the busy main beach. It can also be reached by walking north alongside the main road and then turning into the woods – again, a distance of 600 yards.

Thoreau enthusiasts will wish to visit the **Thoreau Lyceum** in Concord which houses much memorabilia of the great man and where stands a replica of his Walden Pond cabin.

(Concord can quickly "be done" in a couple of hours, but to explore any house usually necessitates joining a guided tour. This often requires a short wait. Most tours take about 40 minutes.)

Continue south from Walden Pond and, after half-a-mile, turn left. Immediately to the right is the prefabricated **Gropius House** which expresses the Bauhaus principles of function and simplicity. This was the first building that the great German architect designed when he arrived in the US in 1937. A further mile leads to the attractive **DeCordova and Dana Museum and Park** (you are now in **Lincoln**) where temporary exhibitions of modern art can be viewed. The 30 acres of grounds, high above **Sandy Point Pond**, are a splendid setting for sculpture. During summer, outdoor concerts are held in the amphitheater.

Also in Lincoln is a gem of a blue, three-story, clapboard house with an Ionic portico. The **Codman House**, which stands in grounds landscaped to resemble an English country estate, is a treasure trove of 18th- and 19th-century furniture and decorative arts.

Shakers and visionaries: To reach **Harvard Village** and the **Fruitlands Museums** return to Concord and drive west on Route 2. After 13 miles, turn south on Route 110 and then immedi-

School children visit Fruitlands Museums.

ately right onto **Old Shirley Road.** This crosses **Depot Road** to become **Prospect Hill** where the entrance to Fruitlands is reached about 2 miles after leaving Route 2. Fruitlands, situated at an altitude of about 600 feet and with magnificent views across the **Nashau River Valley** to **Mount Wachusett** and **Mount Monadnock**, is immaculately maintained and its four museums are a pleasure to visit.

An 18th-century farmhouse where, for some months, Bronson Alcott and his family, an English friend, Charles Lane, and others attempted an experiment in communal living has been made into a **Transcendentalist Museum.** One reason for the break-up of the group was that Lane wished Alcott to abandon his family and to join him at Harvard's Shaker Village. Not surprisingly, Mrs Alcott did not approve. And then who could be an Adamite, as was Samuel Bower, in the harsh Massachusetts winter? (An Adamite is a nudist: presumably an Evite is a female nudist.)

The **Shaker House**, built in 1790s, was an office for the Harvard Shakers Society which flourished until 1918. Shaker handicrafts are displayed and a variety of exhibits offer an insight into the Shaker way of life – celibacy, communal ownership of property and worship joyfully expressed in dance.

The other two museums are the **American Indian** and the **Picture Gallery**. The former houses a selection of North American (not New England) Indian relics, historic Indian arts and industries and dioramas. The west gallery of the latter displays delightful "primitive" portraits by early 19th-century itinerant artists while the east gallery has the works of landscape painters associated with the Hudson River School.

Say "Good morning" or "Good afternoon" to those whom you encounter at **Old Sturbridge Village** (OSV) who are dressed in 19th-century garb and they will counter with a "G'Day" and explain that, in the early 19th century, that was the acceptable greeting. OSV, a living history museum, 55 miles west of Boston on the Massachusetts Turnpike near exit 9, is a complete village and farm from about 1830. (OSV is served by the Peter Pan bus from Boston.)

More than 40 original buildings, which span the period from 1730 to 1840, have been collected from New England and placed here to create a village and a 70-acre farm. Many of the buildings stand around a central green and a lake is spanned by a covered bridge. At OSV the blacksmith and the potter, clad in appropriate garb yet talking contemporary language, work as they would have in the 1830s. A pair of oxen harnessed to a plow are used to turn the sod. Rural life is authentically re-created with a variety of religious and political events punctuating the daily and seasonal rhythm of village life and farm work.

Two small but superb museums, one devoted to clocks and the other to glass, round off a splendid destination.

Interpreters at Old Sturbridge Village.

DAY TRIPS SOUTH

South of Boston is Cape Cod with its glorious beaches. But, even before reaching the canal that separates the Cape from the rest of Massachusetts, several historic towns, some with not to be ignored beaches, await. Mention Pilgrims, and Plymouth and Provincetown are Pavlovian responses.

Start your southern safari by leaving Boston on Route 3 (the Southeast Expressway). Observe the two colorfully painted gas tanks to the left. The more fanciful, the work of a nun, is supposed to conceal the image of Chairman Mao. Take Exit 12 and join the **Quincy Shore Drive** which crosses the **Neponset River** by a drawbridge and, 9 miles after leaving Boston, arrive at **Quincy** which bears the honorific "city of presidents" because here both John Adams and John Quincy Adams were born. (Quincy can also readily be reached on the red line of the "T".)

Home of the Adams: Antiquarians and historians will delight in half-a-dozen buildings associated with the name Quincy. First to be reached on entering the city is the 1770 mid-Georgian **Josiah Quincy House** (20 Muirhead Street) which is furnished with Quincy family heirlooms. Half-a-mile further south is the **Quincy Homestead** (34 Butler Road) whose handsome country mansion dates to the beginning of the 19th century.

Half-a-mile to the west, at 135 Adams Street, is the splendid **Adams National Historic Site,** home to four generations of the Adams family for 140 years and now decorated with their furnishings and memorabilia. The delightful **Stone Library** in the immaculately maintained grounds contains John Quincy Adams' Library of 14,000 books. The **United Parish First Church** (1306 Hancock Street), a few hundred yards south of the Josiah Quincy House, is known as the **Church of the Presidents**

and contains the remains of the two presidents and their wives. About a mile south of here, on **Franklin Street**, are the modest salt-box houses in which the presidents were born. Simple though they may be, Abigail, wife of John, wrote that she preferred the charms of "my little cottage" to the grandeur of the London court.

But Quincy has more to offer than gracious living. Here the **Granite Railway**, the country's first commercial railway, was built in order to transport granite to Charlestown for the Bunker Hill Monument. The Metropolitan District Commission offers tours of the **railway incline** (Mullin Avenue in West Quincy), the **railway terminus** (Bunker Hill Lane) **a quarry** (Ricciuti Drive) and a **turning mill**.

On leaving town on **Washington Street** (Route 3A), observe on the right, as you cross the **Weymouth Fore River** drawbridge, the now defunct **Bethlehem Shipyards**. Here the Thomas W. Lawson, the only seven-

masted schooner ever built, was launched as was the first atomic-powered surface ship.

Continue south on Route 3A to the **Hingham Rotary**. Exit on **Summer Street**, then turn left at **Martin's Lane** for a 1-mile drive to **World's End**, an idyllic 248-acre oasis designed by Frederick Law Olmsted. At different – fortunately not at the same – times, it was proposed as a site for the United Nations and as a nuclear waste disposal site, much to the dismay of the artists and nature lovers who frequent it. Stroll on paths lined with oak, hickory and cedar trees and through rolling fields where prize Jersey cattle formerly grazed and which are now home to pheasant, quails, foxes and rabbits. Herons and egrets populate the 5-mile rugged shoreline and all the while the impressive Boston skyline can be seen in the distance.

Return to Summer Street, turn left and follow the road to **Washington Boulevard**. This leads to **Nantasket Beach**, the best beach close to Boston (16 miles) and to **Hull** from where there are views of the Atlantic and the harbor islands. These islands include the buffeted **Brewsters**, on which stands the **Boston Light**, the nation's first lighthouse. (Both Nantasket and Hull can be reached by ferry from Boston.)

Backtrack from Hull to peaceful **Hingham** where the numbers on the handsome, usually white, clapboard houses on **Main Street** are not to assist the mailman but proudly announce when the houses were built: this was, more often than not, in the 19th century and, occasionally, in the 18th. The town has several inspiring churches, including the **Old Ship Church** on Main Street, the oldest building in the nation in continuous ecclesiastical service. The interior of its roof echoes an inverted ship's hull, reflecting the fact that its builders were ships' carpenters.

Continue south on Route 3A through **Cohasset** where **Jerusalem Road** winds past stately homes overlooking a

The peace of World's End.

244

rocky coast reminiscent of Cape Ann. Fourteen miles further south is **Marshfield**, where the **Daniel Webster Law Office**, standing in the grounds of the 18th-century **Winslow House**, is testimony to the great orator having spent the last 20 years of his life here. Immediately past this **Duxbury**, with its beautiful homes and 9-mile long barrier beach, is a bird-watcher's paradise. The energetic might wish to ascend the 130-foot high **Myles Standish Monument** for a bird's-eye view of the region.

Birth of a nation: And so, 40 miles after leaving Boston, to **Plymouth**, the site of the first permanent American settlement north of Virginia. It was in 1620 that the Pilgrims set foot – or so legend goes – on Plymouth Rock.

Much can be seen at Plymouth relating to the Pilgrims: a trolley runs between the different sights. A stone's throw from the monument over the **Rock** is the *Mayflower II*, a replica of the original *Mayflower*, built in Eng-

land and sailed to Plymouth in 1957. This 104-foot long vessel, peopled with interpreters, vividly conveys the hardships that its 102 passengers undoubtedly suffered on their 66-day voyage.

Across the road from the Rock is **Coles Hill** where, during their first winter, the Pilgrims secretly buried their dead at night. Here, too, is the **Plymouth National Wax Museum** with 26 life-size dioramas illustrating the Pilgrims' story from the emigration of the Separatists from England to Holland in 1607 to the first Thanksgiving celebration in 1621. An imposing statue of **Massasoit**, the Indian chief who helped the Pilgrims survive their first spring, stands in front of the Museum.

Pilgrim Hall Museum on **Main Street**, a Greek revival building designed by Alexander Parris and the oldest public museum in the nation – the Salem Museum is older but began life as a private institution – boasts the country's largest collection of Pilgrim memorabilia. Here the Pilgrims come to

life with such items as John Alden's halbred, Myles Standish's bible and the cradle of Peregrine White who was born aboard the *Mayflower*.

Further east, beyond Main Street, is **Burial Hill** with gravestones dating back to the time of the Colony. "Under this stone rests the ashes of Willm Bradford, a zealous Puritan and sincere Christian, Governor of Plymouth Colony from April 1621–57 (the year he died aged 69) except 5 years which he declined." The hill was the site of the Pilgrims' first meeting house, fort and watch-tower from where friends and foes arriving by sea could be observed. South of Burial Hill is the **Jenney Grist Mill** where corn is still ground as in the days of the Pilgrims. One can also visit half-a-dozen old houses, including the **Jabez Howland House** on **Sandwich Street**, the only surviving house in Plymouth in which a Mayflower Pilgrim actually lived.

The year is always 1627 at **Plimoth Plantation**, 3 miles south of the Rock, where interpreters dressed in authentic Pilgrim costumes and speaking in old English dialects, assume the roles of specific historical residents of the Colony. Query Mistress Alden about Captain Standish and she may well respond: "Oh, he lives next door and there are some, sir, who feel he is not the easiest man with whom to deal." Question the same Mistress Alden or Captain Standish about Paul Revere or George Washington and they will look at you with incomprehension. The interpreters do not simply stand around waiting for questions but go about their 1627 work and interact with one another. Even the livestock is painstakingly backbred to approximate 17th-century barnyard beasts.

Another part of the site is a reconstructed Wampanoag village which recaptures Indian life in Massachusetts in the 1620s. Unfortunately, nothing is perfect, and this magnificent living museum is marred by an incongruous, albeit handsome, reception area.

Plimoth Plantation.

Conclude a visit to Plymouth at **Cranberry World**, down at the waterfront at the north end of town. A handsome, exhaustive museum has displays illustrating the history, lore and commercial development of cranberries.

Cape Cod: Seventeen miles after leaving Plymouth on State 3, the soaring **Sagamore Bridge**, spanning the **Cape Cod Canal**, comes into view. Across it is a land of marshes and meadows, of pines and of cranberry bogs and, above all, of beaches. The region is nirvana for many Bostonians and New Englanders, New Yorkers and Canadians.

First, a word on the geography of Cape Cod which Thoreau called "the bared and bended arm of Massachusetts." The **Upper Cape**, with the towns of Sandwich, Barnstable, Falmouth and Woods Hole, is the part just beyond the canal: **Mid-Cape**, which stretches from Hyannis to Orleans and which includes the towns of Chatham, Harwich, Brewster, Dennis and Yarmouth, is at the base of the concavity, while the

Lower Cape – that part generally likened to the forearm, stretching northwards to end with the "sandy fist" of Provincetown – includes the towns of Eastham, Wellfleet and Truro.

The Sagamore Bridge debouches onto Interstate 6 (the mid-Cape Highway) which runs first east and then north and ends, after 60 miles, at Provincetown. This is the route to take to reach a destination, but much more intriguing is Route 6A (the old King's Highway). It parallels, more or less, Highway 6 and passes through many of the Cape's 15 towns and 70 villages, most with salt-box architecture and a classical white painted church.

Distances between communities are short and it is possible to travel the entire Cape, with frequent stops, in one day. But it's much better take several days and, for those with the time, several weeks. Most visitors make one township their base, though some prefer to mosey around driving from town to town. Each town, each village, is the

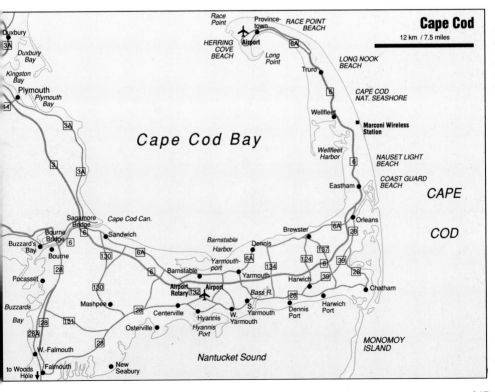

same yet each has its own distinctive character and its devotees who are besotted by their place on the Cape, from where they will never budge. All are close to superb beaches.

The Cape boasts about 300 miles of sandy beaches, some backed by glorious, almost 100-foot high dunes. Thunderous surf is found on the **Outer Cape**, which is washed by the Atlantic, while gentler waters prevail in the concavity of **Cape Cod Bay.** Slightly rougher are the waters in **Buzzards Bay** and **Nantucket Sound**, respectively to the southwest of the Upper Cape and to the south of the Mid-Cape. Because the Cape is exceptionally narrow, it is possible to spend the morning in roaring surf and, half an hour later, loll in placid, shallow waters. If none of this appeals, then innumerable ponds and lakes invite swimming, sailing and wind-surfing, undisturbed by ocean waves. Only snag is that resident parking permits are required at some of the better beaches.

Permits are much more readily ob-tained for fishing in those 20 percent of the Cape's 365 ponds which are home to, among others, brown, rainbow and brook trout, white and yellow perch, black bass and land-locked salmon. Extensive opportunities for salt-water fishing are also available.

Nearly 40 golf courses dot the Cape. The greatest concentration of greens are at the largest two towns of **Barnstable** (seven courses) and **Falmouth** (five courses). Only about a dozen courses are strictly private.

Each community has set aside special areas for bicycling, but pedallers really come into their own on the **Cape Cod Rail Trail**, a paved recreational trail that runs on an abandoned railroad bed for 20 miles from Route 134 in **Dennis** to **Eastham**. It passes en route quintessential Cape scenery and several cultural and historical sites. The **Salt Pond Visitors Center** to the **Cape Cod National Seashore** is only a quarter of a mile from the trail's end in Eastham. **Sandwich**, the town that glass built

Harvesting cranberries.

and the first community reached after crossing the Canal, is an especially good place to be if the weather is inclement. Not that it doesn't have its quota of good beaches - but it also probably has more museums than anywhere else on the Cape. Glass lamps, candlesticks and innumerable other items exhibiting a characteristic lacy pattern that was the vogue in the second half of the 19th century can be enjoyed in the **Sandwich Glass Museum**.

Several interesting historic sites border **Shawne Pond**. These include the **Hoxie House** which, with its 17th-century furnishings, is believed to be the oldest (1637) house on the Cape. In **Dexter's Grist Mill**, in use since the 1650s, demonstrations of old milling skills may be enjoyed. **Yesteryear's Doll and Miniature Museum** fills two floors of the **First Parish Meeting House** with delightful memories.

Best of all is the **Heritage Plantation**, located in 76 acres of gardens rich in rhododendrons and day-lillies. It

houses an eclectic collection of Americana in several buildings. A replica of the round Shaker Barn at Hancock Shaker Village contains a magnificent collection of antique cars dating from 1899 to 1937. Another replica, this time of the "Publick House," a recreation hall for the Continental Army (1783), is filled with antique firearms, flags, Indian artifacts and 2,000 miniature soldiers. The Art Museum houses a glorious collection of folk art, including more than 100 Currier and Ives prints. And, for rambunctious children, there is an 1912 working carousel.

Twenty-eight miles further along Route 6A, at the eastern end of the Mid-Cape, is **Brewster**, another good place to spend a rainy day. The **Stony Brook Grist Mill** still grinds corn as it did in 1663. During April and May, schools of alewives (herring) returning from the Atlantic struggle in the mill-stream to leap up ladders that will lead them to the tranquil mill ponds where they spawn.

Those fascinated by conflagrations will adore the town's **New England Fire and History Museum** which contains one of the world's largest collections of antique fire equipment and memorabilia. All will be intrigued by the **Drummer Boy Museum**, which contains 21 life-size murals dramatizing, with light and sound, the American Revolution.

The **Dillingham House** is probably the Cape's second oldest (1660) house and the **Sydenstricker Glass Factory** provides the opportunity to observe handsome items made in an ingenious manner. For the children, there is **Sealand of Cape Cod** with its aquarium and seal and dolphin shows.

The Lower Cape: In 1961, in order to preserve the beauty of the Cape and to highlight a number of natural and historic sights, six towns – Chatham, Orleans, Eastham, Wellfleet, Truro and Provincetown – became the **Cape Cod National Seashore** (CCNS) under the aegis of the National Parks Services of the Department of the Interior. Visitors

Cape Cod, a bicyclist's paradise.

Centers are at Eastham (**Salt Pond**) and at Provincetown (**Province Lands**). Both are disappointing, although the view of sand dunes and ocean from the upper deck of the latter is spectacular.

Close to a glorious beach is the **Marconi Area (South Wellfleet)** where Guglielmo Marconi built his radio towers and from where, in 1903, he sent the first radio signal across the Atlantic. Further south at **Eastham's Coast Guard Beach** visit the **Old Coast Guard Station**, now a museum displaying the somewhat simple equipment used to rescue mariners from the thousands of vessels that were wrecked on this part of the coast.

However, what attracts most to the ccns are the magnificent beaches and the glorious desert-like dunes. They are at their best at **Nauset Beach (Orleans)**, **Nauset Light Beach (Eastham)**, **Marconi Beach (South Wellfleet)**, **Head of the Meadow Beach (Truro)**, **Provincetown** and, above all, at **Long Nook Beach (Truro)** where, unfortu-

nately, parking is almost impossible.

Provincetown's popular beaches are **Herring Cove**, about a mile from town and whose southeast section, by far the best part, is exclusively gay, and **Race Point**, which is about 6 miles from town. It was at Race Point that Thoreau, after strolling, wrote "here a man may stand, and put all America behind him." Then there is **Long Point**, gained by walking across a mile-long causeway at the south end of the town. Near the start of the causeway a commemorative stone recalls that it was "somewhere near here" that the Pilgrims first landed.

Provincetown, at the very tip of the Cape, is a three-ring, often raucous circus. It has many arts and crafts stores, art galleries, shops (both elegant and tawdry), and restaurants, all of which cater to a large and visible gay population, a much less obvious indigenous colony of Portuguese fishing folk and, during the summer, hordes of tourists. And yet serious artists maintain a tradition which started in 1901 with the

A trio of transvestites in Provincetown.

founding of the Cape Cod School of Art.

Although 117 miles from Boston by road, Provincetown is just 57 miles by sea. During July and August, tourist numbers are swollen by hundreds disembarking from the ferry which leaves Boston at 9.30 a.m. and arrives in Provincetown soon after noon. (A regular air service links Boston and Provincetown: flying time is 20 minutes.)

Commercial Street, invariably referred to as **Front Street**, parallels the shore and is where most activity occurs. Paralleling Front Street is **Back Street** (properly **Bradford Street**). Near Back Street is the Monument which commemorates the Pilgrims' stop in Provincetown in 1620 for six weeks before they moved on to Plymouth because of its more protected harbor and more arable soil. The **Monument**, a slim and stately affair adapted from the Torre del Mangia in Siena and built in the early 1900s, is the tallest granite structure in the country. It towers 352 feet above the town and can be ascended (it is a stiff climb) to enjoy a grand view of the Lower Cape.

The museum at the base of the Monument is a splendid affair with excellent dioramas showing the arrival of the Pilgrims, a fascinating whaling section and eclectic exhibits of the region's culture. On Front Street the **Heritage Museum**, housed in the old **Methodist Church**, displays local artifacts and memorabilia. Works of local artists are on show in the **Art Association** building at the east end of town.

Leave Provincetown, return for 28 miles on Interstate 6 to the traffic circle at **Orleans** and exit on State 28 for the 9 miles south to **Chatham** which is situated at the Cape's elbow. This is the Newport of the Cape, with its large cedar-shingled summer homes. The observation deck above the **Fish Pier** is an excellent place to be in the early afternoon to watch returning trawlers unloading their catches. Railway buffs will enjoy the **Railroad Museum**, housed in a Victorian railroad station.

Psychedelic shopping at Provincetown. Right, finding a room is seldom a problem on the Cape.

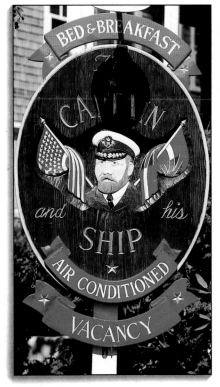

Bird watchers will make their way by boat from Chatham to **Monomoy Island**, an 8-mile stretch of pristine barrier reef, a national wildlife refuge which is an important resting place for birds on the Atlantic Flyway.

From Chatham, continue west on State 28 along the Cape's South Shore, passing **Harwich** where cranberry bogs come into their own and then driving through a honky-tonk area until, after 17 miles, you reach **Hyannis**. It and its port are the commercial center and the transport hub of the mid-Cape with regular scheduled airline services to Boston, Martha's Vineyard and Nantucket and ferries to the two islands. Railroad buffs might enjoy boarding a vintage train for the one-hour ride to Sandwich or to Buzzards Bay.

The magnet at **Hyannisport** is the **Kennedy Compound** which, however, is not visible from the road nor is it open to the public. All you are likely to see is a bronze medallion on a stone wall honoring the President with his words:

"It is better that this country set sail than lie still in the harbor."

A further 17 miles on State 28 leads to elegant **Falmouth**, whose delightful green is surrounded by 18th- and 19th-century houses hidden by graceful elms. The **Julia Wood House** and the **Conant House Museum** are maintained by the Falmouth Historical Society: the former, which dates from 1790, has a genuine widow's walk while the latter features exhibits of whaling times. Eight miles beyond Falmouth, at the southernmost tip of the Cape, is **Woods Hole**, famous for its **Oceanographic Institute** and from where ferries leave for Nantucket and Martha's Vineyard.

Leave Woods Hole on State 28 and travel north for 17 miles to **Bourne** at the canal. Either cross the canal by the **Bourne Bridge** and then drive east for 3 miles on Interstate 6 to join State 3 or travel along State 6 on the south side of the canal which can then be crossed by the Sagamore Bridge. Boston beckons.

Testing the waters at Truro.

WHALE WATCHING

Pegasus and Pepper, Batik and Gemini, Petrel and Ishtar make a great spectacle as they lunge, breach and flipper. You can see them by boarding one of the half-a-dozen large, handsome, white, whale-watching boats which, each day from Easter until the beginning of October, leave Commercial Wharf in Provincetown on a three-hour voyage.

Their destination is the Stellwagen Bank, a shallow underwater deposit of sand and gravel, to which, year after year, Pegasus and her friends, who are hump-backed whales, return after spending the winter in their West Indies breeding grounds. Experts recognize the different humpbacks, which often reach lengths of 40–50 feet and weights of 30 tonnes, by their distinctive body markings, especially those on their tail flukes.

Huge quantities of plankton and an infinite number of small sand eels are the magnets that attract to Stellwagen Bank the world's largest concentration of whales, both in numbers and in species. The vast majority of the 500 or so whales who visit here each year are humpbacks, but their number includes minkes, finbacks and a few right whales. In addition to the whales, visitors are often fortunate enough to be entertained by pods of several hundred frolick-

ing white-sided dolphins and to observe immense basking sharks. Seabirds can also be spotted as they follow the whales, feeding on the fish and plankton that they leave behind.

It's rare for a visitor not to see a whale during a trip and, more often than not, the whale-watching boats approach to within 50 feet of six to 12 of these magnificent mammals. Nothing can be more dramatic than to watch a humpback lunging upwards from the depths to break the surface of the water with dozens of small fish hanging from its mouth.

The humpback is basically a bulk feeder who dives deep below the schools of sand eels and then lunges upwards through the school with its mouth open. In so doing, it engulfs large quantities of fish and water. Its rorquals (folds of skin that begin at the chin and stretch to the whale's navel) balloon up and probably double the capacity of the mouth. This allows the animals to capture hundreds, if not thousands, of fish with every lunge.

Other activities which are certain to thrill watchers are breaching, when the mammals jump out of the water, and flippering, when the whales roll onto their sides and lift their long white flipper out of the water before slamming it down hard on the surface.

Whale watching became popular in 1975 when Captain Al Avellar, who organized deep-sea fishing trips from Provincetown, had the idea that some visitors to the Cape might enjoy watching the whales on Stellwagen Bank. He invited Charles Mayo, a marine biologist based in Provincetown, to act as a guide and so began an attraction which now annually draws more than 100,000 visitors.

On some boats the Provincetown-based Center for Coastal Studies provides a biologist who acts as guide and who also gathers scientific data. Whale watching at Provincetown has, with Yankee ingenuity, become a model for the marriage of science and commerce.

Whales as a source of income are not new to Provincetown, nor is the annual visit of these mammals to Stellwagen Bank. In the 18th century the Portuguese fishermen of Provincetown hunted the right whales which populated Stellwagen and reduced their numbers from 50,000 to the mere 300 which now survive. (Right whales are so-called because they were the right whales to hunt: they were slow swimmers and so the hunters could keep abreast of them in row-boats. Once harpooned, dead whales float right on the surface rather than sink.)

Later Provincetown whale-hunters would set off to the Arctic in search of quarry and, indeed, Provincetown had a whaling fleet in the 18th century which was exceeded in size only by those of Nantucket and New Bedford.

Whale watching boats which visit Stellwagen Bank are also based at Boston, Hyannisport, Gloucester and New Bedford. At the last named, the former whaling capital of the world, visit the superb Whaling Museum.

DAY TRIPS NORTH

The North Shore which, at least as far as Bostonians are concerned, ends at Cape Ann, is far more rugged and its waters much colder, than the South Shore and Cape Cod. And, apart from Rockport, the North Shore, a region of seaports – Salem, Marblehead, Gloucester and Newburyport – and well preserved 18th-century houses, is more sedate, more up-market than the South Shore.

Start your journey by leaving Boston either through the **Callahan Tunnel** or over the **Tobin Bridge**. The traveler who opts for the latter is marginally less likely to encounter traffic snarls and, even if he does, is rewarded by splendid views of the *USS Constitution*. Either way, make for Route 1A and the Lynn roundabout. A detour here, to the south on Route 129, is rewarding. Drive along the 2-mile causeway which, on the left, is bordered by a not too attractive beach, to **Little Nahant Island**.

Continue across this island and a second, shorter, causeway to **Nahant Island** with its winding roads, fishing coves, **Forty Step Beach** with its rocky cliffs and ledges, and a mixture of summer and suburban homes, some humble, some in the style of Greek temples or Victorian mansions. A sign at **Bass Point** at the tip of the island announces that lawn tennis was played here for the first time in the US in August 1874.

Back at the roundabout turn right and drive along **Lynn Shore Drive**; this skirts wide, flat **Lynn Beach**, odoriferous at low tide. After about a mile, one reaches **Swampscott** – the transition is quite marked – and the city is left behind. Lynn Shore Drive now becomes **Humphrey Avenue** which soon becomes **Atlantic Avenue**. The sea is no longer visible and the road now passes some grand, white Federal-style homes standing in beautiful grounds.

Yachties' haven: About 6 miles after the roundabout, turn right on **Ocean Avenue** and drive across the causeway at the base of Marblehead Harbor and arrive at exclusive **Marblehead Neck**. **Harbor Avenue** makes a 3-mile loop around the Neck, passing some splendid homes and, on the harbor side, the **Eastern Yacht Club**, the east coast's most prestigious yacht club – although that statement will certainly be challenged by members of the neighboring **Corinthian Yacht Club. Chandler Hovey Park**, in the lee of the lighthouse at the tip of the Neck, is a glorious windswept point from which to watch dozens of white sails scudding in and out of the deep, protected harbor.

Return across the causeway to Ocean Avenue, turn right onto **Atlantic Avenue** and immediately arrive in **Marblehead** proper, a twisting labyrinth of busy, narrow one-way streets lined by ancient clapboard houses. All is bustle and go. **Washington Square** in the heart of the town is its highest point and provides pleasant views. The

square is surrounded by private mansions which once belonged to sea captains and merchants; it is fronted by **Abbot Hall**, the town hall, which has earned a niche in history by being home to Archibald Willard's renowned painting *The Spirit of '76*.

The **Jeremiah Lee Mansion** on **Washington Street**, built in 1768, is an excellent example of pre-revolutionary architecture. Its exterior is of wood cut to imitate stone while its interior has a grand entrance hall, elegant furnishings and original panelling. Also worth visiting is the **King Hooper Mansion**, an early 18th-century building with slave quarters, ballroom and garden.

Two vantage points from which to enjoy the passing scene are **Crocker Park** and **Sewall Fort** at the south and north end respectively of **Front Street** which borders the bustling harbor. Another splendid view point, just beyond the Fort, is the **Old Burial Hill** where 600 Revolutionary war veterans are interred. Leave the town by **Lafayette Street**; this immediately becomes Route 114 which, in turn, soon joins Route 1A and, after a further 3 miles, enters fascinating Salem.

A bewitched seaport: Salem – the word is derived from the Hebrew *shalom,* meaning peace – was once one of the nation's great seaports. At its apogee, at the end of the 18th century, many in foreign parts believed that New York was a town in a land that was called Salem. Today, it is a shadow, albeit a delightful one, of its former self, rich in museums and historic sites.

The **Salem Maritime National Historic Site** includes a Visitors Center whose excellent 10-minute slide presentation should be seen before visiting, among others, the 1819 **Custom House** with an office once used by Nathaniel Hawthorne, the 1761 **Derby House** (Derby, a ship-owner, was probably the nation's first millionaire) and the desolate 2,000-foot long **Derby Wharf**, one of 40 wharves once crowded with merchantmen. Adjacent

Watching the sails from Marblehead's Chandler Hovey Park.

THE WITCHES OF SALEM

Any historic allusion to the witch-hunts that were enjoyed by Bay State colonists usually brings up the name of the town of Salem. And it's true that Salem, where most of the witchcraft trials were held, racked up a top score for exterminations, executing some 20 victims at the peak of the hysteria in 1692.

However, it was in Boston in 1688 that the wheels of persecution really got rolling, propelled by the most fanatical witch-hunter of them all, the Rev. Cotton Mather. And it was in Boston in 1693 that the order finally was issued by Governor General Sir William Phips, bringing the craziness to an abrupt halt and freeing 150 "witch suspects" from jail – including Phips' own wife.

Witch-killing had been known for hundreds of years before it arrived in America. In the early pages of the Bible, Exodus XXII: 17 demanded: "Thou shalt not suffer a witch to live." Dating from the Roman Inquisition in the year 1200, witch trials were common in Europe. A witch or warlock who confessed under torture would get an "easy" death, like hanging or beheading. But any who refused to confess got burned at the stake.

In the mid-1600s, when the fever blew across the North Atlantic, the colonies of Rhode Island, Connecticut and Massachusetts joined the pack with decrees of death. Connecticut quickly seized and executed nine victims. Bostonians hanged Margaret Jones of Charlestown on a bright June day in 1648, and for an encore on Boston Common they hanged the beautiful and cultured Anne Hibbins, widow of the colony's former representative to England.

Against that lunatic background, Cotton Mather sensed great opportunity for self-promotion and professional success. He was already the colony's most highly acclaimed clergyman. He was learned, brilliant, ambitious, but he yearned for more. He longed to succeed his father, the Rev. Increase Mather, as the president of Harvard. He decided it would boost his reputation and enhance his career if he could identify as-

sorted witches and promote their executions. So he went to work, and soon focused on a witch-suspect named Goodwife Glover, the mother of a North End laundress. With Mather's help, poor Mrs Glover quickly wound up in the noose of a Boston Common gallows rope.

In that same year, the fever struck Salem. The initial case involved a hot-tempered, trouble-making minister named Samuel Parris. He upset the serenity of his neighbors by arriving in town with two black slaves from the West Indies, a man named John and his wife Tituba. Within two years, Tituba was teaching voodoo to a pair of young girls, Ann Putnam and Mercy Lewis. When they had learned all they needed to know from Tituba, they turned against the black woman with hysterical charges of witchcraft. And Tituba wound up in jail.

At this point, Salem's witchcraft surge really took off. Tituba pointed the witch-finger against two other Salem women, Sarah Osburn and Sarah Good. They in turn dragged in Rebecca Nurse and Martha Corey. And the madness kept spreading like infection, with every suspect accusing somebody else, until scores of victims awaited death. Between June and September in 1648, the Salemites executed 14 women as witches and six men as warlocks. And, to leave nothing to chance they also convicted and hanged two dogs.

Throughout the year, Cotton Mather was a frequent visitor to the town. He never missed an execution. He was a roaring orator at all hangings. He was quick to gallop his horse to the front of a crowd of onlookers and to leap from his saddle to the gallows platform. There he would rant and rave, preach and pray, devoting most of his performance to berating and denouncing the victim who was waiting to die, and thereafter adding a modest personal bit calculated to move his steps toward the presidency of Harvard.

Such was the situation in 1693 when William Phips, who had been busy fighting the Indians and the French in the northern woods, returned to his official duties in Boston. Phips took one disgusted look at the witchery set-up and immediately issued a proclamation freeing all suspects who were still incarcerated. The madness braked to an abrupt halt.

Pickering Wharf, with its many restaurants and stores, including several antique shops, will delight those who enjoy Boston's Quincy Market. However, *caveat emptor:* 200 years ago the English were making and exporting to Salem copies of Chinese export-ware.

A few hundred yards northeast from here is the **House of the Seven Gables**, the setting for Hawthorne's novel of that name. Several other houses at the site include the author's birthplace.

In town is the world-class **Peabody Museum** whose wealth stems from the fact that, in 1799, 22 Salem men who had sailed beyond Cape Horn and Cape of Good Hope founded the East India Marine Society, one of whose purposes was to form a "museum of natural and artificial curiosities" to be collected by members on their voyages. How well they succeeded! Ships' models, figureheads, nautical instruments, charts and maps abound in the Museum's Maritime Department, while the Asian Export Department glitters with porcelain, gold, silver, furniture and textiles created by Chinese, Japanese and Indian artisans in the 19th century. Artifacts from the South Pacific (especially the Solomon Islands) and the Far East (especially New Guinea) abound in the Ethnology Department, which also has an unsurpassed Japanese collection. A department of Natural History rounds off the collection of this, the oldest continuously operating museum in the country, which is rich throughout in marine paintings.

Across the road is the **Essex Institute** whose collection of paintings, decorative objects and household items provides a close look at domestic life in early Essex County. Several restored houses in the grounds of the Institute cover the evolution of architecture and furnishings in the region from the 17th to the 19th centuries. Outstanding are the **Gardner-Pingree** (1805) and the **Andrew-Safford** Houses (1819) while the **Derby-Beebe** summerhouse (1799) is a delicious gem.

Children at Salem's House of the Seven Gables.

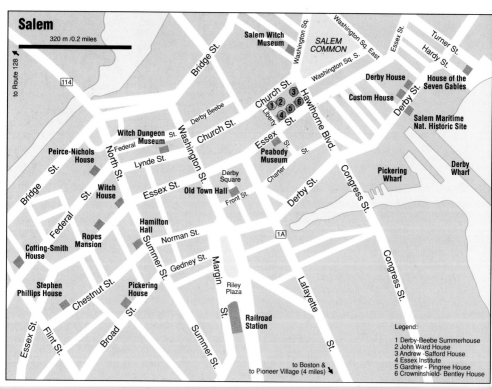

The Institute also owns three other distinguished houses: the **Cotting-Smith**, the **Peirce-Nichols** and the **Ropes**. The last, with its beautiful gardens, houses a rich collection of Nanking porcelain and Irish glass.

West of these museums, elegant homes, many built for sea captains by Samuel McIntire, line **Chestnut**, **Essex** and **Federal Streets**. The first of these streets is a National Historic Landmark and justly deserves its accolade as one of the most beautiful and distinguished streets in the nation.

The **Witch Museum** (Washington Square) and the **Witch Dungeon and Museum** (16 Lynde Street), both in former churches, present their versions of the witch hunts which made Salem notorious in 1692–93. More can be learnt about this agitation in the **Witch House** (310 Essex Street) where Judge Corwin questioned more than 200 who were accused of witchcraft.

All these places can be visited by following the red line painted on the sidewalk. Alternatively, board a trackless trolley for a narrated tour of all the sites, alighting at will and rejoining a later car. Trackless trolleys also make 90-minute trips to the Pioneer Village and Marblehead. Visitors can alight at several stops and rejoin later trolleys. The **Pioneer Village**, 4 miles south of Salem and staffed by interpreters in period costume, introduces visitors to Salem of the 1620s when it was the first capital of Massachusetts. The buildings range from rough dugouts and wigwams to thatched cottages. Crafts demonstrated include making tallow candles and spinning wool.

From Salem, travel north on Route 1A to **Beverly**, from where, in 1775, the schooner *Hannah* was armed and sent out to harass British shipping, thus giving birth to the Continental Navy. Turn east on Route 127 and drive through **Beverly Farms**, **Pride's Crossing** and **Manchester**, all of which were, and are, proper places for dyed-in-the-wool Yankees to have summer retreats or

Ropes Mansion at Salem.

year-round homes. **Singing Beach** at Manchester, 31 miles from Boston, is especially attractive. It derives its name from the crackling sound made when walking on the sands. (There is parking only at the railway station, half-a-mile from the beach.)

Six miles past Manchester, turn right for **Magnolia** and immediately sense the former glory which once attracted the rich and the beautiful from New York, Cincinnati and St Louis. Their palatial homes are now guest houses and **Main Street's** once elegant stores – the street was known as "Robbers' Alley" – are very ordinary. Yet a drive along the seafront where the waves pound the rocks and where many grand buildings still stand is exhilarating.

Continue in Magnolia along **Hesperus Avenue** and, after a couple of miles, stop at **Hammond Castle Museum**. This handsome building was constructed in the mid-1920s with bits and pieces of European châteaux. The eponymous owner was an inventor and the castle was his home, his laboratory and a gallery for his art collection. The castle, which has secret passageways and a 100-foot long hall for the 8,200 pipe organ (advance arrangements can be made for a mini-organ concert), stands on a bluff overlooking the sea and **Norman's Woe**, a surf-pounded rock that is the setting for Longfellow's poem *The Wreck of the Hesperus*.

Hesperus Avenue now rejoins Route 127 and, after 3 miles, arrives at the drawbridge in Gloucester which spans the **Annisquam Canal**, a boon to sailors who do not wish to round Cape Ann. Those who have perished are remembered by a statue of a fisherman, one hand shading his eyes as he peers into the distance, the other firmly gripping the steering wheel over which he is bent, on the other side of the bridge.

Gloucester, the nation's oldest seaport, was founded in 1623 by a group of Englishmen who had come "to praise God and to catch fish." How well they succeeded can be observed at the **Clamming**.

harbor: today's fleet of 250 boats unloads fish, and catches of fishermen from Canada, Iceland, Greenland and Scandinavia are processed in preparation for shipping to cities throughout the nation. Today, the majority of fishermen in this, one of the world's leading fishing ports, are of Portuguese or Italian descent. Whale-watching cruises also leave from the harbor.

In town visit the **Sargent-Murray House**, the handsome 18th-century Georgian home of Judith Sargent and John Murray. The first **Universalist Church** in the country, a movement which Murray founded, is across the street. Displayed in a large neighboring Federal-style house, the headquarters of the **Cape Ann Historical Association**, is an outstanding collection of seascapes by the renowned American marine painter Fitz Hugh Lane. Here, too, is an interesting collection of furniture, silver and porcelains and a Maritime room. Further inland, on **Main Street**, is the **Portuguese Church of Our Lady of Good Voyage**, readily recognizable by its two blue cupolas.

From the church, drive around the harbor to **East Main Street**; this immediately arrives at **Rocky Neck**, an artists' colony looking across the water to Gloucester and containing several lively restaurants. Rudyard Kipling worked on *Captains Courageous* – remember the film with Spencer Tracy? – while staying here.

On leaving Rocky Neck, turn right onto **Eastern Point Road**. After about 3 miles, take the right fork, even though you are entering a private estate. This is the exclusive enclave of **Eastern Point** which boasts a score of magnificent homes. Notable among these, and open to the public, is **Beauport**, built and furnished between 1907 and 1934 by Henry Davis Sleeper, a decorator and collector of American art and antiquities. More than half of the 40 rooms, each designed and decorated to cover a different period of American life, are open to the public.

Relaxing at Cape Ann's Halibut Point.

Some of the most popular rooms in what has been called the most fascinating house in America are the Paul Revere room, the China Trade room, the Pine kitchen, the Strawberry Hill room (a tribute to English Gothic) and the Golden Step room from which there is a breathtaking view of the harbor. Isabella Stewart Gardner and John D. Rockefeller were just two of many American collectors who visited Beauport and who were influenced by Sleeper's taste.

At the end of Eastern Point, just beyond **Niles Beach**, are the half-mile **Long Bar Breakwater** and **Eastern Point Ligh**t, both built with renowned Rockport granite. This is a great place to fish for mackerel, flounder or pollock and to collect colorful sea anemones.

A Cape for a Queen: Return to the entrance to Eastern Point, turn right onto **Framington Avenue** and then left onto **Atlantic Road**. You are now on a counter-clockwise loop of **Cape Ann**, following by land, if not by sea, the exploration made in 1604 by Champlain, the French explorer, and then in 1614 by John Smith who mapped the area and named it in honor of his queen. Cape Ann is a sheer delight, with its sometimes wild, sometimes caressing coast, dotted with delightful sandy beaches, glorious rocky outcrops and secret coves, plus numerous boutiques, galleries and restaurants.

Good Harbor, **Long** and **Pebble beaches** are immediately passed and, after about 7 miles, **Rockport** is reached. It's difficult to believe that this bustling, even frenetic, resort was a tranquil fishing village until the 1920s. Then, it was discovered by artists and subsequently became a day-trippers' paradise. Most of the town's two dozen galleries, which display works of both local and international artists, are on **Main Street** but the lure which attracts nearly all is **Bearskin Neck**. This narrow peninsula, jutting out beyond the harbor, is densely packed with old fishing sheds, many with gardens, that

Fisherman statue at Gloucester. <u>Right</u>, lobster feast.

have been converted into galleries, antique stores and restaurants.

A favorite with camera-buffs is a red lobster shack called **Motif 1** because of the infinite number of times it has been photographed and painted. Magnificent views of the Atlantic Ocean can be enjoyed from the breakwater at the end of the Neck.

Leave Rockport for **Pigeon Cove**, a couple of miles along Route 127A, and turn left to visit the **Paper House**; its walls and furnishings are made of Boston newspapers whose pages were compressed together – 215 sheets for the walls – and then lacquered. One desk is made exclusively of *Christian Science Monitors*, another of accounts of Lindbergh's transatlantic flight.

Return to Route 127A and continue for another couple of miles to **Halibut Point**. A half-mile walk from the parking lot through blueberry bushes leads to the outermost tip of Cape Ann where huge tilted sheets of granite and fascinating tidal ponds have their devo-

tees. A disused quarry near the parking lot can be explored and is testimony to the fact that Rockport and its surrounds were formerly renowned for their granite, seen in many Boston buildings.

Continue on the loop past charming villages and rocky inlets – **Folly Cove**, **Lanesville**, **Plum Cove**, **Lobster Cove** – to **Annisquam**, which borders an inlet at the northern end of the canal of that name. This is a delightful spot with a couple of restaurants and the tang of the ocean. And so back to Gloucester; but, rather than returning to the city, turn west on Route 128 and take Exit 14 to gain Route 133 which leads to the north.

The appearance of **Codman's**, an unsophisticated, self-service restaurant immediately before **Essex**, belies its contribution to mankind. This is where, on a hot July day in 1916, Lawrence Codman tossed some clams into a pan of boiling oil and created the heavenly dish of fried clams. Essex's other main draw is its antique shops, although its most outstanding attraction is the huge

Essex, an antique collector's delight.

redstone town hall which towers above the village playing fields.

Immediately before reaching Ipswich, turn right onto **Argilla Road**, bordered by the estates of bohemians. After about 3 miles, it leads to the **Crane Memorial Reservation**, covering more than 1,400 acres and with more than 5 miles of magnificent white sands and dunes. However, nothing is perfect and the greenfly season from mid-July to mid-August can be sheer hell. The **Pine Hollow Interpretive** (sic) **Trail** is an enjoyable 1-mile stroll over dunes into pine hollows and onto a boardwalk in a red maple swamp. Overlooking the beach is **Castle Hill**, the Crane estate, whose 59-room mansion may be visited and in whose lovely grounds glorious concerts are held on summer weekends.

Return on Argilla Road to **South Main Street** which borders the **Ipswich** village green. On the left is the dark-brown **John Whipple House** with its lovely 17th-century garden furnished in period style. Across the road, the white Federal-period **John Heard House**, built with profits from the China trade, is filled with Chinese and early American artifacts and has a collection of antique carriages in its grounds. These are just two of 40 restored 17th- and 18th-century houses which permit Ipswich to claim that it has more restored houses from this period than anywhere else on the North Shore.

Backtrack from Ipswich by crossing the **Ipswich River** on the **Choate Bridge**, built in 1764 and, after a couple of miles, **Appleton Farms**, open to the public, is passed on the right. This glorious estate which, with its oak trees is reminiscent of the English countryside, has been farmed continuously since 1640 by the same family.

Horsey types might wish to detour from Ipswich on Route 1A for about 5 miles to **Hamilton** and to the **Myopia Hunt Club** with its renowned polo fields. The Club owes its name to the fact that the Prince brothers, who were

Tourists view Rockport's Motif No. 1.

266

its founders, and many of their friends wore spectacles.

Travel north from Ipswich and, after 12 miles, Route 1A becomes **Newburyport's** elegant **High Street**, lined by magnificent clapboard Federal-period houses, many with widow's walks. The **Cushing House** (No. 98), headquarters of the Historical Society, has 21 splendidly furnished rooms, a varied collection of artifacts and a garden with many plants more than a century old.

Turn right from High Street to reach the **Merrimack River** and the waterfront. The story of the town's nautical heritage – difficult to believe that this charming spot was once home to a large merchant fleet and a thriving shipbuilding industry – is told in the **Custom House**, now a **Maritime Museum**.

Between the waterfront and High Street is the reconstructed **Market Square** and **Inn Street Mall**, a pleasing ensemble of early 19th-century three-story brick and granite buildings where it is a delight to stroll, to shop and to dine. Two churches in town are worth visiting. **Old South**, the older (1785), boasts a whispering gallery and a bell cast by Paul Revere; the newer (1801) **Unitarian** is renowned for its delicate wooden spire.

From Newburyport, a 3-mile drive across a causeway leads to **Plum Island**, a 4,700-acre reservation (**Parker River National Wildlife Refuge**) with a 6-mile stretch of superb sands which is nirvana for both bird watchers and beach bums. The dunes, freshwater bogs and fresh and tidal marshes are, according to the season, covered with false heather, dune grass or scrub pine and, after Labor Day, visitors are permitted to pick beach plums and cranberries. Turtles and toads, woodchucks and rabbits, pheasant and deer can all readily be observed; in March and October the skies are black with migrating geese and ducks. Peak season for green flies is mid-July to mid-August.

From Newburyport, it is an easy 35-mile drive back to Boston on Route 1.

Details of Motif No. 1.

TRAVEL TIPS

Getting There

270	By Air
271	By Rail
271	By Bus
271	By Car

Travel Essentials

272	Visas & Passports
272	Money Matters
272	Health Tips
272	Customs
272	Tipping
272	What to Wear

Getting Acquainted

273	Geography & Population
273	Time Zones
273	Climate
274	Weights & Measures
274	Electricity
274	Business Hours
274	Fax Facilities
274	Public Holidays & Events
276	Media

Getting Around

277	Rapid Transit
277	By Bus
279	Commuter Rail
279	Passport Visitor Pass
279	Taxicabs
279	Car Hire
279	Limousine Services
280	Commuter Boat
280	Other Ferries, Buses & Planes
280	Tours

Where to Stay

282	Boston Hotels
284	Greater Boston B&B
285	Hostels & "Ys"
285	Cambridge Hotels
286	Greater Boston Hotels

Food Digest

287	Where to Eat
287	Restaurants

Things to Do

294	High Spots
294	Freedom Trail

Culture Plus

296	Places of Interest
303	Parks
303	Entertainment
305	Theater
306	Movie Theaters

Nightlife

306	Comedy Clubs
307	Dance Clubs
307	Folk Music
307	The Jazz Scene
308	Pubs
308	Gay Scene

Sports

309	Spectator
310	Participant

Shopping

311	

Further Reading

314	Non-Fiction
315	Fiction

Special Information

315	Information Sources
316	Essential Phone Numbers
316	Consulates

Arts/Photo Credits

317	

Index

318	

GETTING THERE

NOTE: Unless a separate exchange code is shown, all telephone numbers are for Boston (US trunk dialing code 617). 800 numbers are toll-free.

BY AIR

Logan International Airport leases space to more than 40 carriers, of which 15 are international airlines. Delta is its largest customer. Currently Logan is the 11th busiest airport in the nation and the 15th busiest in the world. It is the northern terminal of the world's busiest airline market – the New York–Boston run – which handles nearly 3.5 million passengers a year. The Pan Am and the Trump New York shuttles leave hourly throughout the day and guarantee seats.

Although a recent *Traveler's Guide to Major US Airports* called Logan "downright hospitable" it is well to remember that in its annual report for the same year the Massachusetts Port Authority confessed that "no-one wants to spend any more time than they have to at the airport."

Logan has five terminals (A – E). Note that domestic and international flights of the same airline do not necessarily use the same terminal. Free service between the terminals including an Airport Handicapped Van is provided daily between 7 a.m. and 11 p.m. (tel: 561-1769).

Currency may be exchanged at Bay Bank and at Shawmut Bank at terminal E. Telegrams may be sent from Western Union at Terminal B. Rental lockers are available at all terminals except D. (It costs $1 to rent a trolley.) Hotel reservations can be made at the lower levels of Terminals C and E. Other terminals have direct telephone lines. The nearest hotel is the Logan Airport Hilton.

Logan, just 3 miles from downtown Boston, is closer to town than any other major airport in the nation: this refers to distance and not to time. Traffic jams at the two tunnels which go under the harbor to connect the airport and city are eternal. For up-to-date information on airport traffic conditions, call Massport's Ground Transportation Hotline (800-235-6426), Mon–Fri 9 a.m–5 p.m.

The MBTA Blue Line from Airport Station is the fastest way to downtown (about 10 minutes) and to many other places as well. Free shuttle buses run between all the airport terminals and the subway station. Cabs can be hired outside each terminal. Fares should average about $12, including tip, providing there are no major traffic jams. Share-A-Cab (tel: 561-1769) operates from all terminals between 3.30 p.m. and 11.30 p.m: the flat-fare is about half that of the normal taxi fare. Airways Transportation buses leave all terminals every half hour until 10 p.m. (6 p.m. on Sats) for downtown and Back Bay hotels and several major bus companies, including Bonanza, Concord Trailways, Peter Pan and Vermont Transit, serve many outlying suburbs and distant destinations.

A delightful way to approach the city and especially useful for those staying in downtown hotels (Boston Harbor, Boston Marriot Long Wharf, Bostonian, Lafayette and Hotel Meridien) is the Airport Water Shuttle (tel: 800-235-6426). It operates every 15 minutes Mon–Fri 6 a.m.–8 p.m; Sat and Sun every 30 minutes, on the quarter hour, between 12.15 p.m. and 7.45 p.m. The voyage takes 7 minutes and the fare is $7. A free shuttle bus operates between the airport ferry dock and all airline terminals.

Car rentals can be arranged at the ground level of all terminals. The following firms are represented:

Avis (tel: 482-6876, 800-331-1212); Budget (569-4000); Dollar (569-5300, 800-421-6868); Hertz (567-7200, 800-654-3131); National (569-6700, 800-328-4567).

When serious traffic delays occur at the tunnel, take Route 1A North to Route 16 and thus to the Tobin Bridge and into Boston.

Some useful telephone numbers (the appropriate Logan terminal is given in brackets) are:
Aer Lingus (E) 223-6537.
Air Atlantic (E) 565-1800.
Air Canada (E) 422-6232.

Air France (E) 237-2747.
Air Nova (E) 422-6232.
Alitalia (E) 223-5730.
American (B) 542-6700.
American Eagle (B) 443-7300.
Braniff (B) 272-6433.
British Airways (E) 247-9297.
Canadian Air (E) 426-7000.
Catskill Airway (B) 833-0196.
Continental (B) 569-8400.
Delta (C) 567-4100.
Delta Business (C) 345-3400.
Eastern (A) 262-3700.
ElAl (E) 223-6700.
First Air (E) 468-8292.
Hub Express (B) 962-4744.
Lufthansa (E) 645-3880.
Midway (C) 621-5700.
Midwest Express (B) 452-2022.
Northwest (Internatl) (E) 225 2525.
Northwest (Domestic) (B) 225 2525.
Pan Am (B) 221-1111.
Pan AM Express (B) 221-1111.
Piedmont (B) 523-1100.
Piedmont Commuter (B) 251-5720.
Sabena (Internatl) (E) 645-3790.
Sabena (Domestic) (B) 645-3790.
Swissair (E) 423-7778.
Trump Shuttle (A) 247-8786.
TWA (Internatl) (E) 367-2800.
TWA (Domestic) (C) 367-2800.
TAP Air Portugal (E) 221-7370.
United (C) 482-7900.
US Air (B) 482-3160.
Valley Airlines (A) 322-1008.
Westover Air (A) 443-9869.
Some other useful airport phone numbers are:
Public Information Office 561-1800.
Foreign Language Translators 561-1803.
Traveler's Aid 542-7286.

BY RAIL

Boston is the northern terminus of Amtrak's Northeast Corridor ("Shore Line"). Passenger trains arrive at South Station (Atlantic Avenue and Summer Street, tel: 482-3660; 800-872-7245 or, for the hearing-impaired, 800-523-6590) from New York, Washington, DC, and Philadelphia with connections from all points in the nationwide Amtrak system. They also stop at Back Bay Station (145 Dartmouth Street, tel: 482-3660). Nine or 10 trains daily travel between New York

and Boston with average travel time being 5 hours but with some trains making the journey in a tad less than 4 hours. South Station is also the eastern terminus for Amtrak's Lake Shore Limited, which travels daily between Chicago and Boston by way of Cleveland, Buffalo, Rochester and Albany. One train daily makes the journey in 21½ hours.

BY BUS

Several intercity bus companies serve Boston. The two largest, Greyhound and Peter Pan, have frequent daily services from New York City and Albany, NY, as well as services from points within New England. Greyhound serves the entire United States and parts of Canada; its unlimited "Ameripass" is available for 7, 15 or 30-day periods.

The major bus terminals are the Greyhound (10 St James Avenue, tel: 423-5810) and the Peter Pan (555 Atlantic Avenue, tel: 482-6620) across from South Station which is often called "Trailways Terminal." Both are used for state, interstate and Canadian travel. The **Greyhound Terminal** also serves Brush Hill, Plymouth and Brockton, and Vermont Transit bus companies while the **Peter Pan Terminal** serves American Eagle, Bloom Bus, C & J Trailways, Concord Trailways, and Plymouth & Brockton bus companies. The Bonzana (tel: 720-4110, 800-556-3815) and Englander (tel: 292-4700, 413-662-2016) bus companies have their terminal on the Dartmouth Street side of South Station.

Both Greyhound and Peter Pan also have terminals at Riverside in Newton, on the "D" Branch of the Green Line.

BY CAR

Getting to Boston: *From the west*: Route 90 (Mass. Pike) is the most clear route inbound. Three major exits: **Exits 18–20** – Cambridge/Allston – best for Cambridge and Charles River locations: **Exit 22** – Prudential Center/Copley Square – best for Back Bay, Fenway, Kenmore Square and Boston Common (via Boylston, Charles, Beacon, Park and Tremont Streets): **Exit 24** – Expressway/Downtown – best for Downtown, North and South Highway acess.

From the south: Routes 95, 24 and 3 all "feed" into Route 128 East which leads into Route 9 inbound. Two major exits are:

Kneeland Street/Chinatown – best for Back Bay, Theater District and Boston Common Visitor Center (via Kneeland, Charles, Beacon, Park and Tremont Streets); **Dock Square** – best for Airport, North End, Waterfront and Faneuil Hall Marketplace.

From the north: Routes 95,1 and 93 enter Boston on elevated highway structures. Four major exits: **Storrow Drive** – best for Back Bay, Beacon Hill, Cambridge and Boston Common Visitor Center (via Government Center exit and Cambridge Street which becomes Tremont Street); **High Street** – best for Downtown; **Kneeland Street** – best for Chinatown and Theater District.

Getting Out of Boston: *To the west*: Route 90 (Mass Pike) best route. From Downtown, enter the "Pike" at **Kneeland Street**; from the Back Bay take **Arlington Street**, **Copley Square** or **Mass. Avenue** at Newbury Street. *To the south and the north*: Route 93 (South–Southeast Expressway) serves the South Shore and Cape Cod (via Route 3) and Rhode Island and New York (via Routes 128 and 95). Route 93 (North) serves the North Shore and the New England Coast (via Route 1 and 95), New Hampshire (via Routes 93 and 95) and Vermont (via Routes 93 and 89).

TRAVEL ESSENTIALS

VISAS & PASSPORTS

To enter the United States you must have a valid passport. Visas are required for all foreigners except Canadians. Vaccinations are not required for entry.

MONEY MATTERS

The most convenient and safest way to carry large sums of money is travelers checks. The two most widely accepted are American Express and Visa. Almost all stores, restaurants and hotels will accept them. Credit cards (American Express, Visa, Mastercard, Diner's Club and Discover) are also widely accepted, but be sure to double-check with waiters or clerks before you order dinner or have your purchases tallied up.

HEALTH TIPS

In the US, health care is very expensive. If you fall ill or need medical attention, the average cost for one night in a hospital in a semi-private room is $460. If you live in a foreign country and do not have private health insurance, try to obtain insurance for your stay here before leaving home.

CUSTOMS

Those over 21 may take into the US 200 cigarettes, 50 cigars, or 3 lbs of tobacco; 1 US quart of alcohol; duty free gifts worth up to $100. You are not allowed to bring in meat products, seeds, plants, fruits. Don't even think about bringing in narcotics. Customs agents in the US are tough and efficient.

The United States allows you to take out anything you wish, but consult the consulate or tourist authority of the country you are visiting next to learn of its custom regulations for entrance.

TIPPING

Tipping is voluntary. Gratuities are not automatically tallied into the bill. Here are a few tipping guidelines:
Waiters are usually given 15 percent of the bill. For above-average service, tip 20 percent.
Taxi cab drivers usually get 15 percent of the fare.
Doormen, skycabs and porters receive 50 to 75 cents per bag.
Hairdressers, manicurists and masseurs usually receive 10 to 15 percent of the total charge.

WHAT TO WEAR

Even more so than in other parts of the country it might be said that "anything goes." This is in part due to the large number of students in Boston and in part because of its international flavor. Rare are the restaurants which demand "jacket and tie." Remember, however, it can be very cold in winter and very hot during summer.

CLOTHING SIZES

The table below gives a comparison of American, Continental and British clothing sizes. It is always best to try on any article before buying it, however, as sizes can vary.

Women's Dresses/Suits

American	Continental	British
6	38/34N	8/30
8	40/36N	10/32
10	42/38N	12/34
12	44/40N	14/36
14	46/42N	16/38
16	48/44N	18/40

Women's Shoes

American	Continental	British
4½	36	3
5½	37	4
6½	38	5
7½	39	6
8½	40	7
9½	41	8
10½	42	9

Men's Suits

American	Continental	British
34	44	34
–	46	36
38	48	38
–	50	40
42	52	42
–	54	44
46	56	46

Men's Shirts

American	Continental	British
14	36	14
14½	37	14½
15	38	15
15½	39	15½
16	40	16
16½	41	16½
17	42	17

Men's Shoes

American	Continental	British
6½	–	6
7½	40	7
8½	41	8
9½	42	9
10½	43	10
11½	44	11

GETTING ACQUAINTED

GEOGRAPHY & POPULATION

Boston, in the north of the country and the most easterly city in the US, has a population of fewer than 600,000 and covers an area of 40 sq. miles (105 sq. km). Lacking a "main drag," it consists of 14 tight neighborhoods, each of which believes in the territorial imperative. Cambridge, separated from Boston by the Charles River, is a town in its own right but it is impossible for the casual visitor to be aware of this. Greater Boston, with nearly 100 towns, encompasses 3 million people and covers 1,100 sq. miles (2,850 sq. km).

TIME ZONES

Boston runs on Eastern Standard Time. Every spring the clock is turned one hour ahead, and every fall one hour back. Boston is three hours ahead of Los Angeles, one hour ahead of Chicago, five hours behind London and 15 hours behind Tokyo.

CLIMATE

Part of the magic of Boston is that it is a land of seasons. The first snow generally falls in January and intermittent snow accompanied by cold weather – a few degrees below freezing – will usually continue until the end of March. The Charles River freezes over about every second year. Spring, which can be very fleeting, is in April and/or May. This is when magnolias and lilacs bloom and magic fills the air. The summer months – June until September – can be very hot and humid with some real dog-days, although for most of the time the weather is just pleasantly hot – in the 70° to 80° F (21°–27° C) range. The fall is like a hesitant bride, appearing and disappearing to be replaced by glorious Indian Summer days. And this can last through to the beginning of December. Decent fall colors can be enjoyed in the outskirts of Boston but cannot compare to those found in northern New England.

In summary, Boston weather can be described in one word: erratic.

WEIGHTS & MEASURES

The US uses the Imperial system of weights and measures. Metric is rarely used. Below is a conversion chart.
1 inch = 2.54 centimeters
1 foot = 30.48 centimeters
1 mile = 1.609 kilometers
1 quart = 1.136 liters
1 ounce = 28.4 grams
1 pound = 0.453 kilograms
1 yard = 0.9144 meters

ELECTRICITY

Boston homes have "standard" electricity which is 110 volts. European appliances require an adaptor because European countries use 220–240 volts. Some hotel bathrooms have electrical outlets suitable for use with European appliances but it is useful to pack an adaptor.

BUSINESS HOURS

Most offices are open 9 a.m.–5 p.m. Mon–Fri., although some offices open at 8 a.m.

Banks are open Mon–Fri 9 a.m.–3 p.m. and often later. On Thursday they remain open until 5 p.m. and often later. Saturday hours are 9 a.m.–2 p.m.

The main Post Office is at 25 Dorchester Avenue (tel: 223-0072), behind South Station. Post Office hours are 8 a.m.–5 p.m. Mon–Fri and 8 a.m.–noon on Sat. The Post Office at Logan Airport is open until midnight. Stamps are also available in vending machines located in airports, hotels, stores and bus and train stations. If you do not know where you will be staying, mail can be addressed to General Delivery, Main Post Office, Boston.

FAX FACILITIES

Fax machines can be found at most hotels. Public fax companies are located throughout the city so check the phone directory under "Facsimile" for the fax service nearest to you.

PUBLIC HOLIDAYS & EVENTS

A list of some of the major celebrations which will appeal to tourists. Public holidays are marked with an *.

JANUARY

1st – New Year's Day*.
15th – Martin Luther King Day*, ceremony at City Hall.
End of month or early February – Chinese New Year, celebrated in Chinatown with lion and dragon dances and firecrackers.

FEBRUARY

Middle of month – Valentine's Weekend Celebration, romance comes to Boston.
Third Monday – Washington's Birthday*, ceremony at Washington's statue in Public Garden.

MARCH

5th – Boston Massacre/Crispus Attucks Day, parade from the massacre site to City Hall Plaza.
Middle of month – New England Spring Flower Show, the oldest annual flower exhibition in the nation lasts for seven days.
Sunday before March 17th – St Patrick's Day Parade, held in South Boston. (It is fortuitous that St Patrick's Day almost coincides with Evacuation Day, otherwise the St Patrick's Parade would not be permitted.)

APRIL

Easter Sunday* – Parade. Join the throngs who walk to the Common in their finery. Judging of costumes in several categories; music and dancing.
Third Sunday – Eve of Patriot's Day, lantern service at Old North Church
Third Monday – Patriots' Day*, celebrations abound especially in Concord and Lexington.
Third Monday – Boston Marathon, the most renowned annual marathon in the world.

MAY

Mid-May – Boston Pops, commencement of a two-month Tuesday to Saturday (8.30 p.m.) season at Symphony Hall.

Mid-May Sunday (biannual) – Art Newbury Street, festival when art in the galleries is joined by music on the streets: an art lover's nirvana.

Mid-May Sunday – Lilac Sunday, the air at the Arnold Arboretum is redolent with the aroma from 400 varieties of psychedelic lilacs in bloom.

Last Monday in May – Memorial Day*, Parade leaves from Copley Square and terminates with a ceremony at the Rose Garden in the Fenway.

JUNE

First week – Cambridge River Festival, lasts all week culminating on the Sunday with two parades that converge on Memorial Drive. Floats, bands, clowns, food, participatory dancing and all the fun of the fair.

First Monday – Parade. Ancient & Honorable Artillery Company (nation's third oldest standing military organization) celebrates.

First Saturday – Back Bay Street Fair, features food, drink, arts and crafts and great live music.

Sunday before the 17th. – Bunker Hill Day, re-enactment of the Battle of Bunker Hill and parades in Charlestown.

Last weekend – Blessing of the Fleet, takes place at both Gloucester and Provincetown: activities peak on the Sunday.

JULY

Month-long – Boston Pops, free outdoor concerts at the Hatch Memorial Shell on the Esplanade.

July 4th. – Labor Day*, Boston is awash with celebrations including reading of Declaration of Independence from Balcony of Old State House.

July 4th. – Harborfest, waterfront activities marked by the turnaround of the *USS Constitution* and fireworks.

July 4th. – Pops Concert, held at Hatch Memorial Shell on the Esplanade culminates with playing of the *1812 Overture* replete with cannons and fireworks.

Early in month – Chowderfest, an opportunity to sample literally dozens of superb New England chowders.

Most weekends – Religious processions and feasts – the North End lives up to its name of "Little Italy" with the oompah of brass bands and lots of food: best on Sundays.

July 14th. – Bastille Day, celebrated on Marlborough Street in Back Bay with champagne, buffet supper and dancing.

AUGUST

Weekends – The North End continues its religious processions and feasts.

Movable – August Moon (Chinese) Festival, prancing lions and dragons and lots of exotic foods in Chinatown.

SEPTEMBER

First Monday – Labor Day*.

A Sunday (biannual) – Art Newbury Street, the city's major concentration of galleries collectively let their hair down.

Second Saturday – Back Bay Street Dance. Marlborough Street is closed as bands and food move in for an evening of gaiety.

Sunday late in month – Charles Street Fair, traditional fall celebration on Beacon Hill's main shopping thoroughfare.

OCTOBER

Monday closest to the 12th. – Columbus Day*, parade in East Boston or North End.

Second last Sunday – Head of the Charles Regatta, the largest one-day crew race in the world attracts oarspeople from everywhere.

NOVEMBER

Monday nearest the 11th – Veterans Day, parade starts on Commonwealth Avenue in Back Bay.

Fourth Thursday – Thanksgiving*.

DECEMBER

16th. – Re-enactment of Boston Tea Party, takes place at Tea Party Museum.

24th. – Carol Singing, Louisburg Square.

25th. – Christmas Day*.

31st – First Night, city-wide revels concentrated in the Back Bay start in the afternoon and continue until the wee small hours.

MEDIA

NEWSPAPERS & MAGAZINES

Boston Globe: Daily newspaper. Thursday supplement gives complete events listings for the next seven days.

Boston Herald: Daily newspaper. Friday supplement contains listings for following week.

Boston Magazine: A slick and informative monthly of local interest.

Boston Phoenix: A thick Saturday alternative weekly with intelligent articles plus listings and comments on the local entertainment scene.

Christian Science Monitor: A prestigous daily newspaper published in Boston on weekdays. Strong on international news: light on local news.

Where Boston: A free glossy monthly with shopping, dining, entertainment and attraction listings.

The kiosk in the middle of Harvard Square (tel: 354-7777) is *the* place at which to purchase national and international newspapers and magazines.

RADIO & TELEVISION

Radio stations in the area are: WEEI on 590 AM for news; WRKO on 680 AM for talk; WCRB on 102.5 FM for classical music; WBCN on 104.1 FM for rock music; WJIB on 96.9 FM for popular music and WGBH (Public Radio – classical music) on 89.7 FM.

Some TV stations are: channel 2 (WGBH) for public television; channel 25 (WXNE); channel 38 (WSBK) screens sports; NBC can be viewed on channel 4 (WBZ); ABC on channel 5 (WCVB) and CBS on channel 7 (WNEV).

GETTING AROUND

Boston, it is justly claimed, is a walker's city which is certainly a good thing for it is certainly not a driver's city. The city planners, as Emerson noted, were the cows and it has been suggested that the Puritan belief in predestination extended even to urban design. Streets appeared where Providence chose to lay them – along cow paths, Indian paths and colonial wagon tracks – and are linked by crooked little alleys. City planners, however, did come into their own in the middle of the 19th century and the Back Bay and South Boston and, to a lesser extent, the South End have impeccable grid systems.

If, as you attempt to drive in the city, you feel frustrated and inadequate, delight in the fact that many Bostonians feel the same way. Being faced by cars coming the wrong way on a one-way street, being stuck in a traffic jam, getting lost and then being unable to find a parking space is about par for the course. Giving the boot (wheel clamping) is a sport much favored by the police. Conveniently located, but inadequate, public parking facilities are found at **Government Center**; **Post Office Square**; beneath the **Boston Common** (entrance on **Charles Street**); the **Prudential Center** and on **Clarendon Street** near the **John Hancock Tower**.

A number of parking garages are situated close to **Harvard Square** in Cambridge. Try **Charles Square Garage**, 1 Bennett Street; **Church Street Parking Lot**, Church Street; **Harvard Square Garage**, JFK and Eliot Streets; and **Holyoke Center Garage**, access via Dunster and Holyoke Street.

Better by far to use the subway (a.k.a. rapid transit or "T") and bus services of the MBTA (**Massachusetts Bay Transportation Authority**). For general MBTA travel information telephone 722-3200 or 800-392-6100 or, for the hearing-impaired, 722-5146, weekdays 6.30 a.m.–11 p.m., weekends 9 a.m.–6 p.m. For 24-hour recorded service information telephone 722-5050; for customer service telephone 722-5215 and for MBTA police emergency telephone 722-5151.

RAPID TRANSIT

Ever since it was inaugurated in 1897, the subway (nowadays the rapid transit or, as it is usually called the "T") has been a source of amusement for Bostonians. One ditty, *The Man Who Never Returned,* revived by folk-singers in the 1960s, tells of poor Charlie doomed to ride forever 'neath the streets of Boston because he lacked the nickel fare necessary to alight. However, despite severe over-crowding for much of the day the "T" is a fairly efficient, clean and user-friendly system.

The four rapid transit lines – Red, Green, Orange, Blue – that radiate out from downtown Boston cling to the name "subway" even though all lines run above ground for much of their route. There are more than 75 rapid transit stations, usually named for a nearby square, street, or landmark. In addition, Green Line trains stop at many street corners along the surface portion of their routes. All four lines intersect in downtown Boston. Transfers between lines, at no extra charge, are possible at:

Park Street – Red and Green Lines (with underground walkway to the Orange Line at Downtown Crossing).
Downtown Crossing – Red and Orange Lines (with underground walkway to the Green Line at Park Street).
Government Center – Blue and Green Lines.
State – Blue and Orange Lines.
Haymarket and North Station – Green and Orange Lines. (This connection is considerably more convenient at Haymarket than at North Station).

"Inbound" is always towards downtown Boston – Park Street, Downtown Crossing and Government Center. "Outbound" means away from downtown. Outside of central Boston, both the Red and Green Lines have branches. Check the sign on the front of the train. Green Line trains (also called streetcars or simply cars) carry letters to indicate different branches: B – Boston College; C –

Cleveland Circle; D – Riverside; E – Heath Street or Arborway. A red line through the letter on a sign means that the train goes only part way on that branch.

Turnstiles in the underground stations of the "T" accept only tokens. These can be purchased at the collectors' booths. A Token Ten-Pack gives 11 tokens for the price of 10. One token (currently 75 cents) permits the traveler to ride as far as he wishes without extra payment. When boarding the "T" at surface stations one token or the exact change (75 cents) is necessary. Getting there on the "T" can be less expensive than getting back. Although all outbound fares (except to Quincy Adams and to Braintree), irrespective of distance, are 75 cents, an inbound journey from outlying stations can go up to $1.75.

The Rapid Transit operates 20 hours each day – from shortly after 5 a.m. until past 1 a.m. On Sundays, services begin about 40 minutes later than on other days. Last trains leave downtown Boston at 12.45 a.m.

BY BUS

The majority of the MBTA's 162 bus routes operate feeder services linking subway stations to neighborhoods not directly served by the rapid transit system. Some crosstown routes connect stations on different subway lines without going into downtown. Only a few MBTA buses actually enter downtown Boston and most of these are express buses from outlying areas. One service which visitors might wish to use is Route 1 which travels along Massachusetts Avenue (at the western end of the Back Bay) across the Charles River to MIT and onto Harvard Square. MBTA buses also serve Lexington (board the T-62 or T-76 at Alewife) and Marblehead (board the T-441 or T-442 at Haymarket).

The basic MBTA bus fare is 50 cents. On a few relatively long routes, zone fares – 25 cents per additional zone, up to $1.50 – are charged. Express bus fares range from $1.25 to $1.90, depending on the length of the route. Exact change is required on buses and dollars bills are not accepted. MBTA tokens are accepted but change is not returned.

Rapid Transit Lines

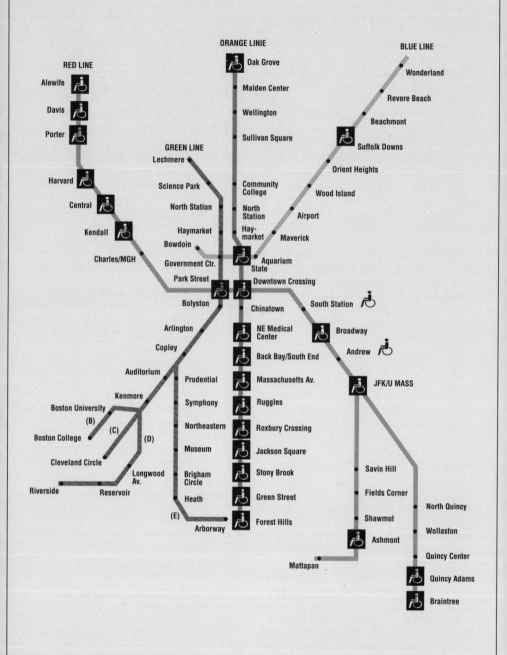

RED LINE
- Alewife
- Davis
- Porter
- Harvard
- Central
- Kendall
- Charles/MGH

ORANGE LINIE
- Oak Grove
- Malden Center
- Wellington
- Sullivan Square
- Community College
- North Station
- Haymarket
- State
- Downtown Crossing
- Chinatown
- NE Medical Center
- Back Bay/South End
- Massachusetts Av.
- Ruggles
- Roxbury Crossing
- Jackson Square
- Stony Brook
- Green Street
- Forest Hills

BLUE LINE
- Wonderland
- Revere Beach
- Beachmont
- Suffolk Downs
- Orient Heights
- Wood Island
- Airport
- Maverick
- Aquarium

GREEN LINE
- Lechmere
- Science Park
- North Station
- Haymarket
- Bowdoin
- Government Ctr.
- Park Street
- Bolyston
- Arlington
- Copley
- Auditorium
- Kenmore
- Boston University (B)
- Boston College
- (C)
- (D)
- Cleveland Circle
- Longwood Av.
- Riverside
- Reservoir
- Prudential
- Symphony
- Northeastern
- Museum
- Brigham Circle
- Heath
- (E)
- Arborway

- South Station
- Broadway
- Andrew
- JFK/U MASS
- Savin Hill
- Fields Corner
- Shawmut
- Ashmont
- Mattapan
- North Quincy
- Wollaston
- Quincy Center
- Quincy Adams
- Braintree

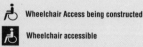

- Wheelchair Access being constructed
- Wheelchair accessible

278

COMMUTER RAIL

MBTA Commuter Rail extends from downtown Boston to as far as 60 miles away and serves such tourist destinations as Concord, Lowell, Salem, Ipswich, Gloucester and Rockport. Trains to the north and the northwest of Boston depart from North Station while trains to points south and west of the city leave from South Station. All south side commuter trains, except the Fairmount Line, also stop at the Back Bay Station. For information call South Station (tel: 345-7456) or North Station (tel: 722-3600).

Commuter rail fares are zoned from a minimum of 75 cents to a maximum of $5.25. A trip from Boston to Salem, for example, costs $2.25. Tickets are sold at the railway stations or can be purchased on the train subject to a surcharge of 50 cents.

PASSPORT VISITOR PASS

A three-day Passport costs $8; a seven-day Passport is $16. Children's Passports (age 5–11) are half the adult price. Passports permit unlimited use on the "T", on MBTA buses up to $1.50 fare (additional fare, if any, payable in cash), and commuter rail zones 1A and 1B. Passports also produce discounts at some tourist attractions and restaurants. Passports are sold at the Airport, at the three railway stations; at the Visitor Information Center on Boston Common and at the Faneuil Hall Marketplace Information Center; at the Harvard subway station and at some hotels. Tel: 722-5218 for further details.

TAXICABS

Some taxi companies – although you will doubt on a rainy day if any exist – are:
Bay State Taxi Service tel: 566-5000;
Boston Cab Association Inc. tel: 536-5010;
Boston City Taxicab tel: 859-0855;
Checker Taxi Co. tel: 536-7000, 536-7500 or, in Cambridge, 497-1500, 497-0700;
Independent Taxi Operators Association tel: 426-8700;
Red Cab tel: 734-5000;
Red & White Cab Association tel: 742-9090;
Town Taxi tel: 536-5000.

Tolls for bridges and tunnels are paid by the passenger. There is no extra fare for additional passengers. The driver may charge extra for trunks or unusual cargo (*e.g.*, crocodiles). For trips over 12 miles from downtown flat rates are charged – currently, $2.10 per mile plus tolls. Tipping is not mandatory but it is a brave soul who does not add 15–20 percent to the fare.

CAR HIRE

There is a wide variety of car hire companies:
American International tel: 800-527-0202, 569-3550;
Avis tel: 800-331-1212, 267-5151, 367-1190, 951-0255 and, in Cambridge, 491-3300;
Budget tel: 800-527-0700, 787-8200;
Dollar Rent A Car tel: 800-421-6878, 367-2654, 523-5098, 723-8312 and, in Cambridge, 354-6410;
Hertz tel: 800-654-3131, 536-0508 and, in Cambridge, 547-0336;
National tel: 800-227-7368, 661-8747;
Rent-A-Wreck tel: 800-535-1391, 720-1136 and, in Cambridge, 628-8800;
Thrifty tel: 800-367-2277, 569-6500;
Ugly Duckling Car Rental tel: 244-3825.

LIMOUSINE SERVICES

A & A Carey Limousine tel: 800-334-4646, 623-8700;
A.C.E. Limousine Inc. tel: 800-356-7877, 356-7877;
Ambassador Services Ltd tel: 800-759-5466, 227-7844;
Cap's Auto Livery tel: 800-621-1096, 523-0727;
Commonwealth Limousine tel: 800-558-LIMO, 787-5575;
Copley Limousine Service tel: 800-634-3807, 338-7731;
Escort Limousine Corporation tel: 800-843-4002, 926-6900;
Fifth Avenue Limousine Service tel: 800-343-2071, 286-1590;
Modern Limousine Service tel: 800-902-6637, 625-4550;
Standard Limousine Service tel: 800-634-0045, 569-3880;
Vintage Limousine Service tel: 738-0044.

COMMUTER BOAT

The Navy Yard Water Shuttle (this is a delightful way to reach the *USS Constitution* and the Bunker Hill Monument) sails from Long Wharf to the Charlestown Navy Yard daily; the voyage takes 10 minutes and the fare is $1.

The Hingham commuter boat sails from Rowes Wharf, Mon–Fri: the one-way fare is $4.

OTHER FERRIES, BUSES & PLANES

The Bay State Cruise Co. (tel: 723-7800) and **Boston Harbor Cruises** (tel: 227 4321) both operate a service to **Georges Island** (time 45 minutes). The service operates from **Long Wharf** daily from mid-June to Labor Day and at weekends only from early-May until mid-June and from mid-September until late-October. Each company has about four sailings daily. During the summer months and at weekends in May and September the Boston Harbor Islands State Park runs a free water taxi service from Georges Island to half-a-dozen of the other Harbor Islands. Each island is visited two or three times daily with the service being increased at the weekends.

A delightful way to reach **Provincetown** during the summer months is to board the **Bay State Cruise Company's** ferry at **Long Wharf** at 9.30 a.m. and arrive at Provincetown 2½ hours later. The ferry leaves Provincetown for Boston at 3 p.m. It runs daily from mid-June to Labor Day and at weekends from Memorial Day to mid-June.

The **A.C. Cruise Line** (tel: 426-8419, 800-422-8419) ferry departs daily (Sundays excepted) at 10 a.m. from late-June to Labor Day and at weekends from Memorial day to mid-June from **Pier One** for **Gloucester** (**Rocky Neck**). The voyage takes 2½ hours boat arrives back in Boston at 5.30 p.m.

For **Plymouth** board the **Plymouth and Brockton** bus at the **Greyhound Terminal** on St James Avenue. The trip takes under one hour. Unfortunately, the majority of buses do not stop in Plymouth itself but at the North Plymouth Bus station which is 2½ miles from the tourist attractions. The same company has a fairly frequent service to

Hyannis: time 2 hours. Connecting buses leave from Hyannis for **Provincetown**, a journey of about 90 minutes. **Bonanza** buses leave from **Back Bay station** and travel via **Falmouth**, **Wareham**, **Buzzard's Bay** to **Woods Hole**.

The **Provincetown–Boston Airline** flies frequently – flight time is 20 minutes – between Boston (Logan airport) and Provincetown.

TOURS

Bus companies run daily tours during the summer months. These cover not only Boston and its environs but venture further afield and visit many destinations mentioned in this book's Day Trips chapters .**Gray Line Tours** (Quality Inn, 275 Tremont Street, tel: 426-8800) and **Brush Hill Transportation Company** (109 Norfolk Street, Dorchester, tel: 287-1900, 800-343-1328) offer tours of Lexington, Concord, Greater Boston, Cambridge, Plimoth Plantation, Salem and Cape Cod. Departure from several downtown hotels.

Throughout the year three companies – **Beantown Trolley** (tel: 236-2148), **Brush Hill Tours** (tel: 287-1900) and **Old Town Trolley** (tel: 269-7010, 269-7150) – run trolley tours which cover Beacon Hill, Newbury Street, Downtown, the Waterfront, the Bunker Hill Pavilion in Charlestown and which pass close to many of the Freedom Trail sites. The uninterrupted tour lasts 90-minutes but passengers can alight as often as they wish and reboard a later trolley of the same company.

Old Town Trolley also runs a **Cambridge** tour which leaves Harvard Square every hour on the hour.

A wide variety of **harbor cruises** ranging from one hour sight-seeing to lunchtime cruises, evening outings and "booze" cruises with dinner and/or musical entertainment are organized by the **Bay State Cruise Company** (tel: 723-7800), **Boston Harbor Cruises** (tel: 227-4321) and the **Massachusetts Bay Lines** (tel: 542-8000). Vessels of the first two companies leave from Long Wharf: those of the Massachusetts Bay line from Rowes Wharf. Cruising and dining can also be enjoyed aboard the state-of-the-art

Spirit of Boston (tel: 569-4055) and the *Gondola Venezia* (tel: 345-0068) which is Boston harbor's answer to Venice's gondolas. Five-hour **whale-watching** cruises, organized by the New England Aquarium (tel: 973-5200) and accompanied by Aquarium naturalists, cast off from Central Wharf daily at 9 a.m. on Mon–Fri and at 8 a.m. and 2 p.m. on Saturdays and Sundays from May until October. They also sail at weekends (departure 11 a.m.) in April and October.

Boston Helicopter Tours: tel: 357-6868. Offer a variety of sight-seeing flights.

Both Boston and Cambridge are ideal for **walking**. Many walking tours, both general and for the specialist, are available.
Boston by Foot: 77 North Washington Street, tel: 367-2345. Offers a wide variety of regular scheduled tours May–October. History and the city's architecture are highlighted. Most tours start at 10 a.m. or 2 p.m. and last for 90 minutes. Also offered "Boston by Little Feet: a Children's Tour" on Sundays at 2 p.m. Meet your guide in front of Faneuil Hall at the statue of Samuel Adams.

Cambridge Discovery Tours: tel: 497-1630. Morning and afternoon tours leave from Cambridge Discovery Information Booth in the heart of Harvard Square.

Cambridge Historical Society: 159 Brattle Street, tel: 547-4252. Offers year-round tours with a variety of themes and routes.

Historic Neighborhoods Foundation: 2 Boylston Street, tel: 426-1885. Has a variety of regular scheduled tours May–November. The Kennedy Roots Tour focuses on North End sites associated with the family roots of John F. Kennedy. Other tours include a Chinatown tour, Financial District tour, Sunset Stroll through Beacon Hill. Tiny tots will adore their "Make Way for Ducklings" stroll in the Public Garden on Saturdays at 11 a.m. It is based on the beloved children's classic *Make Way for Ducklings*.

New England Sights: 18 Brattle Street, Cambridge, tel: 492-6689. Offer custom-tailored tours with multilingual guides. Historic, cultural and educational attractions are highlighted.

Uncommon Tours: 437 Boylston Street, tel: 266-9768. Explore hidden spaces, uncommon places and cover unique events. Some of the walk, ride or sail tours offered on a regular basis include a Pub and Tavern crawl, a Clambake, a Bargains to Baubles shopping tour and a Culinary Tour of the North End.

Victorian Society in America: 137 Beacon Street, tel: 282-9830 (evenings only). Organizes walking tours on spring and fall Sunday afternoons. Emphasis is on architecture, landscape and women's achievements.

The **National Park Service**: 15 State Street, tel: 242-5642. Has frequent free tours of the **Freedom Trail** from mid-Jun to mid-Oct. Half-a-dozen Freedom Trail sites are visited in a tour which lasts about 90 minutes.

Boston Park Ranger Tours: tel: 522-2369. Tours are held during the summer months in the Public Garden. Enjoy their "What's in Bloom" tour, an introduction to the plants in bloom in this historic arboretum. All tours are free.

Fine Arts Tours: Box 206, Newton 02159, tel: 655-8532. Provide an educated visit to the Boston art scene. Reguarly scheduled tours include a Newbury Street gallery tour, visits to artists' studios, Expert's Guide to the Museum of Fine Arts. Tours are for both the expert and the novice: groups are small.

Museum of Fine Arts: 465 Huntington Avenue, tel: 267-9300. Organizes 3-hour Boston architectural tours. Summer, Sat at 10 a.m: Fall, Wed and Sat at 10 a.m.

Boston Beer Company: Samuel Adams Brewery, 30 Germania Street, tel: 522-9080. Tour the brewery and its museum of interesting historical Boston area breweriana. Telephone for details.

WHERE TO STAY

The city of Boston is fairly well endowed with hotels, although one might be tempted to question this during spring and fall when conventions are in full swing. Hard facts are that the metropolitan area boasts more than 21,000 hotel rooms, of which two-thirds are in Boston and Cambridge. Bed and breakfast accommodation is becoming increasingly popular and can be of a high standard. And then, of course, there is the inevitable "Y" and youth hostels.

Some visitors might prefer the rarified atmosphere of Cambridge from which Boston proper is quickly (about 15 minutes) and easily reached by public transport. Another alternative is to stay in one or other of the many hotels in Greater or Metropolitan Boston and join the MBTA (Massachusetts Bay Transportation Authority) commuters for a 30–40 minute journey every morning and evening. These suburban hotels, most of which belong to major chains, are less expensive than city hotels.

A very approximate guide to current room rates (standard double) is: $ = under $100; $$ = $100–150; $$$ = $150–200; $$$$ = over $200.

BOSTON HOTELS

Boston Harbor Hotel, 70 Rowes Wharf, tel: 439-7000. 230 rooms. Board the airport water shuttle at Logan and, seven minutes later, step into the luxury of the city's new signature building. Bedrooms all have either harbor or skyline views and all have windows which may be opened. Eighteen rooms are specially designed for the physically handicapped. A museum-quality art collection decorates the public areas. Across the road is the Financial District while minutes away (on foot) is the Aquarium and Quincy Market. $$$$

Boston Park Plaza Hotel & Towers, 50 Park Plaza, tel: 426-2000. 977 rooms. This excellently located, middle-of-the-road, bustling hotel began life in 1927 as the flagship of the Statler chain. It is within walking distance of the Back Bay Amtrack Station, the Greyhound Bus Terminal and the underground. Several airlines have offices in the hotel which provides an airport shuttle service. $$

Bostonian Hotel, Faneuil Hall Marketplace, tel: 523-3600. 153 rooms. Continental elegance and intimacy are the keynotes here. The Harkness Wing, an original 1824 building, has rooms with working fireplaces, exposed beamed ceilings and brick walls. The newer wing is more contemporary in style. Unfortunately, the hotel is situated exactly between Faneuil Hall Marketplace and Haymarket which can spell trouble for light sleepers. The hotel offers complimenatry limousine service to the airport and other parts of Boston. $$$$

Colonnade, 120 Huntington Avenue, tel: 424-7000. 294 rooms. A charming, European style hotel that prides itself on its multilingual staff. All the bedrooms are L-shaped with distinct sitting, sleeping and dressing areas. Situated very close to the Prudential Center and the Christian Science Complex and with a subway stop at its doorstep. $$$

Copley Plaza, 138 St James Avenue, tel: 267-5300. 393 rooms. It is still, with its European style, "*la grande dame*" of Boston hotels. Some rooms, many decorated with period furniture, are on the small side. Since it opened in 1912, it has been visited by every President in office. Situated in Copley Square, it is close to most tourist attractions and public transport is on the doorstep. $$$$

Copley Square, 47 Huntington Avenue, tel: 536-9000. 150 rooms. This modest and moderately priced hotel, which opened in the 1890s, was recently refurbished. Windows in bedrooms, which vary enormously in size, may be opened. Some rooms do not have *en suite* facilities. Half-a-dozen steps lead to either the Prudential Center or the Public Library. $$

"57" Park Plaza/Howard Johnson, 200 Stuart Street, tel: 482-1800. 360 rooms. A cut above what one usually associates with the second part of the name. A hotel in the heart of the Theater District and within walking distance of most tourist attractions. The hotel complex includes two cinemas. Free-indoor parking with direct access to your room. $$

Four Seasons, 200 Boylston Street, tel: 338-4400. 288 rooms. This 15-story red-brick hotel, which overlooks the Public Garden, is devoted to elegance and sybaritic living. All bedrooms are large and have bay windows which may be opened. $$$$

Hilton Back Bay, 40 Dalton Street, tel: 236-1100. 335 rooms. Across the road from the Hynes Convention Center and the Christian Science Complex. Close to Massachusetts Avenue and bus to Cambridge. $$$

Holiday Inn/Government Center, 5 Blossom Street, tel: 742-7630. 300 rooms. Situated at the foot of the wrong side of Beacon Hill and next to the Massachusetts General Hospital. The River is just a few yards away. A cinema is part of the complex. $$

Inn at Children's/Best Western, 342 Longwood Avenue, tel: 731-4700. 152 rooms. Situated in the heart of the city's major medical complex and adjoining the Longwood Galleria which has a food court and some retail stores. Also close to the Fenway with its colleges and museums. A bus stop at the hotel door means that downtown Boston is only minutes away. Some units are kitchenette studios. $$

Lafayette, One Avenue de Lafayette, tel: 451-2600. 500 rooms. Grand and elegant, this relatively new Swissotel rises above Lafayette Place, a three-level shopping complex of boutiques and restaurants. Upper floors have superb views of the waterfront and Beacon Hill. In the heart of downtown and close to everything. Twenty-five rooms specially designed for the physically handicapped. $$$$

Le Meridien, 250 Franklin Street, tel: 451-1900. 326 rooms. A superb recycling in the early 1980s of the Federal Reserve Bank, which was patterned after a 16th-century Roman palazzo, brought France to Boston. The hotel is in the heart of the Financial District yet close to Quincy Market. $$$$

Lenox Hotel, 710 Boylston Street, tel: 536-5300. 220 rooms. Modest and moderate traditional family hotel built in 1900. Bedrooms, some with functional fireplaces, have recently been redecorated in French Provincial, Oriental or Colonial decor. Just a few steps from the Prudential Center and the Public Library. A subway stop is at the doorstep. $$

Logan Airport Hilton, Logan International Airport, tel: 569-9300. 542 rooms. The only hotel located at the airport. Free limousine service to airlines. Outdoor pool. $$$

Marriott Copley Plaza, 110 Huntington Avenue, tel: 236-5800. 1,039 rooms. Handsome bedrooms in this hotel which has 36 rooms suitable for the handicapped. Not only is the hotel linked to the Copley Place shopping mall with its upmarket stores but it is also connected by a glassed-in walkway with the Prudential Center where there is still more shopping and restaurants. $$$$

Marriott Long Wharf, 296 State Street, Long Wharf, tel: 227-0800. 400 rooms. Situated at the waterfront immediately next to the Aquarium and just across the road from Quincy Market. Ideally situated for all water activities. Most rooms in this architecturally unusual hotel have panoramic views of the harbor. Step out of the hotel and into the subway. $$$

Midtown Hotel, 220 Huntington Avenue, tel: 262-1000. 160 rooms. Near Museum of Fine Arts, Symphony Hall, Christian Science Complex and Prudential Center. Bus to Cambridge and subway to downtown at doorstep. $$

Omni Parker House, 60 School Street, tel: 227-8600. 540 rooms. Although claimed to be the oldest continuously operating hotel in America, the present building, which has frequently been renovated, dates only from 1927. Some rooms have showers only. Malcolm X and Ho Chi Minh both worked here. A favorite with politicians and possibly the most centrally located hotel in the city. $$$

Ritz-Carlton, 15 Arlington Street, tel: 536-5700. 278 rooms. Still, as ever, the city's *numero uno*, with the highest staff-to-guest ratio in town. All bedroom windows may be opened, the better to enjoy the view over the Public Garden. Forty-one of the units are suites, including a presidential suite for kids with specially scaled-down fixtures and the latest toys – including a rubber duck for the executive bath. The Back Bay with its stores, galleries and restaurants is on the doorstep. Complimentary limousine service within the city on weekday mornings. $$$$

Sheraton Boston Hotel & Towers, Prudential Center, tel: 236-2000. 1,300 rooms. New England's largest hotel, adjacent to the Hynes Convention Center and the Christian Science Complex. Do not be put off by the exterior of the twin 29-story towers. The Tower rooms (top four floors) are superior and more expensive than the Hotel rooms. $$$$

Tremont House, 275 Tremont Street, tel: 426-1400. 288 rooms. This "Quality hotel" is situated in the Theater District and within walking distance of most tourist attractions. $$.

Westin Hotel, Copley Place, 10 Huntington Avenue, tel: 262-9600. 804 rooms. Rooms in Boston's tallest hotel – it has 36 stories, starting on the eighth floor – are probably the city's largest and have superb views of the River Charles. Forty rooms are specially designed for the physically handicapped. Hotel is linked by skybridge to the Copley Place shopping mall and is thus suicide for spendthrifts. $$$$

GREATER BOSTON B&B

The Massachusetts Office of Travel and Tourism, 100 Cambridge Street, Boston, MA 02202, publishes a free *Bed-and-Breakfast Guide* which lists guests houses throughout the state.

In Boston and Cambridge B & B accommodation runs from about $50–$100 for a double. Central organizations to contact are: **A Bed & Breakfast Above the Rest**, 50 Boatswains Way, Boston 02150, tel: 277-2292, 800-677-2262. Offers rooms in Boston and Cambridge.

New England Bed and Breakfast, 1045 Centre Street, Newton, MA 02159, tel: 224-2112. Lists homes that are a 10–20 minute drive to Boston or within walking distance of public transportation.

Bed &Breakfast Agency of Boston, 47 Commercial Wharf, Boston, MA 02110, tel: 720-3540, 800-CITY-BNB). Offers turn-of-the-century townhouses, furnished condos and much more to B & B clients.

Bed and Breakfast Associates, Bay Colony, P.O. Box 166, Babson Park Branch, Boston, MA 02157, tel: 449-5302. Lists homes in metropolitan Boston and throughout eastern Massachusetts. Directory $5.

Bed and Breakfast of Cambridge and Greater Boston, P.O. Box 665, Cambridge, MA 02140, tel: 576-1492. Features accommodation in private homes in Boston and Cambridge.

Boston Bed and Breakfast, tel: 332-4199. Features accommodation in private homes in Boston and Cambridge.

Host Homes of Boston, P.O. Box 117, Newton, MA 02168, tel: 244-1308. A moored yacht in the harbor and a Victorian townhouse in the Back Bay are just some of the listings carried by this organization.

A Cambridge House, P.O. Box 211, Massachusetts Avenue, Cambridge, MA 02140, tel: 491-6300. Is a delightful historic-listed home with 22 A/C rooms and shared bath. An exercise room is also available. Breakfast is included and parking is available. This is a reservation center for host homes throughout New England.

Specific B & B accommodation addresses are:
Anthony's Town House, 331 Beacon Street, Brookline 02146, tel: 566-3972. A four-story turn-of-the-century brownstone townhouse with 14 rooms decorated with Queen Anne and Victorian style furnishings. Situated on the Green Line of the "T": 15 minutes to downtown Boston.

Baileys/Boston House, 331 Beacon Street, Boston 02199, tel: 262-4543. A European style B & B home with 10 guests rooms in the heart of the Back Bay.

Beacon Inns & Guest Houses, 248 Newbury Street, Boston 02116, tel: 266-7142. Guest rooms with private bath and kitchenettes in the heart of the Back Bay.

Beacon Street Guest House, 1047 Beacon Street, Brookline 02146, tel: 232-0292, 800-872-7211. 15 rooms. Close to Fenway Park and Boston University and on the Green Line of the "T": 15 minutes to downtown Boston.

Brookline Manor Guest House, 32 Centre Street, Brookline 02146, tel: 232-0003, 800-535-5325. 35 rooms. Close to Fenway Park and Boston University and on the Green Line of the "T": 15 minutes to downtown Boston.

Newbury Inn, 533 Newbury Street, Boston 02215, tel: 266-2583. Nine rooms, some with fireplace. Kitchen facilities. On the western fringe of the Back Bay and close to the Green line of the "T": 15 minutes to downtown Boston.

106 Chestnut Street, Boston 02108, tel: 227-7866. An elegant Federal-style townhouse on Beacon Hill. Some rooms with private baths. Eighteenth-century European furnishings provide a perfect setting for collectibles from more than 90 countries.

27 Brimmer Street, Boston 02108, tel: 523-7376. An elegant 1869 six-story townhouse on historic Beacon Hill. All rooms have fireplace, double or queen-size bed and private bath. Elevator for luggage. Smoking not permitted.

Victorian Bows, 173 West Brookline Street, Boston 02118, tel: 266-1235, 800-225-7001. Restored high-stoop 1860s brownstone on the edge of the increasingly fashionable South End. Private bathrooms. Close to Copley Square.

HOSTELS & "Ys"

Berkeley Residence Club, 40 Berkeley Street, Boston 02116, tel: 482-8850. Superbly located close to Copley Square and South Station this 200 room club run by the YWCA offers single and doubles. Shared bathrooms. Pleasant garden and public rooms. $29 for singles: $40 for doubles.

Boston International Youth Hostel, 12 Hemenway Street, Fenway, tel: 536-9455. Well located at the western fringe of the Back Bay and very close to public transport (both underground and bus). 220 beds in 4–6 bed dormitories: bring or hire sheets. A 10-minute chore is required. Currently $12 a night for members: $15 for non-members.

Garden Halls Residences, 164 Marlborough Street, tel: 267-0079. Empty dorm rooms in the heart of the Back Bay with a bed, dresser and desk. No A/C and no bedding (bring your own linen). Some rooms with private bathroom. Singles, doubles, triples and quads cost $25 per night per person (3-night minimum stay).

Greater Boston YMCA, 316 Huntington Avenue, Fenway, tel: 536-7800. Clean small rooms each with color TV run $29 for singles and $42 for doubles (with double bed). This includes hot breakfast and maid service. Maximum stay is 10 days. Guests have full use of all athletic facilities. The "Y" is superbly situated within walking distance of the Christian Science Complex, the Prudential Center, Museum of Fine Arts and Symphony Hall. The Green Line of the "T" stops at the door and downtown is only 10 minutes away.

CAMBRIDGE HOTELS

The majority of Cambridge hotels are situated near Harvard University or at the extreme eastern end of the MIT campus.

In the former group are:

Charles, 1 Bennett Street, tel. 864-1200. 299 rooms. A touch of class is provided on the edge of Harvard Square: Cambridge's answer to the Ritz-Carlton. Its Regattabar is consistently rated as the best jazz scene in the region. A shopping mall is attached to the hotel and shops and restaurants are all around. $$$

Harvard Motor House, 110 Mount Auburn Street, tel: 864-5200. 72 rooms. A six-floor modern motel in the heart of Harvard's

Cambridge. All rooms with picture windows: complimentary continental breakfast. That the hotel lacks restaurants does not present a problem: myriad eateries are within a stone's throw. $

Kirkland Inn, 67 Kirkland Street, tel: 547-4600. Fairly basic accommodation close to Harvard Square. Many rooms without private facilities. Reservations not accepted. More a hostel than a hotel. $

Quality Inn, 1651 Massachusetts Avenue, tel: 491-l000. 135 rooms. A moderately priced hotel in the heart of Harvard's Cambridge. Public transport at the door. $

Sheraton Commander, 16 Garden Street, tel: 547-4800. 176 rooms. An old fashioned but recently renovated hotel near Cambridge Common and Harvard Yard. Some rooms have Boston rockers and four-poster beds and some have kitchenettes. $$$

Among the hotels at the extreme eastern end of the MIT campus are:
Marriott Cambridge, Two Cambridge Center, tel: 494-6600. 43l rooms. A new 25-story hotel with a modest adjacent shopping complex. A subway stop at the hotel entrance means that both Downtown Boston and Harvard Square are just minutes away. $$$

Royal Sonesta, 5 Cambridge Parkway, tel: 491-3600. 400 rooms. On the banks of the Charles and offering great views of the Boston skyline. Closest of all hotels to the Science Museum. Practically next door is the Cambridge Galleria, metropolitan Boston's newest shopping mall. Free shuttle service into Boston. $$$

Other Cambridge hotels include:
Guest Quarters Suites, 400 Soldiers Field Road, Boston, tel: 783-0090. 310 suites. All accommodation is in two-room suites with two telephones and two TV sets. Great for families because the living rooms contain sofa-beds and children under 18 are free. Breakfast is included in room rate. Next to the Harvard Business School and on the banks of the Charles. A 15-minute stroll leads to Harvard College. $$

Howard Johnson Hotel Cambridge, 777 Memorial Drive, tel: 492-7777. 204 rooms. This attractive, modern motel, popular with tour groups, is situated on the Cambridge side of the Charles river about equidistant from Harvard College and MIT and across the river from Boston University. Rooms have splendid views of Boston skyline. $$

Hyatt Regency, 575 Memorial Drive, tel: 492-1234. 500 rooms. The "pyramid on the Charles" is situated on the Cambridge side of the river about equidistant from Harvard College and MIT and across the bridge from Boston University: great views of the Boston skyline. Fifteen rooms specially designed for the physically handicapped. $$$$

GREATER BOSTON HOTELS

Holiday Inn-Boston at Brookline, 1200 Beacon Street, Brookline, tel: 277-1200. 208 rooms. Small, comfortable rooms and free underground parking in a residential neighborhood which is 15 minutes from downtown Boston on the Green Line of the "T" which passes the hotel. Coolidge Corner with excellent shopping and a variety of restaurants is only a short stroll. $$

Howard Johnson Hotel, 575 Commonwealth Avenue, Brookline, tel: 267-3100. 179 rooms. Practically situated in the outfield of Fenway Park, home of the Red Sox and close to Boston University, this typical Howard Johnson's is near Kenmore Square with all its stores and a terminus for public transport. From here a mere 15 minutes to downtown Boston. $

Terrace Motor Lodge, 1650 Commonwealth Avenue, Brighton, tel: 566-6260. 75 rooms. A complex of motel units suitable for families because of two-room suites and because children under 16 are free. Free use of kitchenettes, although dishes and utensils are not provided. Boston University is nearby and Downtown Boston is reached in 20 minutes on the Green Line of the "T". $

FOOD DIGEST

WHERE TO EAT

Many claim that Boston has the best seafood in the nation and it is certainly a great town in which to soak your fingers in steamers and lobsters. Some Boston specialities are clam chowder (made without adding tomatoes), scrod (not a separate species of fish but the name given to small tender haddock or cod) and steamers (clams served with two dipping sauces). Baked beans, once synonymous with Boston, and Boston brownbread are no longer that popular and may be rather difficult to find.

In the late 1980s a renaissance of Boston cuisine occurred which was spearheaded by half-a-dozen imaginative chefs – Jasper White of Jasper's, Lydia Shire of Biba, Gordon Hamersley of Hamersley's, Michela Larson of Michela's, Chris Schlesinger of East Coast Grill and Todd English of Olives. Contemporary New England cuisine was born and made its impact on the American scene.

The Back Bay, especially Newbury and Boylston Streets, has many sidewalk cafés and restaurants but none of these has the panache of their European counterparts. A recent hot-bed of *haute cuisine*, mainly contemporary American, is the South End, home to many yuppies and gays. Some other hot spots where restaurants are concentrated are Faneuil Hall Marketplace, Chinatown and the North End. Also, excellent international dining can be enjoyed in nearly all major hotels. Over in Cambridge, restaurants are concentrated around both Harvard and Central Squares. Many of these are small, inexpensive, ethnic eateries. However, not all the enormous floating student population is impecunious and, especially as many are from abroad, they significantly contribute to the restaurant scene.

As time passes, the dress code at restau-rants becomes less and less formal, although a few bastions remain. Traditionally, Bostonians are not late diners and restaurants are fairly busy by 7 p.m. Some restaurants have introduced "early bird dinners" – usually from 5 p.m.–7 p.m. when meals are much less expensive than later dining.

In a recent survey of the average price of a meal in 17 major American cities, Boston was two-thirds as expensive as New York and, as near as mattered, no dearer, no less expensive, than Los Angeles, Philadelphia, Washington DC, San Francisco or Chicago. However, Boston's culinary fame is generally agreed to reside at the high end of the price range with extremely few mid-range restaurants offering a positive "dining experience."

RESTAURANTS

Rough guide to prices for a three-course dinner excluding beverages, tax and tip: $ = under $15; $$ = $15–$28; $$$ = $28-$40: $$$ = over $40. As a general rule, a tip of 15 percent on checks less than $70 is practically mandatory: above that, better leave 20 percent. On top of this there is a 5 percent state meal tax.

LANDMARK

Anthony's Pier 4, 140 Northern Avenue (on Pier 4), tel: 423-6363. This 1,000-seat restaurant, situated on the waterfront, probably attracts more tourists than any other Boston restaurant. Portions are large; excellent wine list. Jacket and tie. No reservations and lines can be long. Limited outdoor dining if weather suitable. Free parking. $$$

Durgin Park, 340 North Market Street (Faneuil Hall Marketplace), tel: 227-2038. Yankee cooking attracts flocks of tourists to this legendary old dining hall where they are seated with others at long, picnic-cloth-covered tables and insulted by the waiters. Try Brontosaurus-sized prime ribs. No reservations: long waits. $$

Jacob Wirth, 31 Stuart Street, tel: 338-8586. A time-warp in the Theater District. Since 1868 wurst, sauerkraut and beer have attracted visitors to this institution with sawdust on the floor. $ – $$

Locke-Ober Café, 3 Winter Place, tel: 542-1340. This "Bastion of Brahmins" with a gentlemen's club atmosphere opened in 1875. Some of the waiters may have been there since then. People die for the Lobster Savannah and the Baked Alaska (order ahead). Outstanding wine card. Naturally, jacket and tie. If this is your scene, the place is a "must." $$$$

Union Oyster House, 41 Union Street (near Faneuil Hall), tel: 227-2750. Daniel Webster dined here where traditional steaks and seafoods are served in the old-fashioned way in atmospheric rooms with creaky floors, low ceilings and wooden booths. "A great raw-bar." No reservations and an irritating PA system. $$$

Wursthaus, 4 John F. Kennedy Street, Harvard Square, Cambridge, tel: 491-7110. Traditional German dishes in a multi-roomed, boothed restaurant have been served to Harvardians since 1917. They claim the largest selection of beers in the world. No reservations. $$

RESTAURANTS WITH A VIEW

Several restaurants offer superb panoramic views of the city and surrounds. As ever, when the view is great, the food falters.

Boston Sail Loft Café and Bar, 1 Memorial Drive, Cambrige, tel: 225-2222. Seafood served overlooking the river and the Boston skyline. $$

Bay Tower room, 60 State Street, tel: 723-1666. Beautiful glass-walled room on the 33rd floor. Tables arranged so that all enjoy view of Faneuil Hall Marketplace, the harbor and airport. One visits this restaurant for the view rather than for the contemporary American cuisine. Jacket and tie. Reservations advised. $$$$

Rowes Wharf Restaurant, Boston Harbor Hotel, 70 Rowes Wharf, tel: 439-3995. Excellent contemporary American cuisine served in a luxurious dark-paneled dining room with superb views of the hotel's marina and harbor. Jacket and tie. Reservations advised. $$$$

Sally Lings, Hyatt Regency Hotel, 575 Memorial Drive, Cambridge, tel: 492-1234. Stunning views of the river and the Boston Skyline can be enjoyed from this fancy Chinese restaurant serving *nouvelle cuisine*. Reservations advised. $$$$

Top of the Hub, Prudential Center, Back Bay, tel: 536-1775. Glass walls on three sides of the 52nd-floor restaurant offer grand views of Boston with, in the distance, the harbor and airport. Seafood is best bet. Reservations advised. Great place for Sunday brunch. $$$

SEAFOOD

Boston prides itself in having the best seafood in the nation. However, those with a tight schedule might be disappointed, for rare is the seafood restaurant that accepts bookings. Lines are often so long that adversity results in your making new friends.

Anthony's Pier 4, 140 Northern Avenue (on Pier 4), tel: 423-6363. (See *Landmark Restaurants*.)

Atlantic Fish Company Restaurant, 777 Boylston Street, tel: 267-4000. Excellent service in this unpretentious bistro-like Back Bay restaurant. No reservations. Limited outdoor dining. $$

Daily Catch, 323, Hanover Street, North End, tel: 523-8567. Also at 261 Northern Avenue (adjacent to Boston Fish Pier), tel: 338-3092 and 1 Kendall Square, Cambridge, tel: 225-2300. Small cramped "Little Italy" outlet is redolent with garlic. $$ – $$$

Jimmy's Harborside, 242 Northern Avenue (adjacent to Boston Fish Pier), tel: 423-1000. Great harbor views from downstairs main dining room where all rooms enjoy unobstructed harbor view and sunny Merchant's Club on upper level. A fun place. Simplify life by ordering one of the shore dinners. No reservations. Valet parking. $$$

Legal Seafoods, Park Plaza Hotel, Park Square, tel: 426-4444. Also at 5 Cambridge Center, Kendall Square, Cambridge, tel: 864-3400. Also at Copley Place, 100 Huntington Avenue. What started as a small Cambridge fish store now has a justly deserved international reputation. Enormous variety. No reservation and lines can be interminable. $$ – $$$.

No Name, 15½ Fish Pier (off Northern Avenue), tel: 338-7539. In spite of the name, an extremely popular, modestly priced restaurant. No frills: just large portions. Majority of dishes are fried. No reservations. $$

Skipjack's, 500 Boylston Street, tel: 536-3500. Also at 2 Brookline Place (off Boylston Street, Route 9), Brookline, tel: 232-8887. The downtown outlet with bright and cheery decor is in one of Boston's newest buildings. Specializes in cajun grilling. No reservations. $$ – $$$

Turner Fisheries, Westin Hotel, 10 Huntington Avenue, Copley Place, tel: 424-7425, 262-9600. On a par with Legal Seafoods (*see above*), although slightly more expensive. Reservations accepted. $$$

Union Oyster House, 41 Union Street, tel: 227-2750. (See *Landmark restaurants*.)

AMERICAN

Biba's, 272 Boylston Street, tel: 426-7878. Bold flavors of this contemporary New England cuisine match the bold decor and make this the most talked-about restaurant in town. Some tables overlook the Public Garden. A fun place. Reservations essential. $$$

Black Rose, 160 State Street, near Faneuil Hall, tel: 742-2286. Also at 50 Church Street, Harvard Square, Cambridge, tel: 492-8630. Irish pub-restaurant with lively atmosphere. Entertainment in evenings may be Irish but the food, including prize-winning chowder, is American. The Cambridge outlet is quite attractive. $.
Under same ownership and with same menus are **The Claddagh**, 355 Columbus Avenue, South End, tel: 262-9874 and the **Purple Shamrock**, 1 Union Street, near Faneuil Hall, tel: 227-2060. All four restaurants serve inexpensive Sunday brunch.

Blue Diner, 215 South Street, tel: 338-4639. Blueplate specials served in genuine restored diner from 1947. Vintage rock on the juke box and a music selector at each booth. No reservations. $ – $$

Bosworth's Boston Baked Beans, 37 Union Street, tel: 248-0880. Baked beans, brown bread and Indian pudding star in a menu focused on traditional New England favorites. Beans baked daily in view of visitors. $

Boston Chicken, 745 Boylston Street, Back Bay, tel: 859-0015. Boston's reply to Kentucky Fried – and its succulent and inexpensive. Self-service and plastic plates – rotisserie chicken, real potatoes and yuppie salads. Outdoor dining. $

Club Café, 209 Columbus Avenue, tel: 536-0966. Innovative dishes, served until 1.30 a.m., in a bright restaurant which is part of a gay complex. $$

Commonwealth Brewing Company, 138 Portland Street (near North Station), tel: 523-8383. Light meals among glistening copper kettles and pipes. Draught beer at cellar temperatures and bottles frosty cold. Seasonal brews. $

Division 16, 955 Boylston Street, Back Bay, tel: 353-0870. Long lines gather outside this former police station not so much for the food, which is mostly burgers and the like, as for the ambience. Trendy. No reservations. $$

Grill-23, 161 Berkley Street, tel: 542-2255. The city's best steakhouse. Clubby type upmarket dining room with a high noise level. Excellent wine list. Valet parking. $$$$

Hamersley's Bistro, 578 Tremont Street, South End, tel: 267-6068. A South End charmer where friendly service accompanies exciting and delightful contemporary New England cuisine. Reservations essential. $$$ – $$$$

Hard Rock Café, 131 Clarendon Street, tel: 424-7625. Good hamburgers and the like served among rock 'n' roll memorabilia. Lots of decibels. Long lines. $

Harvest, 44 Brattle Street, Harvard Square, Cambridge, tel: 492-1115. Contemporary New England cuisine served in an academic ambience: the best restaurant on campus. Excellent wine list. Outdoor courtyard. Reservations advised. $$$

Hilltop Steakhouse, 855 Broadway, Saugus, tel: 233-7700. Drive north on Route 1 for 20 minutes and stop at the herd of plastic life-sized cattle on the left. The five dining rooms in this 1,500-room steakhouse are always full and the line often long. Basic no-nonsense menu. An inexpensive experience. No reservations. Cash only. $

Hungry I, 71½ Charles Street, tel: 227-3524. Tiny, romantic, some say claustrophobic, downstairs restaurant which serves contemporary American cuisine. Imginative menu. Delightful courtyard. Reservations required. $$$ – $$$$

Jasper's, 240 Commercial Street (near the waterfront), tel: 523-1126. Contemporary New England cuisine at its very best. Flawless professional service in two elegant but different dining rooms. Outstanding wine list. Reservations advised. $$$$

J.C. Hillary's Limited, 793 Boylston Street, Back Bay, tel: 536-6300. Pleasant, inexpensive brasserie-type restaurant with no-nonsense food. Limited outdoor dining. No reservations. $$

Morton's of Chicago, 1 Exeter Place, Back Bay, tel: 266-5858. The place for those who love red meat. Waiters present a trolley laden with enormous cuts. Corny decor. Closed Sundays. $$ – $$$

Parker's, Omni Parker House, School Street, tel: 227-8600. A New England tradition since 1854: home of Parker rolls and Boston Cream Pie. Extremely comfortable Yankee room with lots of silverware. Excellent food with formal and attentive service. $$$ – $$$$

Rarities, Charles Hotel, 1 Bennet Street, Harvard Square, Cambridge, tel: 661-5050. One of Boston's great restaurants: superb food, exquisite service in a stunning setting. Outstanding wine list. *Prix fixe* menu. Jacket and tie. Reservations advised. $$$$

Seasons, Bostonian Hotel at North and Blackstone Streets, near Faneuil Hall, tel: 523-3600. Many tables overlook Faneuil Hall Marketplace. Curtains covering the arched ceiling are parted at sunset to reveal a skylight which makes a stunning room even more stunning. Service and presentation superb. Excellent wine list (American only). A dining experience. Jacket and tie. Reservations advised. $$$$

St Cloud's, 557 Tremont Street, South End, tel: 353-0202. One of the restaurants that has put the South End on the culinary map. Somewhat small portions of contemporary New England cuisine in a romantic little jewel. Reservations advised. Closed Mondays. $$$

Stage Deli, 275 Tremont Street, Theater District, tel: 523-3354. Also at 725 Boylston Street, Back Bay, tel: 859-9747. Claims to be the only genuine New York deli in "The Hub." Expensive.

SOUTHERN

Cajun Yankee, 1193 Cambridge Street, Cambridge, tel: 576-1971. Cajun at its best. Small menu written on blackboard in snug dining room. No reservations can lead to long lines. Closed: Sun and Mon. $$$

Chef Chandler's Commonwealth Grille, 111 Dartmouth Street, tel: 353-0160. Red-hot Creole-cajun food in a black-and-chrome restaurant. A fun place. Reservations suggested. $$

Cottonwood Café, 1815, Massachusetts Avenue, Cambridge, tel: 661-7440. Southwest American *nouvelle* in Cambridge. Innovative food in an exciting atmosphere. No reservations can lead to long lines. $$

East Coast Grill, 1271 Cambridge Street, tel: 491-6568. Long lines testify to the high regard in which this restaurant's barbecues are held. Open grill in view of diners. Laid back with rock and country music. A fun place. No reservation. $$$

The Loading Zone, 150 Kneeland Street, tel: 695-0087. Southern barbecue served in a factory like room with your table placed atop works of art. A noisy, funky place with good food. $$

Porterhouse Grill, 2046 Massachusetts Avenue, Cambridge, tel: 354-9793. Texas heaven in the booths of a Porter Square bar. Food is heavily smoked, Texas style. Closed: Mon. $

MEXICAN

Casa Romero, 30 Gloucester Street, tel: 536-4431. Delightful romantic ambience. Mission-style decor. No tacos or burritos here but unusual well prepared, non-greasy dishes. $$$

Mexican Cuisine, 1682 Massachusetts Avenue, Cambridge, tel: 661-1634. A crowded, smoky, hole-in-the-wall which serves the "best Mexican food within hundreds of miles." Remarkable seafood dishes. No reservations. $$

Sol Azteca, 914A Beacon Street, Brookline, tel: 262-0909. Explosively hot food in a casual basement restaurant. Ignore the Tex-Mex and traditional Mexcian food here and go for the specialities. $$$

CONTINENTAL

Difficult to decide when "French" or "American" becomes "Continental" but continental is how the following restaurants classify themselves.
Locke-Ober Café, 3 Winter Place, tel: 542-1340. (See *Landmark restaurants*.)

St Botolph, 99 St Botolph Street, tel: 266-3030. Casual urban dining in a restored, turreted 19th-century South End townhouse frequented by the upwardly mobile. No standard entrées but extensive list of appetizers, soups, salads, pastas and grilled pizzas. Café on ground floor less expensive than upstairs dining room. Valet parking. $$$

Harvard Bookstore Café, 190 Newbury Street, tel: 536-0095. Dining among bookstacks or dining outside and watching the world go by. Limited menu. $$

Café Plaza, Copley Plaza Hotel, Copley Square, tel: 267-5300. Dining in a 1900s classic dining room – "one of the most beautiful dining rooms in Boston" – is an experience for that special occasion. Fabulous wine collection. Jacket and tie. Dinner only: never on a Sunday. $$$$

FRENCH

The majority of Boston's best French restaurants are found in hotels.
Aujourd'hui, 200 Boylston Street, tel: 451-1392. Some truly superb contemporary dishes accompanied by excellent wines in an opulent dining room overlooking the Public Garden. Jacket and tie. Sunday brunch "the finest in Boston." Valet parking. $$$$

L'Espalier, 30 Gloucester Street, tel: 262-3023. Imaginative cuisine served in three elegant, intimate dining rooms – each different – in a 19th-century Back Bay townhouse. *Prix fixe* menu available. Excellent wine list. Valet parking. Dinner only. Closed: Sun. $$$$

Le Marquis de Lafayette, 1 Avenue de Lafayette, tel: 451-2600. A superb experience. Impeccable service, distinguished wines, outstanding cuisine in a grand dining room. Jacket and tie. *Prix fixe* menu available. The place for an occasion. Jazz on Saturday evenings. $$$$

Maison Robert, 45 School Street, tel: 227-3370. Romantic elegance and fine classic French cuisine in **Bonhomme Richard**, the upstairs dining room in the French Second Empire Old City Hall building. Jacket and tie. $$$$ **Ben's Café**, on ground floor and with patio dining, is half the price.

Olives, 67 Main Street (Monument Avenue), Charlestown, tel: 242-1999. Great chefs have converted a small shop in this trendy part of town into a Provence-like restaurant. No-reservations policy usually results in long lines. $$$

Ritz-Carlton Dining Room, Ritz-Carlton Hotel, 15 Arlington Street, tel: 536-5700. For that special occasion visit this elegant, under-stated dining room with all expansive windows which provide view of Public Garden. Superb wines. You may dine better elsewhere but not more graciously. *Prix fixe* menu. Jacket and tie. Wonderful but expensive ($$$) Sunday brunch. $$$$ – and more.

Veronique, Longwood Tower, 20 Chapel Street, Brookline, tel: 731-4800. (Green line of the "T" stops at the door.) Beautiful room in mock-Tudor castle. The place for a romantic evening. Some innovative dishes but generally old-fashioned classic French food. Jacket and tie. Valet parking. $$$

ITALIAN

Not surprisingly, the majority of Italian restaurants are situated in "Little Italy" (the North End). However, most aficionados of Italian food find their delights in less touristy areas.

Allegro, 313 Moody Street, Waltham, tel: 891-5486. Outstanding Northern Italian food including scrumptious pastas make the trip to this small suburban bistro rewarding. Reservations advised. $$$

Bnu, 123 Stuart Street, Theater District. tel: 367-8405. An Italian hilltown trattoria in downtown Boston serving *nuova cucina* food, mostly pizzas and pastas. $$

Ciaobella, 240A Newbury Street, tel: 536-2626. Upscale spot for the trendy crowd serving some excellent Southern Italian cuisine. Outdoor dining. Valet parking. $$

European, 218 Hanover Street, North End, tel: 523-5694. Massachusett's oldest Italian restaurant, practically a landmark, serves generous portions of southern specialities in an informal and cavernous dining room. $$

Felicia's, 145A Richmond Street, North End, tel: 523-9885. Southern Italian home cooking in a small well-established upstairs restaurant. $$$

G'Vanni's, 2 Prince Street, North End, tel: 523-0107 or 720-FOOD: Crowded, popular, romantic restaurant serving inconsistent Southern cuisine. Reservations necessary. Free limousine service an attraction. $$$ – $$$$

Mamma Maria, 3 North Square, North End, tel: 523-0077. Unconventional *nuova cucina* menu served in several charming small rooms in a three-story townhouse. Upstairs rooms have best ambience and view. Reservations advisable. Valet parking. $$$ – $$$$.

Michela's, 1 Athenaeum Street, Cambridge (near Kendall Square) tel: 225-2121. An elegant, unique and outstanding cuisine all make this Boston's *numero uno* Italian restaurant. Fabulous wine list. $$$$. **Michela's Caffé** in the atrium of the building has a limited innovative menu that is less expensive ($$) – and you'll still be able to order from the wine list.

Pastavino, Heritage on the Public Garden, 73 Park Plaza, tel: 482-0010. A new, art deco trattoria with an abundance of mirrors. Serves ambitious Northern Italian cuisine. Large portions. Outdoor dining. $$$

Piccola Venezia, 63 Salem Street, North End, tel: 523-9082. Large helpings with lots of red sauce attract gourmands rather than gourmets to this small restaurant. $$

Ristorante Toscano, 41 Charles Street, tel: 723-4090. Boston's "only authentic Italian restaurant" produces wonderful food in a Tuscan ambience. $$$ – $$$$

Spaghetti Club, 93 Winthrop Street, Harvard Square, Cambridge, tel: 576-1210. Straightforward menu dominated by pastas and grilled entrées. Concentrate on the specials. Value for money. No reservations. $$

Upstairs at the Pudding, 10 Holyoke Street, Harvard Square, Cambridge, tel: 864-1933. Romantic dining in the beautiful dining room of Harvard's Hasty Pudding Club. A definite experience. Northern Italian cuisine. *Prix fixe* menu. Semi-formal. Reservations suggested. $$$$

GERMAN

Jacob Wirth, 31 Stuart Street, tel: 338-8586. (See *Landmark restaurants*.)

Wursthaus, 4 John F. Kennedy Street, Harvard Square, Cambridge, tel: 491-7110. (See *Landmark restaurants*.)

CHINESE

Restaurants in Boston's Chinatown have a good reputation throughout the nation but most are fairly basic with formica-topped tables. For more elegant Chinese dining the visitor must venture further afield.

Carl's Pagoda, 23 Tyler Street, Chinatown. tel: 357-9837. Non-pretentious upstairs restaurant serves great Cantonese food. Ask Carl to choose the menu. BYOB. No reservations. $$

Golden Palace, 14 Tyler Street, Chinatown, tel: 423-4565. Cavernous, crowded Cantonese restaurant whose main attraction is *dim sum* which is served from 9 a.m.–3 p.m. $ – $$

Hong Kong Cuisine, 27–29 Beach Street, Chinatown, tel: 451-2006, 451-2647. Dinner menu leans towards poultry and pork. $$

Imperial Tea House, 70 Beach Street, Chinatown, tel: 426-8439. Large busy Cantonese restaurant where the main act is *dim sum* served from 9 a.m–3 p.m. $ – $$

Mary Chung, 447 Massachusetts Avenue, Cambridge, tel: 864-1991. Cozy, unpretentious spot for Mandarin and Szechuan specialities. $$

New House of Toy, 16 Hudson Street, Chinatown, tel: 426-5587. Specializes in Cantonese cuisine. Serves good quality but limited selection of *dim sum*. $$

Sally Ling, Hyatt Hotel, 575 Memorial Drive, Cambridge, tel: 868-1818. (See *Restaurants with a View*.)

Taiwan Cuisine, 63 Beach Street, Chinatown, tel: 451-5222. Concentrates on Cantonese seafood and Taiwan–Mandarin dishes. No liquor. $ – $$

JAPANESE

Genji, 327 Newbury Street, tel: 267-5656. Well-established, serene, somewhat upmarket Back Bay restaurant with good sushi bar. $$

Goemen Japanese Noodle, 1 Kendall Square (Building 100), Cambridge, tel: 577-9595. Genuine Japanese noodle house. Pleasant surroundings; simple yet effective menu. Mix and match ample portions of delicious noodles with less ample meat and vegetable toppings. $

Restaurant Suntory, 212 Stuart Street, tel: 338-2111. As one expects with the name Suntory, the best in formal Japanese dining. Three exquisite floors, each different, devoted to Japanese delights. Valet parking. Jacket and tie. $$$$

Roka, 1001 Masssachusetts Avenue, Cambridge, tel: 661-0344. Pleasant, modest restaurant. $$

Tatsukichi-Boston, 189 State Street (near Quincy Market), tel: 720-2468. Also at 308 Harvard Street, Brookline, tel: 566-0200. Consistently one of top Japanese restaurants in town. Most pleasant of the three floors is the ground floor. Interesting house specials. $$$

THAI

Bangkok Cuisine, 177A Massachusetts Avenue, Boston, tel: 262-5377. The daddy of Boston's Thai restaurants. Small shop-restaurant usually given nod as best Thai in Boston. Decor somewhat garish. No reservations. $$

King and I, 259 Newbury Street, tel: 437-9611. Also at 145 Charles Street, tel: 227-3320. Subtly spiced food. Reasonably subdued decor. Outdoor dining at Newbury Street outlet. $$

Singha House, 1105 Massachusetts Avenue, Harvard Square, Cambridge, tel: 451-0247. Impressive food in contemporary decor. $$

Thai Cuisine, 14A Westland Avenue (near Symphony Hall), tel: 262-1485. Same ownership as and similar to Bangkok Cuisine (*see above*). No reservations. $$

INDIAN

Elegant Indian restaurants have yet to find their way to Boston.

Indian Pavilion, 17 Central Square, Cambridge, tel: 547-7463. A hole-in-the-wall restaurant frequented by both Indians and students who enjoy the tandooris. $$

Kebab-N-Curry, 30 Massachusetts Bay, Back Bay, tel: 536-9835. Pleasant intimate ambience with helpful waiters. Good tandooris. $$

Shalimar of India, 546 Masssachusetts Avenue, Cambridge, tel: 547-9280. Friendly service and wailing music behind the curtained windows of a shopfront. $

KOSHER

Milk Street Café, Milk Street (Devonshire Street), tel: 542-2433. Breakfast and lunch only at this strictly kosher place popular with businessmen. Vegetarian as well as meat dishes. 2–8 for entrée. $

Rubin's, 500 Harvard Street, Brookline, tel: 566-8761. Strictly kosher. Best chopped liver in town. No reservations: line can be long on Sundays. $

PIZZA

Bertucci's, 799 Main Street, Cambridge, tel: 661-8356. Also at Harvard Square, tel: 864-4748 and Faneuil Hall Marketplace, tel: 227-7889. A pizza chain which cooks great thin crust pizza in traditional brick ovens and puts almost anything on it. Inexpensive decent house wine. Atmospheric. Some outlets have a bocce court in the restaurant. $

Pizzeria Uno's, 731 Boylston Street, Back Bay, tel: 267-8554. Also at Faneuil Hall Marketplace, tel: 523-5722 and 22 John F. Kennedy Street, Harvard Square, Cambridge, tel: 497-1530. Deep dish crust with fresh and gooey toppings. Good appetizers. No reservations leads to long lines. $

THINGS TO DO

HIGH SPOTS

A view from the top is a good way to "case the joint." The two in the heart of the city are especially worth visiting.

John Hancock Observatory: Copley Square, tel: 247-1977. The observatory on the 60th floor (740 ft) of New England's tallest building has "Funscopes" focused on famous landmarks, high-power telescopes and a series of exhibits. And all the while the sonorous voice of the late Walter Muir Whitehill narrates a historical commentary. Open: Mon–Sat 9 a.m–11 p.m. and Sun 10 a.m.–11 p.m. (May–Oct) or noon–11 p.m. (Nov–Apr). Last ticket sold at 10.15 p.m.

Prudential Skywalk: 800 Boylston Street, tel: 236-3318. Situated on the 50th floor of the city's second tallest building provides the only 360 degree panorama of the city and beyond. Open: Mon–Sat 10 a.m.–10 p.m., Sun noon–10 p.m. The lounge and restaurant on the 52nd floor are well worth visiting at sunset. Sunday brunch is not to be sneezed at.

Air Traffic Control Tower: Logan International Airport, tel: 569-6710. This, the world's tallest airport control tower, offers an outstanding look at the city, the harbor and the beaches of Boston. The observation deck on the 16th floor is open: 9 a.m.–6 p.m. and until 9 p.m. in summer. The lounge, one floor above, is open: Mon–Thur 3 p.m.–11 p.m., Fri and Sat 3 p.m.–midnight.

FREEDOM TRAIL

Ben Franklin's Statue and Site of First Public School: School Street, tel: 536-4100
.

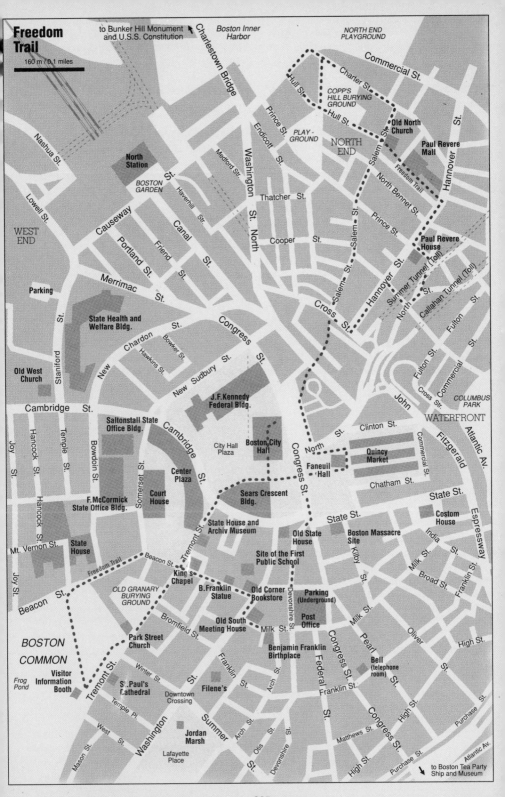

Freedom Trail

160 m / 0.1 miles

to Bunker Hill Monument and U.S.S. Constitution

Boston Inner Harbor

NORTH END PLAYGROUND

Charlestown Bridge

Commercial St.

Charter St.

COPP'S HILL BURYING GROUND

Hull St.

PLAY-GROUND

Prince St.

Endicott St.

Medford Str.

Washington St. North

Thatcher St.

Cooper St.

NORTH END

Old North Church

Salem St.

North Bennet St.

Prince St.

Freedom Trail

Hannover St.

Paul Revere Mall

Paul Revere House

North Square

Hannover St.

Summer Tunnel (Toll)

Callahan Tunnel (Toll)

Cross St.

Salem St.

Salem St.

Salem St.

North St.

Fulton St.

Fulton St.

Commercial St.

Cross Str.

COLUMBUS PARK

WATERFRONT

Nashua St.

Lowell St.

WEST END

North Station

BOSTON GARDEN

Causeway St.

Portland St.

Friend St.

Canal St.

Haverhill Str.

Merrimac St.

Parking

State Health and Welfare Bldg.

Staniford St.

Chardon St.

Hawkins St.

Bowker St.

New Sudbury St.

New St.

Congress St.

Congress St.

John F. Fitzgerald

Atlantic Av.

Old West Church

Cambridge St.

Joy St.

Hancock St.

Temple St.

Bowdon St.

Somerset St.

Saltonstall State Office Bldg.

J.F. Kennedy Federal Bldg.

Cambridge St.

City Hall Plaza

Boston City Hall

Center Plaza

Court House

North St.

Clinton St.

Quincy Market

Chatham St.

Faneuil Hall

Fitzgerald

Atlantic Av.

Espressway

F.McCormick State Office Bldg.

Hancock St.

Mt. Vernon St.

State House

Joy St.

Beacon St.

Freedom Trail

Beacon St.

Tremont St.

Sears Crescent Bldg.

State House and Archiv Museum

King's Chapel

OLD GRANARY BURYING GROUND

B.Franklin Statue

Old Corner Bookstore

Congress St.

Old State House

State St.

Boston Massacre Site

Kilby St.

Devonshire St.

Site of the First Public School

Costom House

India St.

State St.

Milk St.

Broad St.

Franklin St.

BOSTON COMMON

Frog Pond

Visitor Information Booth

Park Street Church

Bromfield St.

Old South Meeting House

Milk St.

Parking (Underground)

Post Office

Benjamin Franklin Birthplace

Federal St.

Congress St.

Franklin St.

Pearl St.

Bell (telephone room)

Oliver St.

High St.

Tremont St.

St. Paul's Cathedral

Temple Pl.

Winter St.

Filene's

Franklin St.

Arch St.

Summer St.

Congress St.

High St.

Mason St.

West St.

Washington St.

Jordan Marsh

Lafayette Place

Downtown Crossing

Arch St.

Otis St.

Devonshire St.

Matthews St.

Purchase St.

Purchase St.

to Boston Tea Party Ship and Museum

Atlantic Av.

Boston Massacre Site: Congress and State Streets, tel: 242-5642. Where five patriots were killed by the British.

Bunker Hill Monument: Monument Square, Charlestown, tel: 242-5641. Daily 9 a.m.–4.30 p.m. Obelisk, whose 294 stairs can be climbed, marks site of first major battle of the Revolution. Small museum.

Copp's Hill Burial Ground: Mill Street, North End, tel: 725-4505. Daily 9 a.m.–5 p.m. Distinguished Americans, including blacks, buried here. Gravestones show marks of British bullets.

Faneuil Hall: Quincy Market, Congress Street, tel: 725-3105. Daily 9 a.m.–5 p.m. Meeting hall on second floor dubbed "Cradle of Victory" because protests of British policy voiced here.

Globe Corner Bookstore: corner of School and Washington Streets, tel: 523-6658. Mon–Fri 9 a.m.–6 p.m; Sat 9.30 a.m.–6 p.m; Sun noon–5 p.m. Center of 19th-century literary Boston: Emerson, Longfellow, Hawthorne and Oliver Wendell Holmes met here.

King's Chapel and Burying Ground: 58 Tremont Street, tel: 523-1749. Tues–Sun 10 a.m.–4 p.m. Present church building dates from 1754. Many notables interred here.

Old North Church: 193 Salem Street, North End, tel: 523-6676. Daily 9 a.m.–5 p.m. From steeple two lanterns hung to warn that British crossing harbor on way to Concord.

Old Granary Burying Ground: Tremont Street, tel: 536-4100. Daily 8 a.m.–5 p.m. Many notables buried here, including Paul Revere, signatories of Declaration of Independence and "Mother Goose."

Old South Meeting House: 310 Washington Street, tel: 482-6439. Apr–Oct, daily 9.30 a.m.–5 p.m; Nov–March, Mon–Fri 10 a.m.–4 p.m; Sat, Sun 10 a.m.–5 p.m. Often used as town meeting site. From here enraged citizens set off to the "Boston Tea-Party."

Old State House: 206 Washington Street, tel: 720-3292. Nov–Mar, Mon–Fri 10 a.m.–4 p.m; Sat 9.30 a.m–5p.m; remainder of year daily 9.30 a.m.–5 p.m. Oldest public building in Boston. Place where Declaration of Independence first read to citizens of Boston.

Park Street Church: One Park Street, tel: 523-3383. Jul and Aug, Tues–Sat 9.30 a.m.–3.30 p.m. William Lloyd Garrison gave his first anti-slavery speech here and, in 1831, *America* was sung publicly for the first time.

Paul Revere House: 19 North Square, North End, tel: 523-2338. Nov to mid-April, daily 9.15 a.m.–4.15 p.m.; mid-Apr to Oct, daily 9.30 a.m.–5.15 p.m. The "man" and family lived in this, the oldest house in downtown Boston.

State House: Beacon and Park Streets, tel: 727-3676. Mon–Fri 10 a.m.–4 p.m. Bulfinch masterpiece. Frequent tours.

U.S.S Constitution: Charlestown Navy Yard, tel: 242-5670. Daily 9.30 a.m.–3.50 p.m. Thousands want to explore "Old Ironsides" which means long lines.

CULTURE PLUS

PLACES OF INTEREST

IN BOSTON

Alexander Graham Bell Room: New England Telephone Company Building, 185 Franklin Street, tel: 743-7691. Mon–Fri 8.30 a.m.–5 p.m. Where the telephone began.

Athenaeum: 10½ Beacon Street, tel: 227-0270. Mon–Fri 9 a.m–5 p.m; Sat 9 a.m.–4 p.m. A bibliophile's delight in an Italian palazzo.

Boston Marine Society: National Historic Park, Building No. 32, Charlestown Navy Yard, tel: 242-0522. Telephone for hours.

Maritime history of the region with lots of model ships.

Bunker Hill Pavilion: 55 Constitution Hill, Charlestown, tel: 241-7575. Daily, Apr–Nov 9.30 a.m.–4.30 p.m; Jun, Jul and Aug till 5.30 p.m. A 25-minute multimedia show recreates the Battle of Bunker Hill.

Children's Museum: Museum Wharf, 300 Congress Street, tel: 426-8855. Sept–Jun, Tues–Sun 10 a.m.–5 p.m, Fri 10 a.m.–9 p.m; July–Aug, daily 10 a.m.–5 p.m, Fri 10 a.m.–9 p.m; holidays 10 a.m.–5 p.m. Laid-back, hands-on, fun museum.

Computer Museum: Museum Wharf, 300 Congress Street, tel: 423-6758 (talking computer). Sept–Jun, Tues–Sun 10 a.m.–5 p.m, Fri 10 a.m –9 p.m; Jul–Aug, daily 10 a.m.–5 p.m; Fri 10 a.m.–9 p.m. Open Mon when public holiday. All you ever wanted to know about computers.

Dorchester Heights National Historic Site: Thomas Park near G Street, tel: 269-4212. Open in summer; telephone for hours. Impressive tower, which may or may not be open, in small park.

First Church of Christ, Scientist, Huntington and Massachusetts Avenues, tel: 450-2000. Guided tours May–Oct 9.30 a.m.–4 p.m; Sun noon–4.45 p.m; rest of year 10 a.m. (Sun 11.15 a.m.) to 3.45 p.m. The **Mapparium** permits the visitor to walk through the world on a glass bridge. Tours of the church.

Frederick Law Olmsted National Historic Site: 99 Warren Street, Brookline, tel: 566-1689. Fri–Sun 10 a.m.–4.30 p.m. Buildings in which Olmsted lived and worked together with his drawings and plans.

Gibson House Museum: 137 Beacon Street, tel: 267-6338. Sat and Sun tours at 2, 3 and 4 p.m. Guided tours of only historic Back Bay house open to visitors: Victorian furnishings.

Harrison Gray Otis House: 141 Cambridge Street, tel: 227-3956. Tues–Fri noon–5 p.m; Sat 10 a.m.–5 p.m. Tours on the hour with last tour at 4 p.m. Enter this Bulfinch house, the headquarters of the Society for the Preservation of New England antiquities and be transported to 18th-century Boston.

Institute of Contemporary Art: 955 Boylston Street, tel: 266-5151. Tues–Sun 11 a.m.–5 p.m; Thur and Fri 11 a.m.–8 p.m. Temporary art exhibits: no permanent collection.

Isabella Stewart Gardner Museum: 280 The Fenway, tel: 566-1401. (For concert information tel: 734-1359). Sept–Jun, Tues noon–6.30 p.m; Wed–Sun noon–5 p.m; July–Aug, Tues–Sun noon–5 p.m. Free admission on Wednesdays. A glorious Venetian palazzo filled with an idiosyncratic art collection.

John F. Kennedy National Historic Site: 83 Beals Street, Brookline, tel: 566-7937. Daily 10 a.m.–4.30 p.m. Closed on public holidays. Birthplace of John F. Kennedy.

John F. Kennedy Library and Museum: Columbia Point, tel: 929-4523. Daily 9 a.m.–5 p.m. The President's papers and memorabilia.

Massachusetts Archives: Columbia Point, tel: 727-2816. Mon–Fri 9 a.m.–5 p.m., Sat 9 a.m.–3 p.m. All you ever wanted to know about Massachusetts.

Mugar Memorial Library: Boston University, 771 Commonwealth Avenue (5th floor), tel: 353-2000. Mon–Fri 9 a.m.–5 p.m. Personal papers and memorabilia of more than 300 great 20th-century figures, including Theodore Roosevelt, Bette Davis and Martin Luther King Jr.

Museum of Afro-American History/African Meeting House: 46 Joy Street, tel: 742-1854. Mon–Fri 10 a.m.–4 p.m. Information on Black Heritage Trail and Boston's black history.

Museum of Fine Arts: 465 Huntington Avenue, tel: 267-9300. Tues–Sun 10 a.m.–5 p.m; Wed 10 a.m.–10 p.m. West Wing only Thur and Fri 10 a.m.–10 p.m. (Telephone for free admission hours.) Tours: Tues–Fri 11 a.m. and 2 p.m., Sat 11 a.m. and 1.30 p.m. Rates second only to New York's Metropolitan Museum: superb paintings: magnificent Oriental and Old Kingdom Egyptian collections. Excellent restaurant and gift shop.

Museum of the National Center for Afro-American Artists: 300 Walnut Avenue, Roxbury/Jamaica Plain, tel: 442-8014. Sept–May, Tues–Sun 1 p.m.–5 p.m; Jun–Aug, Wed–Sun 1 p.m.–6 p.m.

Museum of Science, Hayden Planetarium and Mugar Omni Theatre: Science Park, tel: 723-2500. Tues–Sun 9 a.m.–5 p.m.; Fri 9 a.m.–9 p.m. Closed Mon except when Mon is public holiday and during Massachusetts school vacations. Exciting and exhausting look-and-touch museum. Splendid shop.

Museum of Transportation: Larz Anderson Park, Brookline, tel: 522-6140. Early-Apr to mid-Oct, Wed–Sun 10 a.m.–5 p.m. (Call for information on winter hours.) Superb collection of vintage automobiles.

New England Aquarium: Central Wharf, tel: 973-5200. Sept–Jun, Mon–Thur 9 a.m.–5 p.m; Fri 9 a.m.–8 p.m; Sat, Sun and hols 9 a.m.–6 p.m; Jul–Aug, Mon, Tues and Thur 9 a.m.–6 p.m; Wed and Fri 9 a.m.–8 p.m; Sat and Sun 9 a.m.–7 p.m. Watch scuba-divers feeding sharks and their friends in giant tank. Dolphin and sea lion shows.

New England Historic Genealogical Society: 99 Newbury Street, tel: 536-5740. Tues–Sat 9 am.–5 p.m., Thur until 9 p.m. Trace your family tree.

New England Sports Museum: 1175 Soldiers Fields Road, tel: 78-SPORT. Wed–Sat 10 a.m.–6 p.m; Sun noon–6 p.m. Sports memorabilia of the local scene. Magnificent life-size and life-like wooden carvings of local deities.

Nichols House Museum: 55 Mt Vernon Street, tel: 227-6993. Tours 1 p.m.–5 p.m. on various days depending on time of year. House attributed to Bulfinch: mid-Victorian furnishings.

Public Library: Copley Square, tel: 536-5400. Mon–Thur 9 a.m.–9 p.m; Fri and Sat 9 a.m.–5 p.m; Sun 2 p.m–6 p.m. Closed: legal hols and Sun, Jun–Sept. Tours on Mon 2.30 p.m., Tues and Wed 6.30 p.m; Thur and

Sat 11 a.m. Relax in tranquil courtyard after viewing ornamentation of the interior.

Tea Party Ship and Museum: Congresss Street Bridge, tel: 338-1773. Daily 9 a.m.–dusk. Toss a tea chest into the harbor from a replica of *Beaver II*.

Trinity Church: Copley Square, tel: 536-0944. Daily 8 a.m.–6 p.m. Closed: holidays. H.H. Richardson's masterwork enriched by the work of great contemporary artists.

U.S.S. Constitution Museum: Charlestown Navy Yard, tel: 242-0543. Daily, spring and fall 9 a.m.–5 p.m; summer 9 a.m.–6 p.m; winter 10 a.m.–4 p.m. Meet members of the crew; take the wheel; climb into a sleeping hammock and much more.

IN CAMBRIDGE

Arthur and Elizabeth Schlesinger Library on the History of Women in America: Radcliffe Quadrangle, 3 James Street, tel: 495-8647. Mon–Fri 9 a.m.–5 p.m. Country's top research center devoted to women's studies. Culinary library.

Harvard University: Holyoke Center, 1350 Massachusetts Avenue, tel: 495-1573. Campus tours in Oct–May, Mon–Fri 10 a.m., 2 p.m; Sat 2 p.m; Jun–Aug, Mon–Sat 10 a.m., 11.15 a.m., 1.30 p.m. and 3 p.m.; Sun 1.30 p.m and 3 p.m.

Harvard University Museums: 32 Quincy Street, tel: 495-9400. Tues–Sun 10 a.m.–5 p.m. Closed: major holidays. The **Fogg**, the **Sackler** and the **Busch-Reisinger** have, among them, outstanding and varied art from most periods.

Harvard University Museums of Natural History: 26 Oxford Street, tel: 495-1910. Mon–Sat 9 a.m.–4.30 p.m.; Sun 1 p.m.–4.30 p.m. Closed: major holidays. Four museums including the oldest Archaeology and Ethnology Museum in the nation. See the Glass Flowers in the Botanical Museum.

Harvard Semitic Museum: 6 Divinity Avenue, tel: 495-5656. Mon–Fri 11 a.m.–5 p.m; Sun 1 p.m.–5 p.m. Main attraction: old Middle East photographs.

Hart Nautical Museum: Massachusetts Institute of Technology, 77 Massachusetts Avenue, tel: 253-5942. Daily 9 a.m.–9 p.m. Model craft.

Hooper-Lee-Nichols House: 159 Brattle Street, tel: 547-4252. Tues and Thur 2 p.m.–5 p.m. Home of the Cambridge Historical Society.

List Visual Arts Center: Weisner Building, Massachusetts Institute of Technology, tel: 253-4680. Weekdays noon–6 p.m; weekends 1 p.m.–5 p.m. Closed: in summer. Temporary exhibits of contemporary art. No permanent exhibition.

Longfellow House: 105 Brattle Street, tel: 876-4491. Daily 10 a.m.–4.30 p.m. Virtually as it was in Longfellow's time.

MIT Museum, Massachusetts Institute of Technology: 265 Massachusetts Avenue, tel: 253-4444. Tues–Fri 9 a.m.–5 p.m; Sat, and Sun noon–4 p.m. Treasures that have made MIT great. Gift shop.

Mount Auburn Cemetery: 580 Mt Auburn Street, tel: 547-7105. Daily 8 a.m.–4.30 p.m; summer till 7 p.m. Progenitor of all Garden cemeteries. Many "greats" are interred here.

Scientific Instruments: Undergraduate Science Center, Harvard University, tel: 495-2779. Sept–Jun, Tues–Fri 11 a.m.–5 p.m. Exhibits illustrating the history of instrumentation in a broad range of subjects.

IN THE WEST

American Jewish Historical Society: Brandeis University, Waltham, tel: 891-8110. Sun 2 p.m.–5 p.m; Mon–Thur 9 a.m.–5 p.m; Fri 9 a.m.–2 p.m.

Battle Road Visitors Center: Route 2A, Concord, tel; 508-862-7753. Sept–May, daily 8.30 a.m.–5 p.m; Jun–Aug 9 a.m.–5.30 p.m. Closed: Mon and Tue Nov–Mar.

Buckman Tavern: Lexington Green, Lexington, tel: 861-0928. Mid-Apr to Oct, Mon–Sat 10 a.m.–5 p.m; Sun 1 p.m.–5 p.m. Where the Minute Men waited the arrival of the Redcoats.

Cardinal Spellman Philatelic Museum: 235 Wellesley Street, Weston, tel: 894-6735. Tues, Wed and Thur 9 a.m.–3.30 p.m; Sun 1 p.m.–5 p.m. Custom-built museum for display of stamps. Also Lincoln memorabilia and tributes to John F. Kennedy.

Charles River Museum of Industry: 154 Moody Street, Waltham, tel: 893-5410. Thur–Sun 10 a.m.–5 p.m. History of American Industry from 1800 to the present, with emphasis on steam.

Codman House: Codman Road, Lincoln, tel: 259-8843. Jun to mid-Oct, Wed–Sun noon–5 p.m. Eighteenth-century house and furnishings; tours on the hour: last tour at 4 p.m.

Concord Museum: 200 Lexington Road, Concord, tel: 508-369-9609. Mon–Sat 10 a.m.–4.30 p.m; Sun 1 p.m.–4 p.m. Jan and Feb varied times. Ralph Waldo Emerson's study with original furnishings; Paul Revere's lantern; decorative arts and domestic artifacts from Concord area.

DeCordova Museum: Sandy Pond Road, Lincoln, tel: 259-8355. Tue–Fri 10 a.m.–5 p.m; Fri 10 a.m.–9 p.m; Sat noon–5 p.m; Sun 1.30 p.m.–5 p.m. Rotating bi-monthly exhibits. Sculpture exhibited in ground. Summer weekend concerts.

Emerson House: 28 Cambridge Turnpike, Concord tel: 508-369-2236. Mid-Apr to mid-Oct, Mon–Sat 10 a.m.–4.30 p.m; Sun 2 p.m.–4.30 p.m; holidays 1 p.m.–5 p.m. Home of Ralph Waldo Emerson from 1835 to 1882.

Fruitlands Museums: 102 Prospect Hill Road, Harvard, tel: 508-456-9028. Mid-May to mid-Oct, Tues–Sun 10 a.m.–5 p.m. Closed: Mon except holidays. American Indian Museum, 19th-century American paintings, 1794 Harvard Shaker House, memorabilia of Bronson Alcott's Con-Sociate Family.

Gore Place: 52 Gore Street, Waltham, tel: 894-2798. Apr 15–Nov 15, Tues–Sat 10 a.m.–5 p.m; Sun 2 p.m.–5 p.m. Guided tours only. One of New England's great Federal homes and estates.

Gropius House: 66 Baker Bridge Road, Lincoln. June–Oct 15, Fri, Sat and Sun noon–5 p.m; rest of year Sat and Sun noon–5 p.m. Guided tours only. The first building designed by Gropius when he arrived in the US.

Hancock-Clarke House: 36 Hancock Street, Lexington, tel: 862-5598. Mid-Apr to Oct, Mon–Sat 10 a.m.–5 p.m; Sun 1 p.m–5 p.m. Where Paul Revere met up with John Hancock and Samuel Adams.

Jewett Arts Center: Wellesley College, Route 135, Wellesley, tel: 235-0320, ext: 205l. Mon and Thur–Sat 10 a.m.–5 p.m; Tues and Wed 10 a.m.–9 p.m; Sun 2 p.m.–5 p.m. Distinguished historical art collection.

Lyman Estate: The Vale, Lyman and Beaver Streets, Waltham, tel: 893-7232. Main house open mid-Jun to mid-Sept, Wed and Thur noon–5 p.m. A McIntire house and conservation center.

Munroe Tavern: 1332 Massachusetts Avenue, Lexington, tel: 862-1703. Mid-Apr to Oct Mon–Sat 10 a.m.–5 p.m; Sun 1 p.m.–5 p.m. Headquarters of the Redcoats during Revolutionary War.

Museum of Our National Heritage: 33 Marrett Road, Lexington, tel: 861-0729. Mon–Sat 9.30 a.m.–4.30 p.m; Sun noon–5.30 p.m. Frequently changing exhibits of history and development of the US.

Nashoba Valley Winery: 100 Wattaquadoc Hill Road, Bolton, tel: 508-779-5521. Daily, Jun–Oct 9 a.m.–6 p.m. Tours Fri, Sat and Sun 11 a.m.–5.30 p.m. Taste exotic wines made from peaches and pears, cranberries and blueberries.

National Historical Park North Bridge Visitors Center: 174 Liberty Street, Concord, tel: 508-369-6993, 508-484-6156. Daily 8.30 a.m.–5 p.m. All you wish to know about "the shot heard round the world."

Old Manse: Monument Street, Concord, tel: 508-369-3909. Mid-Apr to end-May, Sat 10 a.m.–4.30 p.m, Sun 10 a.m.–4.30 p.m); Jun–Nov, Mon 10 a.m.–4.30 p.m, Sun 1 p.m.–4.30 p.m. Closed: Tues. Home of Rev. William Emerson. Nathaniel Hawthorne and

Ralph W. Emerson also lived in this house which contains furnishings from the Revolutionary War period.

Old Sturbridge Village: Route 20, Sturbridge, tel: 508-347 3362 and, for the deaf, 508-347-5383. May–Oct, daily 9 a.m.–5 p.m; Nov–Apr, Tues–Sun 10 a.m.–4 p.m. Sights, sounds and smells of New England village in the 1830s.

Orchard House: 399 Lexington Road, Concord, tel: 508-369-4118. Apr–Nov, Mon–Sat 10 a.m.–4.30 p.m; Sun 1 p.m.–4.30 p.m. Louisa May Alcott wrote *Little Women* here. Also home of School of Philosophy.

The Wayside: 455 Lexington Road, Concord, tel: 508-369-6975. Mid-Apr to Oct, Fri–Tues 9.30 a.m.–5.30 p.m. The Alcotts, Hawthrone and Margaret Sidney lived here – not at the same time.

Rose Art Museum: Brandeis University, Waltham, tel: 736-3434. Tues–Sun 1 p.m.–5 p.m., Thur 1 p.m.–9 p.m. Permanent collection and exhibits of outstanding contemporary American art.

Thoreau Lyceum: 156 Belknap Street, Concord, tel: 508-369-5912. Apr–Dec, Mon–Sat 10 a.m.–5 p.m; Sun 2–5 p.m. Memorabilia of the great man and a replica of his Walden Pond cabin.

Visitor Center: 1875 Massachusetts Avenue, Lexington, tel: 862-1450. Jul–Oct, daily 9 a.m.–5 p.m.; Nov–Jun, daily 10 a.m.–4 p.m.

Wayside Inn: Boston Post Road (Route 20, 5 miles west of Route 126), tel: 508-443-4661. America's oldest operating inn.

IN THE NORTH

Abbot Hall: Washington Square, Marblehead, tel: 617-631-0528. May–Nov, Mon and Fri 8 a.m.–5 p.m; Tues, Wed and Thur 8 a.m.–9 p.m; Sat 9 a.m.–6 p.m., Sun 11 a.m.–6 p.m. A.M. Willard's painting *The Spirit of '76*.

Addison Gallery of American Art: Phillips Academy, Andover, tel: 508-475-7515. Sept–Jul, Tues–Sun 10 a.m.–4 p.m. American paintings and sculpture.

Beauport Sleeper-McCann House: 75 Eastern Point Boulevard, Gloucester, tel: 508-283-0800. Mid-May to mid-Oct, Mon–Fri 10 a.m.–4 p.m; Mid-Sept to mid-May Sat, Sun 1 p.m.–4 p.m. Twenty-six rooms furnished with American and European decorative arts.

Cape Ann Historical Museum: 27 Pleasant Street, Gloucester, tel: 508-462-8681. Tues–Sat 10 a.m.–5 p.m; Sun noon–4 p.m. Closed: Feb. Renowned Fitz Hugh Lane collection, antique furniture and silver in historic house.

Cushing House Museum: 98 High Street, Newburyport, tel: 508-462-2681. Tues–Sat 10 a.m.–4 p.m. Furnished rooms with collection of artifacts, a carriage house and a French garden.

Custom House Maritime Museum: 25 Water Street, Newburyport, tel: 508-462-8681. Tues–Sat 10 a.m.–4 p.m. Exhibits on maritime history, tools and paintings.

Essex Institute Museum and Neighborhood: 132 Essex Street, Salem, tel: 508-744-3390. Mon–Sat 9 a.m.–5 p.m; Thur 9 a.m.–9 p.m; Sun 1 p.m.–5 p.m. Closed: Mon Nov–Jun. Paintings and domestic life in early Essex county. Restored houses in ground showing architecture and furniture of 17th to 19th centuries.

Hammond Castle: 80 Hesperus Avenue, Gloucester, tel: 508-283-2080. Daily 9 a.m.–5 p.m. Medieval castle with collection of Roman, Medieval and Renaissance art and giant pipe organ.

House of Seven Gables: 54 Turner Street, Salem, tel: 508-744-0991. Sept–Jun, daily 10 a.m.–4.30 p.m; Jul–Labor Day, daily 9.30–5.30 p.m. Made famous by Hawthorne's classic tale. Center of complex of waterfront houses and gardens.

Jeremiah Lee Mansion and Museum: 161 Washington Street, Marblehead, tel: 617-631-1069. Mon–Sat 10 a.m.–4 p.m. Colonial furnishings and decorations in Georgian house.

John Heard House: 40 South Main Street, Ipswich, tel: 508-356-2811. Seasonal Tues–Sun. Eighteenth-century China trade mansion with Chinese and early-American furnishings. Collection of restored carriages.

John Whipple House: 53 South Main Street, Ipswich, tel: 508-356-2811. Seasonal Tues–Sun. Seventeenth-century house filled with antiques. Delightful herb garden.

King Hooper Mansion: 8 Hooper Street, Marblehead, tel: 617-631-2068. Tues–Sun 1 p.m.–4 p.m. Closed: Jan and Feb. Eighteenth-century house.

Lawrence Heritage State Park: 1 Jackson Street, Lawrence, tel: 508-794-1655. Daily 8.30 a.m.–5 p.m. Story of industrial revolution in Lawrence.

Lowell National Park and Heritage State Park: 246 Market Street, Lowell, tel: 508-459-1000. Daily 8.30 a.m.–5 p.m. Remains of the nation's most significant planned industrial city have become the nation's first industrial state park.

Museum of American Textile History: 800 Massachusetts Avenue, North Andover, tel: 508-686-0191. Tues–Fri 10 a.m.–5 p.m; Sat and Sun 1 p.m.–5 p.m. Exhibits demonstrate the evolution of woolen textile manufacture.

New England Quilt Museum: 256 Market Street, Lowell, tel: 508-452-4207. Tues–Sat 10 a.m.–4 p.m; Sun noon–4 p.m. Historic and contemporary examples of the art of quilting.

Peabody Museum of Salem: East India Square, Salem, tel: 508-745-1876. Mon–Sat 10 a.m.–5 p.m; Thur 10 a.m.–9 p.m; Sun noon–5 p.m. Superb museum with comprehensive maritime, ethnological, Asia export and natural history collections.

Rockport Paper House: 50A Pigeon Street, Pigeon Cove, Rockport., tel: 508-546-2629. Any reasonable hour. House and furnishings completely built from paper.

Ropes Mansion and Garden: 318 Essex Street, Salem, tel: 508-744-0718. Jun–Oct, Tues–Sat 10 a.m.–4 p.m., Sun 1 p.m.–4.30 p.m. Important collections of Nanking porcelain and Irish glass.

Salem Maritime National Historic Site: 174 Derby Street, Salem, tel: 508-744-4323. Daily 8.30 a.m.–5 p.m. Waterfront wharves and buildings from Salem's years as foremost American seaport.

Salem Witch Museum: 19½ Washington Square North, Salem. tel: 508-744-1692. Daily 10 a.m.–5 p.m; Jul and Aug 10 a.m.–7 p.m. Multi-sensory presentation recreating 1692 witch hysteria.

Saugus Iron Works National Historic Site: 244 Central Street, Saugus tel: 233-0050. Apr–Oct, daily 9 a.m.–5 p.m; Nov–Mar, daily 9 a.m.–4 p.m. America's first successful integrated iron works.

Witch Dungeon Museum: 16 Lynde Street, Salem, tel: 508-744-9812. May–Nov 10 a.m.–5 p.m. Live presentations of witch trials and recreated dungeon.

Witch House: 310½ Essex Street, Salem tel: 508-744-0180. Mid-Mar to Jun 10 p.m.–4.30 p.m; Jul–Aug 10 a.m.–6 p.m; Labor Day–Dec 10 a.m.–4.30 p.m. Restored home of Jonathan Corwin, one of judges of Salem witch trials.

Whistler House Museum of Art: 243 Worthen Street, Lowell, tel: 508-452-7641. Tues–Sat 11 a.m.–4 p.m; Sun 1 p.m.–4 p.m. Whistler's father's home and the artist's etchings.

IN THE SOUTH

Adams National Historic Site: 135 Adams Street, Quincy, tel: 773-1177. Mid-Apr to mid-Nov 9 a.m.–5 p.m. Guided tours. Home of the Adams family for 140 years, now decorated with their furnishings and memorabilia.

Cape Cod and Hyannis Railroad: 252 Main Street, Hyannis, tel: 508-771-1145. Telephone for schedules. Travel and dine aboard a vintage rail coach.

Cranberry World Visitor Center: Water Street, Plymouth, tel: 508-747-1000. Apr–Nov 9.30 a.m.–5 p.m. Also Jul and Aug, Mon–Fri 5 p.m.–9 p.m. All there is to learn about cranberries. Free juice tastings.

Daniel Webster's Law Office: Winslow House, Careswell and Webster Streets, Marshfield, tel: 837-9527. Seasonal Wed–Sat.

Drummer Boy Museum: Route 6A, West Brewster. tel: 508-896-3823. May–Oct, daily 10 a.m.–4 p.m. Contains 21 life-size murals dramatizing, with light and sound, the American Revolution.

Heritage Plantation of Sandwich: 130 Grove Street, Sandwich, tel: 508-888-3300. Daily 10 a.m.–5 p.m. Eclectic collection of Americana in several buildings among 76 acres of gardens rich in rhododendrons and day-lilies.

Jabez Howland House: 33 Sandwich Street, Plymouth, tel: 508-746-0590. Late-May to mid-Oct (except Wed) 10 a.m.–5 p.m. The only surviving house in Plymouth in which a Mayflower Pilgrim lived.

John Adams and John Quincy Adams Birthplaces: 133 and 141 Franklin Street, Quincy, tel: 773-1177. Mid-Apr to mid-Oct 9 a.m.–5 p.m. Guided tours.

New England Fire and History Museum: Brewster, tel: 508-896-5711. Mid-May to mid-Sept 10 a.m.–5 p.m; mid-Sept to mid-Oct Sat and Sun. Outstanding collection of antique fire equipment and memorabilia.

Old Ship Church: 90 Main Street, Hingham, tel: 749-1679. Seasonal Tues–Sun. Oldest building in the nation in continuous ecclesiastical use.

Pilgrim Hall Museum: 75 Court Street, Route 3A, Plymouth, tel: 508-746-1620. Daily 9.30 a.m.–4.30 p.m. Oldest public museum in the nation. Pilgrim memorabilia.

Pilgrim Monument and Provincetown Museum: Winslow Street, off Bradford Street, Provincetown, tel: 508-487-1310. Apr–Jun, daily 9 a.m.–5 p.m; Jul–Sept, daily

servation tower can be ascended. Exhaustive museum with dioramas showing arrival of Pilgrims, whaling section and much more.

Plimoth Plantation: Plymouth, tel: 508-746-1622. End-Mar to Nov, daily 9 a.m.–5 p.m. The Wampanoag campsite is open, at the same hours, only from May–Oct. A recreation of the Pilgrims' village populated by interpreters dressed and speaking as pilgrims. The campsite recreates an Indian village in the 1620s.

Plymouth Wax Museum: 16 Carver Street, Plymouth, tel: 508-746-6468. Mar–Nov 9 a.m.–5 p.m; until 6.30 p.m. late-Jun to Labor Day. Twenty-six life size dioramas illustrating Pilgrims' story.

Provincetown Art Association and Museum: 460 Commercial Street, Provincetown, tel: 508-487-1750. Summer, daily noon–5 p.m. and 7 p.m.–10 p.m. Exhibitions by emerging and established artists.

Provincetown Heritage Museum: 356 Commercial Street, Provincetown, tel: 508-847-0666. Daily 10 a.m.–5 p.m. Eclectic exhibits of the region's culture.

Sandwich Glass Museum: 129 Main Street, Sandwich, tel: 508-888-0251. Apr–Oct, daily 9.30 a.m.–4.30 p.m; Nov, Dec, Feb and Mar, Wed–Sun 9.30 p.m.–4 p.m. Late 19th-century glass on display.

Sealand of Cape Cod: Route 6A. tel: 508-385-9252. Daily. Dolphins and sea lions go through their paces.

United First Parish Church: 1306 Hancock Street, Quincy. Mid-May to Labor Day, 10 a.m.–4 p.m. daily except Sun. Contains remains of John Adams and John Quincy Adams and their wives.

Yesteryear's Doll Museum: Main and River Streets, Sandwich, tel; 508-888-1711. Mid-May to Nov, Mon–Sat 10 a.m.–4 p.m., Sun 1 p.m.–4 p.m. Two floors of beautifully costumed dolls, tiny shops and miniature rooms.

PARKS

Arnold Arboretum: 125 Arborway, Jamaica Plain, tel: 524-1718. Daily sunrise to sunset. Visitor center open Mon–Fri 9 a.m.–6 p.m; Sat and Sun 10 a.m.–6 p.m. The jewel of Olmstead's "Emerald Necklace" dates from 1872. Over 7,000 kinds of trees and shrubs cover the Arboretum's 265 acres. Bonsai pavilion has dwarfed trees, some of which predate the Revolution.

Franklin Park Zoo: Blue Hill and Columbia Avenues, tel: 442-2002, 442-0991. Nov–Feb, daily 9 a.m.–4 p.m; Mar–Oct, daily 9 a.m.–5 p.m. Situated in Boston's largest public park, the Zoo includes the Children's Zoo, Birds' World and Rainforest exhibit.

Georges Island: Boston Harbor, tel: 727-5293. Jun–Oct, daily 9 a.m.–sunset. Ferries leave from Long and Rowes Wharf on the waterfront. Picnicking, fishing, tours of Fort Warren (a Civil War landmark) and a free water taxi (late-Jun to Labor Day) to other harbor islands. No alcohol.

Lovells Island: Boston Harbor, tel: 727-5295. Jun–Labor Day, daily 9 a.m.–sunset. Take ferry from Long or Rowes Wharf to Georges island and then free water taxi. Swimming, picnicking and free water taxi to other islands. No alcohol.

World's End: Martin's Lane, Hingham, tel: 749-5780. 10 a.m.–sunset. This 250-acre peninsula, 14 miles south of Boston, was landscaped by Frederick Law Olmsted. Stroll over 200 acres of magnificent landscaping, examine shells on the shore, look for horseshoe crabs in the water. Grand spot for birdwatchers and for great views of the Boston skyline.

ENTERTAINMENT

CLASSICAL AFFAIRS

Boston, as befits the "Athens of the North," is, considering its size, the most musical city in the nation. This it owes to tradition and also to its many educational institutes. Chamber music groups and choral groups abound. Among the former are the Cambridge Society for Early Music and the Boston Camerata; among the latter is the Handel and Haydn Society, America's oldest musical organization who first performed in 1815, and the upstart Boston Cecilia whose chorus first sang in 1875. (Not to be forgotten are the choirs of churches such as Emmanuel Church, King's Chapel and First Church in Cambridge Congregational.) Then there is the Boston Symphony Orchestra or simply Symphony, the most illustrious of the city's musical organizations, and the Boston Philharmonic Orchestra.

The city's premier dance company is Boston Ballet whose repertory includes classical and modern works. Other dance groups include Concert Dance Company, which soon celebrates its 25th birthday and which presents the works of both masters and innovators and Dance Umbrella, the most active New England presenter of contemporary and culturally diverse dance from around the world. Dance Express, which was formerly in Boston under the name of Dinosaur Dance Company and which has moved to New York, returns annually to "The Hub" with a contemporary dance program.

The renowned Sarah Caldwell and her Opera Company of Boston have been bringing innovative and popular opera to Boston for nearly half a century. A new company is the Boston Opera Company, while Boston Concert Opera has been performing four operas annually with a 50-piece orchestra, without sets or costumes.

And, all the while, playing, singing and dancing, as much for your pleasure as for their own, are students from most of the 50 colleges and universities in Greater Boston.

Some venues where classical performances can be enjoyed are:

Berklee Performance Center: 136 Massachusetts Avenue, tel: 266-7455. Owned by the Berklee School of Music this 1,200-seat auditorium, which has recently been renovated is best known for its jazz concerts. A multitude of excellent musical events, at very reasonable prices, are mounted by college students and faculty.

Boston Center for the Arts: 539 Tremont Street, tel: 426-500. This 1,850-capacity center in the South End is used for a wide variety of productions.

Concert Dance Company of Boston: Zero Church Street, Cambridge, tel: 661-0237. In its third decade this professional modern dance company commissions and performs works by a variety of internationally acclaimed artists.

Gardner Museum: 280 The Fenway, tel: 734-1359. Chamber music concerts in the Tapestry Room at 3 p.m. on Sun, 6 p.m. on Tues and 12.15 p.m. on Thur.

Hatch Memorial Shell: the Esplanade, tel: 5727-9547. Renowned for its free May–Sept concerts and dance performances. Most famous are the Boston (Symphony) Pops concerts in July.

Jordan Hall: 30 Gainsborough Street, tel: 536-2412. Considered an acoustic marvel, this hall is home to the Boston Philharmonic Orchestra who present a number of concerts throughout the winter. Many other classical performances are presented.

Longfellow House: 105 Brattle Street, tel: 876-4491. Chamber music in the garden in summer on alternate Sunday afternoons 3 p.m.–4.30 p.m.

Museum of Fine Arts: 465 Huntington Avenue, tel: 267-9300. A resident trio and numerous guest artistes play throughout the year in the Remis Auditorium.

New England Conservatory of Music: 290 Huntington Avenue, tel: 262-1120, ext: 257 or 536-2412. This is the site of more than 300 annual concerts – soloists, groups and full orchestra – most of which are free, given by faculty and students of the Conservatory and guest artistes.

Opera House: 539 Washington Street, tel: 426-5300. Pop, classical and opera performed at the home of Sarah Caldwell's opera company.

Sanders Theatre: Memorial Hall, Cambridge & Quincy Streets, Cambridge, tel: 495-2420. This 1,200-seat theatre is renowned for its Gothic architecture and for holding, for over a century, a wide variety of musical and literary events.

Symphony Hall: 301 Massachusetts Avenue, tel: 266-1492. Home of the Boston Symphony Orchestra who present Friday afternoon and Saturday evening concerts in the winter and Pop concerts in May and June. The hall is also used for a variety of other classical performances including a celebrity series.

Wang Center for the Performing Arts: 268 Tremont Street, Theater District, tel: 482-9393. A big stage and a big auditorium mean that this is a favorite venue for ballet, opera, concerts and Broadway plays. It is the home of the Boston Ballet, the strongest and most artistic dance company in the area.

THEATER

Boston theater runs the entire gamut from Broadway shows to amateur and very professional college productions by way of repertory and experimental theater. It has long played the role of a tryout town for pre-Broadway productions. Rare is the day when the visitor cannot attend some stage show, although student productions are mounted only in term time.

Note that theatre tickets for major theaters can be purchased, subject to availability, for half-price on the day of performance at the Bostix booth at the Faneuil Hall Marketplace. Credit cards are not accepted. Bostix is open Mon–Sat 11 a.m.–6 p.m. and on Sun noon–6 p.m. Call 723-5181 for recorded information on the day's offerings.

Alley Theater: 1253 Cambridge Street, tel: 491-8166. Home of an innovative group who produce new and experimental plays, including premieres.

Boston Shakespeare Company: 17 Harcourt Street, Back Bay, tel: 267-5600. A professional resident company performs works of the Bard and a variety of new works.

Boston University Theatre: Huntington Avenue, Back Bay, tel: 266-3913. In this theatre the Huntington Theatre Company annually mounts five professional productions, which include such varied delights as Gilbert and Sullivan and Henry Miller.

Charles Playhouse: 74 Warrenton Street, Theater District, tel: 426-5225. Little doubt that *Shear Madness*, the longest running non-musical play in US history (12 years), will be playing here when you visit town.

Charlestown Working Theater: Hill Street, Charlestown, tel: 242-3534. Productions at this non-profit community theatre focus on social themes and concerns. Special events throughout the year include cabaret, jazz and comedy performances.

Colonial Theatre: 106 Boylston Street, Theater District, tel: 426-9366. Boston's oldest theatre with a richly restored turn-of-the-century proscenium. Features pre- and post-Broadway productions.

Emerson Majestic Theater: 219 Tremont Street, Theater District, tel: 578-8727. This jewel box of a theatre which belongs to Emerson College was recently lovingly restored. Presents very professional productions of musicals by Emerson students and other non-commercial non-profit groups including Dance Umbrella, Boston Lyric Opera, Ballet Theatre of Boston.

Loeb Drama Center: 60 Brattle Street, Cambridge, tel: 547-8300. Home of the long established resident American Repertory Theatre which presents neglected works of the past, new American plays and modern interpretations of the classics.

Lyric Stage: 54 Charles Street, tel: 742-8703. Boston's oldest residential professional theatre company presents serious 20th-century plays including New England and American premieres.

Mystery Café Dinner Theatre: 736 Massachusetts Avenue, Cambridge tel: 262-1286. Whodunit Dinner Theatre in Boston. Solve a murder over a four-course dinner.

New Ehrlich Theater: Boston Center for the Arts, 539 Tremont Street, South End, tel: 482-6316. Serious stage plays include the works of international writers such as Pinter, Goldoni, Rebeck and Blumenthal. Reservations can only be made on day of show.

Publick Theater: Herter Park, 1175 Soldiers Field Road, Brighton, tel: 720-1007 or, for the deaf, 720-2789. Light-hearted frolics can be enjoyed under the stars May–Sept at Boston's summer theatre. Showtime is 8 p.m. Wed–Sun.

Shubert Theatre: 265 Tremont Street, Theater District, tel: 426-4520. This theatre is frequently the setting for pre-Broadway tryouts and for touring Broadway companies.

Wilbur Theatre: 246 Tremont Street, Theater District, tel: 423-4008. Opened in 1914 this intimate and elegantly restored theatre can boast several world premieres, including *A Streetcar Named Desire* and *Our Town*.

MOVIE THEATERS

The city and suburbs have a fair number of cinemas, many with multiple screens. On occasions the Boston Public Library, tel: 536-5400, and the Museum of Fine Arts, tel: 267-9300, show oldies. Some commercial cinemas in the center of the city are:
Beacon Hill: 1 Beacon Street, tel: 723-811. Three screens.
Charles: 195 Cambridge Street, tel: 227-1330. Three screens.
Cheri: 50 Dalton Street (near the Convention Center), tel: 536-2870. Four screens.
Cinema 57: 200 Stuart Street, Theater District, tel: 482-1222. Two screens.
Copley Place: 100 Huntington Avenue, tel: 266-1300. Nine screens.
Paris: 841 Boylston Street, tel: 267-8181. One screen.

IN CAMBRIDGE

Brattle Theatre: 40 Brattle Street, Harvard Square, tel: 876-6837. *Casablanca* with Bogie and Bacall will probably be playing when you visit. It is a legendary favorite at this recently renovated cinema which plays reruns of the classics and frequently mounts film festivals. One screen.
Janis Cinema: Galleria, 57 John F. Kennedy Street, tel: 661-3737. Shows many revivals and foreign films. One screen.
Nickelodeon Theatre: 10 Church Street, tel: 864-4580. Four screens.

NIGHTLIFE

Although Boston does not have an extremely exciting night life its 250,000 students ensure that it has a busy one. Bars and nightclubs, discos and comedy clubs abound in both Boston, especially in the Back Bay, and in Cambridge. Most remain open until 2 a.m. on weekdays and 1 a.m. on Saturdays, although Cambridge nightspots tend to close earlier than their Boston counterparts. Those under 21 cannot be served liquor, but this does not necessarily mean they will be denied admission.

(The distinction between the different categories in which the following nightspots are listed is often blurred.)

COMEDY CLUBS

Nowhere in the nation are Comedy Clubs more popular than in Boston. Those over 35 might feel uncomfortable, for nearly all who visit these clubs are students. Some clubs serve light snacks as well as drinks (bar and tables); all have a cover charge and at some the show is continuous while at others there are discrete showtime hours, especially when big names perform. Most clubs have an "Open Mike" night when the audience may take to the stage. Some clubs are:

Catch a Rising Star: 30 John F. Kennedy Street, Harvard Square, Cambridge, tel: 661-9887. Showtime Sun–Thur, 8.30 p.m; Fri 8.30 p.m. and 11 p.m; Sat 7.30 p.m., 9.45 p.m., midnight. All ages admitted. Local and Harvard groups occasionally appear as well as comedians of national stature. "Open Mike" comedy Sun and Mon.

Comedy Connection at Duck Soup: Wilbur Theatre, 246 Tremont Street, Theater District, tel: 542-8511. Most upscale comedy club. Showtime Sun–Thur 8.30 p.m; Fri 8.30 p.m., 10.30 p.m; Sat 7 p.m. 9 p.m., 11 p.m.

Comedy Vault: 124 Boylston Street, tel: 267-6626. Set in an old bank vault below Remington's Eating and Drinking Exchange. Shows Thur–Sat.

Nick's Comedy Stop: 100 Warrenton Street, Theater District, tel: 482-0930. The largest comedy shop around. Now a nightclub as well as a restaurant and comedy club. Showtime Sun–Thur 8.30 p.m; Fri 8.30 p.m., 10.30 p.m; Sat 8 p.m., 10 p.m. and 11.30 p.m. "Open Mike" night on Mon.

Stitches: 835 Beacon Street, tel: 424-6995. Mostly local talent but always a good show. Showtime Wed, Thur 9 p.m; Fri 9 p.m., 11 p.m; Sat 8 p.m., 10 p.m. and midnight.

DANCE CLUBS

Citi: 15 Landsdowne Road, near Fenway Park, tel: 262-2424. Huge bars and dance floor. The ultimate spot for dancing to loud music, videos and lasers. Live music on occasions. Young crowd often in bizarre dress. Thur–Sun 9 p.m.–2 a.m. Telephone for gay night.

Hard Rock Café: 131 Clarendon Street, tel: 424-7625. The Massachusetts Institute of Rock 'n' Roll, with a remarkable selection of memorabilia of the great, will appeal to both young and old, although it is mainly the former who form long lines. Lots of souvenirs on sale. Daily 11 a.m.–2 a.m.

Nightstage: 823 Main Street, Cambridge, tel: 497-8200. Considered one of the best live performance rooms. Intimate showcase for blues, rock 'n' roll, country and more. Small dance floor but mainly a place for listening. Telephone for showtime.

Nine Landsdowne Street: tel: 536-0206. A converted warehouse with lots of strobes and decibels. Extremely popular with the very young. Mon–Sat 9 p.m.–2 a.m.

Paradise: 967 Commonwealth Avenue, tel: 254-9831. National pop, rock, jazz, cajun and more bands regularly perform here in a clean tropical atmosphere. Young college crowd. Dress wild. Mon 8 p.m.–2 a.m; Tues–Sun 8 p.m.–2 a.m.

Rathskeller (The Rat): 528 Commonwealth Avenue, tel: 536-2750. Enjoys a reputation for discovering new bands. Youngsters enjoy two or three bands nightly. Loud bands get louder and youngsters get boozier. 8 p.m.–2 a.m.

The Roxy: 279 Tremont Street, Theater District, tel: 227-7699. Dancing in a ballroom to the big band sound. Balcony overlooking the dance floor which is lined by tables. Jacket and tie essential. Oldsters will not feel out of place. Light fare to maintain energy. Thur–Sat 8 p.m.–2 a.m.

Venus de Milo: 7 Landsdowne Street, tel: 421-9595. You'll love or hate this stylish place featuring hip-hop and house music and a sophisitcated, multicultural crowd. 8 p.m.– 2 a.m.

Zanzibar: 1 Boylston Place, tel: 451-1955. Cocktails and dancing in a South Pacific setting. The second floor looks down upon the dance floor on the first. Jackets and ties required. Wed–Sat 8 p.m.–2 a.m.

FOLK MUSIC

Passim: 47 Palmer Street, Cambridge, tel: 492-7679. A survivor from the 1960s which has given many greats their first chance and on which much of Boston's reputation as a folk mecca rests. No alcohol. Mon–Sat 11.30 a.m.–11 p.m.

THE JAZZ SCENE

Bay Tower Room: 60 State Street, tel: 723-1666. Spectacular views rather than the music are the attraction at this tower lounge, 300 feet above downtown Boston. Mon–Sat 4.30 p.m.–1.30 a.m.

Plaza Bar: Copley Plaza Hotel, 138 St James Avenue, Copley Square, tel: 267-5300. Sophisticated entertainment for sophisticates at this cabaret-style club. Top names. Showtimes 9 p.m. and 11 p.m. nightly.

Regattabar: Charles Hotel, Bennett and Eliot Streets, Harvard Square, Cambridge, tel: 864-1200. Consistently obtains the nod as the best jazz club in the region. Great *hors d'ouevres*. Frequented by thirtysomething crowd. Top names. Tues–Sun 8 p.m.–1 a.m. Showtime Mon–Sat 9 p.m. and 11 p.m.

Ryles: 212 Hampshire Street, Inman Square, Cambridge, tel: 867-9330. For many years a favorite featuring the best of New England's jazz musicians in both its upstairs and downstairs lounges. Dinner served 5.30 p.m.–11 p.m. weeknights and until midnight Fri and Sat.

Scullers Lounge: Guest Quarters Suite Hotel, 400 Soldiers Field Road, Brighton, tel: 783-0090, ext: 7290. Hotel jazz club which attracts big names. Showtimes Thur–Sat 8 p.m. and 10 p.m., Tues and Wed jazz series 7.30 p.m–11.30 p.m.

Zachary's Bar: Colonnade Hotel, 120 Huntington Avenue, tel: 424-7000. Dance to live jazz and sip wine in elegant surroundings. Live entertainment Tues–Thur 8 p.m.–midnight, Fri and Sat 9 p.m.–1 a.m.

PUBS

(These establishments serve food as well as drink.)

Black Rose: 160 State Street, tel: 742-2286. This classic Irish pub which is close to Faneuil Hall Marletplace, teems with Boston businessmen released from the office. Live Irish music nightly and weekend afternoons. Daily 11.30 a.m.–2 a.m.

Bull & Finch Pub: Hampshire House, 84 Beacon Street, tel: 227-9605. Mobbed with tourists who come to gawk at what is, in reality, nothing like what they see on their TV screen in *Cheers*. The place to buy *Cheers* souvenirs. Daily 11 a.m.–1.15 a.m.

Casablanca: 40 Brattle Street, Harvard Square, tel: 876-0999. "Here's looking at you, Kid" seated in rickshaw-shaped wicker booths around copper tables among other beautiful people. A Harvard institution. No food but restaurant upstairs. Sun–Thur 6 p.m.–1 a.m., Fri and Sat 6 p.m.–2 a.m.

Claddagh: corner Dartmouth Street and Columbus Avenue, South End, tel: 262-9874. Under same managment and has same character as Black Rose (*see above*). Live

entertainment Wed–Sat evenings. Lots of sing-alongs. Daily 11.30 a.m.–12.30 a.m.

Daisy Buchanan's: 240A Newbury Street, Back Bay, tel: 247-8516. Although there's no cover, proper dress is required at this well-established bar and restaurant with a great rock juke-box. Thirtysomething crowd. Daily 11.30 a.m.–2 a.m.

Division 16: 955 Boylston Street, Back Bay, tel: 353-0870. Yuppies line up to enter this dimly lit up-beat restaurant and bar. Daily 11.30 a.m.–1.30 a.m.

Eliot Lounge: 370 Commonwealth Avenue, tel: 262-1078. Well-established lively lounge bar popular with an older crowd. Daily 3 p.m.–2 a.m.

Friday's: 26 Exeter Street, Back Bay, tel: 266-9040. Yuppies and preppies flock here at weekends to enjoy the upbeat social life. Daily 11 a.m.–1 a.m.

Purple Shamrock: 1 Union Street, tel: 227-2060. Under same management and has same Irish character as Black Rose (*see above*). Irish entertainment is featured nightly and on weekend afternoons. Starmakers sing-along on Tues evenings and comedy show on Wed. Daily 11.30 a.m.–2 a.m.

Wursthaus: 4 John F. Kennedy Street, Cambridge, tel: 491-7110. Serious beer drinkers make for the fun and cozy upstairs bar. One of the largest selection of beers in the world. Sun–Thur 4 p.m.–midnight, Fri and Sat 4 p.m.–1 a.m.

GAY SCENE

Boston Ramrod Room: 1254 Boylston Street, tel: 266-2986. Popular with the leather crowd. Daily until 2 a.m.

Buddies: 51 Stuart Street, Theater District, tel: 426-3772. A jumpin' dance bar and neighborhood club popular with the young crowd. Daily noon–2 a.m.

Chaps: 27 Huntington Avenue, tel: 266-7778. Levi-clad clones frequent this disco. Daily 2 p.m.–2 a.m.

Indigo: 823 Main Street, Cambridge, tel: 497-7200. A lively Lesbian club playing anything from House and progressive to Top 40. Wed 8 p.m.–2 a.m., Thur and Fri 4 p.m.–2 a.m., Sat 10 p.m.–2 a.m.

Metropolitan Health Club and Club Café: 209 Columbus Avenue, tel: 536-3066. A gay complex with good restaurant, cocktail bar, cabaret and gym.

Napoleon Club: 52 Piedmont Street, tel: 338-7547. The oldest gay club in the nation. Aging patrons will feel at ease in the wrinkle room. Piano bar nightly and disco on Fri and Sat 9 a.m.–2 p.m.

Sporters: 228 Cambridge Street, Boston, tel:742-4048. A dance club for young gays featuring modern music. Daily noon–2 a.m.

1270 Club: 1270 Boylston Street, tel: 437-1257. Well-established large gay disco on three floors with a basement piano bar and two upper levels for dancing. In summer outdoor roof deck opens at 1 p.m. Young crowd. Daily 4 p.m.–2 a.m. (Jun–Sept 1 p.m.–1 a.m.)

SPORTS

Sports-mad Boston has major league teams in baseball, football, basketball and hockey. Tickets for the last two sports are difficult to obtain, although 2,500 general admission tickets are available for every game. Baseball does not present too much of a problem and football billets are practically given away, possibly because of the inept performances of the New England Patriots who many prefer not to consider to be a Boston team: they play 25 miles outwith the city.

Tickets can be purchased at Bostix, Faneuil Hall Marketplace, tel: 723-5181, Mon–Sat 11 a.m.–6 p.m., Sun noon–6 p.m: at Out of Town Tickets, tel: 492-1900 in the concourse of the subway in Harvard Square, Mon–Fri 9 a.m.–7 p.m., Sat 9 a.m.–6 p:m: or at Ticketron, tel 720-3400, Mon–Fri 8.30 a.m.–5.30 p.m.

Baseball: Boston Red Sox, Fenway Park, Yawkey Way, tel: 267-8661. This cozy park which was built in 1912 still has grass rather than artificial turf. Kenmore Square (Green line of the "T" – branches B, C, D) and Fenway stations (Green line – branch D) are only a short distance from the Park. Box office open Mon–Fri 9 a.m–5 p.m., Sat 9.30 a.m.–2 p.m.

Basketball: Boston Celtics, Boston Garden, 150 Causeway Street, tel: 523-3030. Travel to the Garden on the Green or Orange lines of the "T". Box Office open: Mon–Sat 11 a.m.–7 p.m; Mon–Fri 11 a.m.–5 p.m. in summer; Sun and holidays year-round 1 p.m –7 p.m. when event scheduled.

Hockey: Boston Bruins, Boston Garden, 150 Causeway Street, tel: 227-3200. Travel to the Garden on the Green or Orange lines of the "T". Box office open: Mon–Sat 11 a.m.– 7 p.m; Mon–Fri 11 a.m.–5 p.m. in summer; Sun and holidays year-round 1 p.m.–7 p.m. when event scheduled.

Football: New England Patriots, Sullivan Stadium, Foxboro, tel: 800-543-1176. Special "T"-Commuter trains to all Patriots home games from South Station, Back Bay Station, Hyde Park, Route 128 Station. By car taken Route 3S (the Southeast Expressway) to Route 128N on to Route 95S. Take exit 9 and follow route 1S for about 3 miles to the stadium. (Total distance about 25 miles.) Box office open: Mon–Sat 9 a.m.–5 p.m. during season; off-season hours are Mon–Fri 9 a.m.–5 p.m.

Each year Boston is host to three major sporting events.
Boston Marathon (tel: Boston Athletic Association at 236-1652). Held on third Monday (Patriot's Day) in mid-April. The finish line is at Copley Square but Copley Station of the "T" is closed on Marathon day. To reach the final stretch take the Orange Line to Back Bay Station or the Green Line

Auditorium or to Kenmore or the Green Line (C branch) to any stop on Beacon Street.
Head of the Charles Regatta, tel: 421-4356. Held on the second last Sunday of October when thousands of oarspeople from throughout the world race their shells on the Charles River. Take the Red Line of the "T" to Harvard Square and walk south on J.F. Kennedy Street to the River. Alternatively, board the Green line (B branch) to Boston University campus and walk across the Boston University Bridge.
United States Pro Tennis Championships, tel: 731-4500. Held at the Longwood Cricket Club during the second week in July. Men professionals from throughout the world. The Green line (D branch) of the "T" stops next to the Club.

PARTICIPANT

Golf: The Massachusetts Golf Association, tel: 891-4300, represents more than 200 clubs in the state and will provide up-to-date information on which courses are open to the general public. Two public 18-hole golf courses supervised by the Parks and Recreation Department are:
Franklin Park, 1 Circuit Drive, tel: 265-4084.
George Wright Golf Course, 27 West Street, Hyde Park, tel: 364-0679.
Other public courses close to the city are:
Fresh Pond Golf Course, 691 Huron Avenue, West Cambridge, tel: 354-8876. Nine-holes.
Newton Commonwealth Golf Course, 212, Kenrick Road, Newton, tel: 244-4763. Telephone for weekend reservations.
Pine Meadows Country Club, 255 Cedar Street, Lexington, tel: 862-5516. Nine-holes.

Bicycling: Lots of opportunities to cycle along the banks of the River Charles or through Olmsted's Emerald Necklace. For details of the former, the Dr. Paul Dudley White Charles River Bike Path, telephone 727-5215. For the latter contact the Boston Park Rangers, tel: 522-2639. For more information on bicycling in and around Boston contact Boston Area Bicycle Coalition, tel: 491-7433. Bicycles can be rented at:
Community Bike Shop, 490 Tremont Street, tel: 542-8623. Mon–Fri 10 a.m.–5.30 p.m., Sat. 10 a.m.–5 p.m.
Surf and Cycle, 1771 Massachusetts Av-

enue, Porter Square, Cambridge, tel: 661-7659. Mon–Sat 10 a.m.–7 p.m.; Sun noon–5 p.m.

Sailing: Boston has produced some great yachtsmen and sailing on the Charles is sheer bliss. Less blissful, but possibly more exciting, is sailing in the harbor.
Boston Sailing Center, 54 Lewis Wharf, tel: 227-4198. A varied 45 boat fleet. "Learn to Sail Vacation Week" is exactly that.
Community Boating Inc. 21 Embankment Road, tel: 523-1038. Become a temporary member; prove you can sail and 100 boats await you from April to November. No reservations required. Mon–Fri 1 p.m.–sunset, Sat and Sun 9 a.m.–sunset.
Jamaica Pond Boathouse, 507 Jamaica Way, tel: 522-6258. Sailboats available during summer months for sailing on a pretty suburban lake.
Courageous Sailing Center, Charlestown Navy Yard, tel: 725-3263). A wide variety of sailboats availabe for charter.

Canoeing: Charles River Canoe Service, 2401 Commonwealth Avenue Newton, tel: 965-5110. Canoes, kayaks and rowing shells for hire. Instruction available. April–Oct, Mon–Fri 10 a.m.–8 p.m., Sat and Sun 9 a.m.–8 p.m.
South Bridge Boat House, 496 Main Street, Concord, tel: 369-9438. Canoes and rowboats for exploring the Sudbury, Assabet and Concord rivers. Apr–Oct 9.30 a.m.–sundown.

Billiards: Boston Billiards, 126 Brookline Avenue, near Kenmore Square, tel: 536-POOL. Impressive rack and roll club with championship Brunswick Gold Crown tables. Light menu and non-alcoholic beverages available. Daily 11a.m.–2 a.m.
Jillina's Billiard Club, 145 Ipswich Street, near Fenway Park, tel: 437-0030. Features 39 Brunswick Gold Crown tables. Café serving snacks. Mon–Sat 11 a.m.–1 a.m., Sun noon–1 a.m.

For public tennis courts, swimming pools and skating rinks, contact the Metropolitan District Commission, 20 Somerset Street, tel. 727-5215.

SHOPPING

Chic and funky, trendy and traditional, state-of-the-art and second-hand, antique and ethnic, bargain-basement and rarified gentility: it's all to be found when shopping in Boston. Three major shopping areas attract strollers as well as serious shoppers. They are the Back Bay which is anchored by Newbury Street, the Downtown Crossing and Faneuil Hall Marketplace. Most stores open between 9 a.m. and 10 a.m. and close at 6 p.m. or 7 p.m. although some, especially at Faneuil Hall Marketplace, stay open later. Some stores, especially those in malls and tourist areas, are open on Sundays from noon until 5 p.m. The state sales tax does not apply to clothing.

Faneuil Hall Marketplace: More than 150 shops and restaurants attract more than a million visitors each month. Food stalls fill the Quincy Market Building while the Bull Market has colorful pushcarts from which handmade crafts and souvenirs are sold. The North and South Markets are bursting with shops and still more restaurants, as is the newer Marketplace Center with its soaring steel, glass and neon canopy.

Many of the stores sell clothing. Men can buy comfortable sportswear from **ACA Joe**, while designer sportswear and suits and shirts are tailor-made at **Alan Lawrence**. **Dupre** features funky junior sportswear while **The Narraganset**, **The Lodge** and **Pappagallo** all offer sport and casual clothes and footwear with a flair for the traditional and contemporary. **Siam Malee** stocks sophisticated Thai silks. And no fashionable wardrobe is complete without nightwear or lingerie from **Dalliance** or **Victoria's Secret** whose selections range from demure to provocative. Heading for colder climes? Visit the **Celtic Weavers** with their wide array of imported caps and capes, kilts and shawls and handknitted fisherman sweaters.

Folklore has an excellent collection of antique and ethnic designer jewelry and exquisite silver and turquoise jewelry. **Cuoio** features costume jewelry and accessories as well as imported Italian shoes and boots. The **Body Lab** and **Faux & Funky** are popular for their jewelry and hair accessories. Other accessories with an exotic flair can be found at **AfricArt** which carries African skin goods, jewelry, belts and bags.

The Limited, in its own architecturally attractive building at the north end of the Marketplace, is a seven-floor department store with trendy, colorful, vaguely European-looking clothes for women, men and children.

Turning to the home rather than self, there's a **Touch of Lace** which proves that the Victorian era is alive and well – teddy bears dressed with lace! the **Faneuil Hall Heritage Shop** with magnificent pewter sculpture, and scrumptious scrimshaw at **Boston Schrimshanders**. And for those that have everything there is always **Brookstone** and the **Sharper Image**.

Downtown Crossing is a brick pedestrian zone, the heart of which is at the intersection of **Washington** and **Winter Streets** where souvenirs and jewelry are sold from pushcarts. A number of well-established jewelry shops – **DePrisco**, **De Scenza Diamonds**, **The E.B. Horn Company** – can also be found here. And here, dominating a score of small stores, is **Filene's** with its world-renowned bargain basement, and **Jordan Marsh**, the largest department store in New England. Here too is what is said to be the world's largest **Woolworth**. Somewhat to the west of this is the relatively new **Lafayette Place** where shopping can be enjoyed at 150 stores on three floors.

Back Bay, with eight-block long Newbury and Boylston Streets, is considered to be Boston's premier shopping area. The young and the not-so-young make for the ultra-trendy, yet historic, **Newbury Street** not only to shop but to sit at the many chic sidewalk cafés and to watch the world pass by. Although the out-of-town part of Newbury Street (the Massachusetts Avenue) end has a not inconsiderable number of not so chic stores, the same cannot be said of the that section closest to the Public Garden and Arlington Street.

Start your safari at **Firestone and Parson**,

a gem of a jewelry store, in the lobby of the **Ritz-Carlton** hotel. On exiting from the hotel further gems can be found in **Dorfman Jewelers** and then one passes, in short order, **Burberry's**, **Charles Sumner**, **Ann Taylor** and **Brooks Brothers**. Cross **Berkeley Street** to reach **Louis**, the most elegant men's stores in Boston, which occupies a handsome free-standing building that was originally the Museum of Natural History. Priceless furnishings surround shoppers in this elegant legend in menswear. The clothes are trendy but not gimmicky: the service is impeccable: the prices are outrageous. There is also a just as elegant, just as expensive **Louis for Women** division. *Haute couture* on this part of the street is amply represented by **Tatiana** and **Divino** for women and **Martini Carl** for men. **Laura Ashley** specializes in fashion with that homespun look.

Across **Clarendon**, Newbury drops a notch in the dignity department and starts pouring on the glitz. One last holdout, **The Lodge**, housed in a splendid old mansion on the corner lot, is now stuffed with the latest in preppie-wear. Across the street, stunning contemporary and modern art are showcased in **Bloch**, **Judi Rotenburg** and **Dyansen** galleries. Several boutiques, including **Pappagallo**, **Serenella** and **Country Road**, hold up the fashion front and both **Rodier** and **Pierre Deux** take a last stab at the chi-chi crowd with ultra-elegant, ultra-expensive watches, jewelry, china and housewares.

Beyond **Dartmouth** the shops tend to get smaller and more specialized. **Alianza Crafts Gallery** features innovative ceramics, glassware and jewelry; **El Paso** carries western duds for the well-dressed cowpoke and **Anokhi**, located next door, stocks hand-printed Indian clothing. The **Society of Arts and Crafts** is a wonderful showcase for American artists working with glass, wood, ceramics and about 100 other less conventional media and the **Harvard Bookstore Café** is a favorite among local literati, who come for the food – although the menu is somewhat limited – as much as the books.

Beyond **Exeter** are several fine galleries specializing in contemporary and modern works, including the **Morgan Gallery**, **Paul Sorota Fine Arts**, **Pucker Safrai** and the **Arden Gallery**. Relax and satisfy the inner person at **Ciaobella** or **Davio's** which are sufficiently pricey for the upscale gang and

make great outposts for people-watching. Freshen up in the most delightful way at **Essense** where an enthusiastic perfumer will custom-blend your scent without charging an arm and a leg. Speciality shops here include **Iguana** which offers an interesting selection of primitive and folk art. **Anaconda** sells nothing but reptile-skin clothing, footwear and accessories and **The Finest Hour** specializes in vintage watches.

Across **Hereford Street**, **Emack & Bolio's Ice Cream** draws a crowd even on the coldest winter nights. The **Avenue Victor Hugo Book Shop**, with its comfortable clutter of used books and magazines, makes for a great afternoon of browsing. Beyond this the street ends with **Tower Records** (open till midnight) which is one of the largest record stores in the nation.

(Those who fail to find on Newbury Street that painting or piece of sculpture for which they are looking might wish to make their way to Downtown's **South Street** which, over the past few years, has attracted some of Boston's best galleries such as **Bromfield**, **Howard Yezerski** and **Robert Klein**.)

One street over (to the south) from Newbury and lacking that street's charm is **Boylston Street**, dominated by the soaring **Prudential Tower**. Here can be found ever dependable **Lord & Taylor** and **Saks Fifth Avenue** and a score of other shops. Closer to town the action heats up and becomes quite rarified. **Bonwit Teller** is followed by **FAO Schwartz** for children of all ages and **Shreve, Crump & Low**, long New England's favorite jewelry store, which also carries antique furniture, silver, porcelain and more. Readily ignored in this elevated company are the boutiques of the non-profit **Women's Education and Industrial Union** which sell delightful gifts, cards, needlework and even antiques and other collectibles.

Cross **Arlington Street** and arrive at the **Heritage on the Garden** complex where **Hermes** elegantly displays absurdly expensive items. Attempting to keep pace are **Yves St Laurent** and **Escada**. Jewelry to enhance that perfect clothing can be obtained at **Raphael Jewellers.**

A relatively new shoppers' delight is **Copley Place**, an indoor shopping mall, at the southeast corner of **Copley Square**. Built at the start of the 1980s, this elegant and glitzy cornucopia houses about 100 stores and restaurants and a nine-screen cinema and links the Westin and Marriott hotels. The stores radiate from a skylight atrium with a 60-ft-high waterfall sculpture circled by pink marble floors. **Nieman-Marcus** is the anchor tenant: other outstanding tenants are **Bally of Switzerland**, **Gucci**, **Ralph Lauren**, **Louis Vuitton**, **Saint Laurent** and **Rizzoli Book Shop**. Jewelers are headed by **Tiffany** while the less traditionally inclined will "ah" and "oh" at the pieces at **The Goldsmith**, **Karten's**, **Riki** and **Ylang Ylang**. Then there are **Crabtree & Evelyn**, **Brookstone** and **Sharper Image**. All this may be enjoyed while nibbling **Godiva** chocolates, which are purchased by the unit rather by weight.

Bookshops are ubiquitous in the city. The handsome **Boston University Mall** in **Kenmore Square**, with three floors of stacks, is the largest bookshop in New England. Smaller, and invariably playing superb background music, is the just as handsome, extremely sedate **Rizzoli Book Shop** in **Copley Place**. Somewhat different is the **Harvard Bookstore Café** on **Newbury Street** in the **Back Bay** where food is served adjoining the stacks. It remains open until 11 p.m. Gays and lesbians flock to the well-stocked **Glad Day Gay Liberation Bookshop** at 673 Boylston Street while whodunit lovers turn the corner to 314 Newbury Street and **Spencer's Mystery Bookshop**.

BEACON HILL

Charles Street, on the flat side of the hill, is Beacon Hill's only commercial street. Its brick sidewalks and gas-lit street lamps correctly suggest that it is the place to look for antiques. You might also wish to check out the handcrafted furniture, toys and utensils at **Charles Street Wood Shop** and the Japanese art at the **Kiki Sun Gallery**. Less frivolous is **Helen's Leather Shop**, with New England's largest selection of genuine leather goods, and **Linens on the Hill** with beautiful items from around the world. **Communications** carries a flashy assortment of jewelry, clothes and knick-knacks. **Rouvalis Flowers**, with its witty and tasteful arrangements of gorgeous fresh blooms, gets the nod as Boston's best florist.

CAMBRIDGE

The area in and around **Harvard Square** is choc-a-bloc with stores, most of which, not unexpectedly, have a youthful appeal. Some stores are gathered in mini-malls. Five such covered complexes are **The Garage** and the **Galleria**, both on **John F. Kennedy Street**, **Truc** and **Atrium Arcade** on **Brattle Street** and **The Shops at Charles Place** which stands on **Bennet** and **Eliot Streets**.

Gentlemen will make for the long-established **Andover Shop** and **J. Press** while those who absolutely demand the Harvard look will enter the **Crimson Shop** and **J. August Co**. Women will find elegant wear at **Ann Taylor**, **Clothware**, the almost ubiquitous **Laura Ashley** and **Talbot's**. The last named specializes in items for *petites*. Armchair travelers and others will enjoy exploring the **Banana Republic.**

Bernheimer's Antique Arts is crammed with pre-Columbian, Greek and Roman, Islamic and Asian antiquities as well as antique jewelry. Downstairs from Bernheimer's is **Fleur de Lys** which carries an exotic collection of French and European china and Victorian and vintage jewelry from the early 1900s. Next door is the magnificent **Crate and Barrel** with all one could wish for the home: yuppiedom in a nutshell.

Those who wish to show that they have been to Harvard – even if only as a tourist – will delight in the **Harvard Shop**, which is crammed with Harvard insignia merchandise. More of the same and practically everything else can be found in the **Harvard Coop Society,** which began in 1882 as a nonprofit service for students and faculty, in the heart of the Square.

Then there are the book stores. It is claimed – and who will contest it? – that here is the greatest concentration of bookshops in the nation. Most are in and around the Square and some are open until midnight. Some of the more unusual bookshops are **Grolier**, which carries the largest selection of poetry books in the country, **Robin Bledsoe** for out-of-print books on art, architecture and design, and a large selection on women artists, and **The Bookcase** with its splendid selection of used foreign-language books. For more foreign books, used as well as new, visit **Schoenhof's Foreign Books**, more an institution than a bookstore.

Stroll a little further and reach **Ahab Rare Books** with antique volumes on eclectic subjects, **The Million-Year Picnic** whose comic book selection plus books on rock 'n' roll, T-shirts and unusual cards will blow your mind, **Asian Books** whose name announces its stock, and **Arsenic and Old Lace** with its collection of books on witchcraft, positive magic and the occult (they also stock herbs and oils, vintage clothing and magical artifacts). Still further out on Huron Avenue is the **Bryn Mawr Bookshop**, the cream of the used bookshop crop.

Stores are not restricted to the region close to the Square but extend eastwards along Massachusetts Avenue to Central Square, with the quality falling as the rents fall. Worth noting is **Act II** which, with its New Orleans ambience, stocks vintage clothing and wigs and where one can have palm and psychic readings. Further along is **Oona's**, crammed with an intriguing selection of "experienced" clothing. **Bowl and Board** has an extensive selection of skirts, blouses and sweaters. The small and readily passed **Hubba Bubba** will entice those aficionados of fetish and bondage who must wear leather gear and a satin G-string. The **Great Eastern Trading Co** at **Central Square** has the best vintage clothing in Cambridge: a dazzling display of dress for tasteful bohemians.

A cluster of stores around 1750 Massachussets Avenue (the northern arm of this thoroughfare) near **Porter Square** will delight those – men and women – searching for vintage clothing and collectibles. Try **Astoria**, **Atlanta**, **Reddog** (furniture also) and **Vintage etc**. In the same neck of the woods, the tailored bohemian will make for **Susanna**, while even more elegant and expensive women's garments can be found at **Pepperweed**.

Over in **East Cambridge** (alight at **Kendall Square** on the Green Line of the "T") is the handsome **Cambridgeside Galleria**, the region's newest shopping mall. Anchor tenants here are **Sears**, **Filene's** and **Lechmere Sales**. More appealing to the dilettante is the very definitively upmarket **Abercrombie and Fitch**, tops for after-shave lotions. Those who enjoy the feel of cotton will make for **The Gap**. **The Limited** carries a wide colorful variety of trendy, vaguely European clothing.

Another Abercrombie and Fitch outlet can be found in the most under-used and most handsome shopping mall in Greater Boston. The **Atrium** on **Route 9** at **Chestnut Hill** may be a financial disaster for its developers but is a joy to visit. **Forgotten Woman**, **Potpourri Designs** and the **Disney Store** are a trio of attractions, while the **Godiva Chocolatier** will assuage hunger pangs.

FURTHER READING

NON-FICTION

Garland, Joseph. *Boston's North Shore* (Little Brown and Company 1978).

Garland, Joseph. *Boston's Gold Coast* (Little Brown and Company,1981).

Hall, Max. *The Charles – The People's River* (David R. Godine, 1986).

Harris, John. *Historic Walks In Old Boston* (The Globe Pequot Press, 1989).

Harris, John. *Historic Walks in Cambridge* (The Globe Pequot Press, 1986).

Hitchcock Jr, Henry Russell. *The Architecture of H.H. Richardson and his Times* (New York Museum of Modern Art, 1936).

Kay, Jane Holtz. *Lost Boston* (Houghton Mifflin, 1980).

Lukas, J. Anthony. *On Common Ground: A Turbulent Decade in the Lives of Three American Families* (Alfred A. Knopf, 1985).

McCord, David. *About Boston* (Little, Brown and Company, 1973).

Daniel, L. Marsh & Clark William H. *The Story of Massachusetts* (American Historical Society, 1938).

O'Connor, Thomas H. *Bibles Brahmins and Bosses* (Trustees of the Public Library of the City of Boston, 1976).

Schama, Simon. *Death of a Harvard Man* (Pelican, 1990).

Schofield, William. *Freedom By the Bay* (Branden Publishing Company, 1988).

Southworth, Susan & Michael. *A.I.A. Guide To Boston* (The Globe Pequot Press, 1989).

Wiencek, Henry. *The Smithsonian Guide to*

Historic America – Southern New England (Stewart, Tabori & Chang, 1989).

Wood, Donald *Cape Cod – A Guide* (Little, Brown and Company, 1973).

Whitehill, Walter Muir. *Boston: A Topographical History* (Harvard University Press, 1968).

FICTION

Atwood, Margaret. *The Handmaid's Tale* (Fawcett, 1986).

Alcott, Louisa May. *Little Women* (Collins, 1987).

Amory, Cleveland. *The Proper Bostonians* (E. P. Dutton, 1947).

Cook, Robert. *Coma* (New America Library, 1977).

Forbes, Esther. *Johnny Tremain* (Buccaneer Books, 1981).

Green, Gerald. *The Last Angry Man* (Seaview Books, 1980).

James, Henry. *The Europeans* (Penguin, 1985).

James, Henry. *The Bostonians* (Penguin, 1984).

Hawthorne, Nathaniel. *The Blithedale Romance* (Norton, 1978).

Hawthorne, Nathaniel. *The Scarlet Letter* (Norton 1978).

Higgins, George. *The Friends of Eddie Coyle* (Penguin, 1987). Also several other mysteries such as *Cogan's Trade*, *Impostors*, *Outlaws*, *Penance for Jerry Kennedy* in "his unfolding masterpieces of contemporary Boston."

Howell, William Dean. *A Modern Instance* (Norton, 1982).

Howell, William Dean. *The Rise of Silas Lapham* (Norton, 1982).

Langton, Jane. *Memorial Hall Murder* (Gollancz, 1990).

Miller, Sue. *The Good Mother* (Dell, 1987).

Marquand, John P. *The Late George Apley* (Simon & Schuster, 1982).

O'Connor, Edwin. *The Last Hurrah* (Little Brown and Company, 1985).

Plath, Sylvia. *The Bell Jar* (Faber, 1967).

Santayana, George. *The Last Puritan* (MacMillan, 1981).

Sarton, May. *Faithful are the Wounds* (Norton, 1986).

Stafford, Jean. *Boston Adventure* (Hogarth, 1986).

Turow, Scot. *One L* (Sceptre, 1988).

White, E.B. *Trumpet of the Swan* (Trophy Books, 1973).

For children:

McCloskey, Robert. *Make Way for Ducklings* (Penguin, 1976).

SPECIAL INFORMATION

INFORMATION SOURCES

Citywide Reservation Services: 25 Huntington Avenue, tel: 267-7424 or 800-HOTEL-93. One-step hotel, B & B and guest house reservation service.

Boston Common Visitor Information Center: Tremont Street side of Boston Common. The booth here marks the start of the Freedom Trail and provides visitor information about Greater Boston, Massachusetts and New England. Open: daily from 9 a.m.–5 p.m.

Faneuil Hall Marketplace Information Center: on the south side of Quincy Market.

Massachusetts Tourism Office: 13th floor, 100 Cambridge Street, tel: 727-3201. The Office can supply details on the state and day trip information. Open: Mon–Fri 9 a.m.–5 p.m.

Prudential Visitor Center: on the west side of the Prudential Plaza, tel: 536-4100, 800-858-0200. The center is operated by the Greater Boston Convention & Visitors Bureau and provides information on Greater Boston, Massachusetts and New England. Open: Mon–Sat 9 a.m.–5 p.m., Sun 1 p.m.–5 p.m.

Massport International Information Booth: Logan International Airport (terminal E). Provides visitors assistance to international visitors. Open: summer noon–8 p.m; winter noon–6 p.m.

National Park Service Visitors Center: 15 State Street, opposite Old State House, tel: 242-5642. Starting point for free Freedom Trail walks (allow 90 minutes). The Center offers services, including information, displays and sales on historic Boston and Massachusetts; rest rooms; public telephones and handicapped accessiblity. Open: daily 9 am.–5 p.m.

Cambridge Discovery Inc: Located at booth in the center of Harvard Square, tel: 497-1630. Source of comprehensive Cambridge-specific information. Tours for groups by appointment. Open: Mon–Sat 9 a.m.–6 p.m.

Harvard University Information Office: Holyoke Centre in Harvard Square, tel: 495-1573. Source of Harvard-specific information. Open: Mon–Sat 9 a.m.–4.45 p.m. Also Sun 1 p.m.–4.45 p.m. in summer.

Travelers Aid Society: Offices at 17 East Street near South Station, tel: 542-7286. Booths at Greyhound Bus Terminal and at Logan Airport, Terminals A and E.

Bostix Ticket Booth: Faneuil Hall, tel: 723-5181. This is Boston's official entertainment and cultural information center, providing tickets and information for more than 100 attractions. Half-price theatre tickets on day of performance are sold here. Open: Tues–Sat 11 a.m.–6 p.m., Sun 11 a.m.–4 p.m.

ESSENTIAL PHONE NUMBERS

Police in Boston/Cambridge: tel: 911.
Pharmacy open 24 hours: tel: 523-4372 (Phillips Drugs, 155 Charles Street).
Medical Hot Lines: Beth Israel Hospital, tel: 735-3300.
Boston Evening Medical Center: tel: 267-7171.
Eye & Ear Infirmary: tel: 523-7900.
Massachusetts General Hospital: tel: 726-2000.
Disabled Information Center: tel: 727-5540.
Credit Cards Lost or Stolen: American Express tel: 800-528-2121; Diners Club/Carte Blanche tel: 800-525-9150; MasterCard tel: 800-826-2181; Visa 800-227-6811.
Weather: tel: 936-1234.

CONSULATES

Austria: 211 Congress Street, tel: 426-0330.
Belgium: 28 State Street, tel: 523-7493.
Canada: Copley Place, tel: 262-3760.
Cape Verde: 535 Boylston Street, tel: 353-0014.
Chile: 79 Milk Street, tel: 426-1678.
Colombia: 535 Boylston Street, tel: 536-6222.
Denmark: 581 Boylston Street, tel: 266-8418.
Dominican Republic: 20 Park Plaza, tel: 482-8121.
Ecuador: 60 State Street, tel: 227-7200.
Finland: 77 Franklin Street, tel: 451-0750.
France: 3 Commonwealth Avenue, tel: 266-1680.
Germany: 100 Huntington Avenue, tel: 536-4414.
Great Britain: 4740 Prudential Towers, tel: 437-7160.
Greece: 20 Park Plaza, tel: 542-3240.
Haiti: 262 Washington Street, tel: 723-5211.
Ireland: 535 Boylston Street, tel: 267-9330.
Israel: 1020 Statler Office Building, tel: 542-0041.
Italy: 100 Boylston Street, tel: 542-0483.
Japan: Federal Reserve Plaza, tel: 973-9772.
Korea: 1 Financial Center, tel: 348-3660.
Mexico: 20 Park Plaza, tel: 426-4942.
Pakistan: 745 Boylston Street, tel: 267-9000.
Peru: 745 Boylston Street, tel: 267-4050.
Portugal: 899 Boylston Street, tel: 536-8740.
Spain: 545 Boylston Street, tel: 536-2506.
Sweden: 6 St James Avenue, tel: 426-5558.
Switzerland: 535 Boylston Street, tel: 266-2038.
Venezuela: 545 Boylston Street, tel: 266-9368.

ART/PHOTO CREDITS

INDEX

A

Acorn Street 107
Adams, Charles Francis 25
Adams, Henry 8
Adams, John 83
Adams, Samuel 29,41, 45, 113, 146, 231
African Meeting House 104
Alcott, Louisa May 102, 108, 144, 234, 235
Allen's Alley 140
Allston, Washington 87
American Tropical Forest 200
Ames Mansion 167
Ames-Webster Mansion 167
Anderson Street 104
Andover 236
Andros, Sir Edmund 34,142
Annisquam 265
Annisquam Canal 262
architecture 149
Arlington Street Church 165
Armenian Library & Museum of America 193
Arnold Arboretum 199
Athenaeum, The 84, 106
Atlantic Avenue 153
Auerbach, Arnold (Red) 77
Avery Street 139

B

Babson College 68
Back Bay 48, 163–174
Barnstable 248
basketball 75
Battery Street 154
Bay State Lobster 154
Bay Street 184
Bay Village 184
Beach Street 140
Beacon Hill 101–112
  development of 42
  founding of 40
  social mix 101
Beacon Street 101, 107
Beauport 264
Beaver II 158
Beck, Ken 85
Bell, Alexander Graham 139
Bellingham Place 109
Berklee College of Music 68–70, 115
Bird, Larry 77
Beverly 261
Black Heritage Trail 103, 104

Blackstone Block 148
Blackstone Square 182–183
Blackstone Street 120, 125
Blackstone, Rev. William 31, 105, 112
Boston
  early growth 31, 48
  naming of 31
Boston Architectural Center 169
Boston Center for the Arts 181
Boston College 65
Boston Common 112, 114
Boston Early Music Festival 115
Boston Garden 74, 77, 190
Boston Harbor 40, 42, 95
Boston Latin School 60–61, 144
Boston Light 157
Boston Marathon 79
Boston Marine Society 131
Boston Massacre 40, 158
Boston Museum 86
Bourne Bridge 252
Boston Opera Company 115
Boston Patriots 78
Boston Philharmonic 115
Boston Pops 115
Boston Public Library 171
Boston Redevelopment Authority 53
Boston Sailing Club 154
Boston Stone 148
Boston Symphony 69, 115
Boston University 64–65, 175
Botanical Museum 217
boutiques 111
Boylston Street 166, 169–170
Boylston Street Bridge 197
Braddock Place 180
Brahmins 23, 42, 53
Brandeis University 64–65
Brattle Theatre 209
Brattle, William 209
Brimmer Street 111
Broad Street Riot 49
Brookline 198
Brooks, Rev. Phillips 171
Bruins 74, 78
Buckman's Tavern 45, 231
Bulfinch, Charles 42, 84, 105, 107, 108, 110, 123, 147, 149, 157, 183, 211, 213, 214, 226
Bull & Finch bar 111
Bunker Hill, Battle of 41, 114, 124, 189
Bunker Hill Monument 131–132
Bunker Hill Pavilion 131
Burrage Mansion 167
Burton, Gary 70
Busch-Reisinger collection 217
Buzzards Bay 248

C

Caldwell, Sara 115
Cambridge 60, 205–226
  Aggasiz House 206
  Biological Laboratories 219
  Brattle Street 208
  Brattle Theatre 209
  Byerly Hall 206
  Cambridge Historical Society 210

Carpenter Center for the Visual Arts 218
Christ Church 205
Divinity Hall 219
Earth Sciences Building 224
Episcopal Divinity School 209
Farlow Herbarium 219
Fay House 206
Harkness Graduate Center 222
Harvard Hall 214
Harvard Law School 221–222
Henry Vassal House 209
Hilles Library 207
Holden Chapel 214
Houghton Library 216
Kresge Auditorium 223
Loeb Drama Center 208
Longfellow House 209
Longfellow Park 210
MacLaruin Building 224
Massachusetts Hall 214
Massachusetts Institute of Technology 223–225
Memorial Hall 220
MIT Museum 223
Mount Auburn Cemetery 211
Murray Research Center 207
Old Burying Ground 205
origins of 205
Radcliffe Dance Center 207
Robinson Hall 216
Rogers Building 224
Sackler Museum 218
Science Center 220
Semitic Museum 219
Sever Hall 215, 216
Stoughton House 209
Technology Square 225
Thayer Hall 214
Town Hall 223
Tozzer Library
University Hall 211
Widener Library 215–216
William James Hall 218
Cambridge Street 110
Cambridgeshire Galleria 190, 226
Cape Ann 257, 262–265
Cape Cod 247-252
Cape Cod National Seashore 249
Cardinal Spellman Philatelic Museum 194
Cathedral of the Holy Cross 182
Celtics 77–78
cemeteries
    Central Burying Ground 114
    Copp's Hill Burial Ground 125
    King's Chapel Burying Ground 144
    Mount Auburn Cemetery 211
    Old Burying Ground, Cambridge 205
    Old Granary Burial Ground 45, 113
    Phipps Street Burying Ground 132
    Sleepy Hollow Cemetery 234
Central Wharf 157
Champion, Albert 181
Channing, Rev. William Ellery 43
Charles II 33
Charles Paine Houses 107
Charles River 31, 95, 109, 115, 189–195
Charles River Information Center 190
Charles River Museum of Industry 194
Charles River Square 112

Charles Street 105, 107, 110–111
Charles Street Meeting House 104, 110
Charlesgate Yacht Club 190
Charlestown 41, 95, 129–132
Charlestown Bridge 189
Charlestown Navy Yard 129–130
Chatham 251
Cheers 111
Chester Square 183
Chestnut Street 107
Child, Lydia Maria 44
Children's Museum 158–159
Chinatown 140
Christ Church 123–124
Christian Science 173
Christian Science Complex 25, 53, 172–174
Christian Science Monitor 173
churches
    Cathedral of the Holy Cross 182
    Christ Church, Cambridge 205
    Concord Baptist Church 180–181
    Emmanuel Church 168
    First Baptist Church 168
    King's Chapel 87, 142
    New Old South Church 171
    Old North Church 123–124
    Old West Church 110
    Park Street Church 113
    St Stephen's Church 123
    Trinity Church 48, 170–171
Church Court 166
Citgo sign 175
City Hall Plaza 141
Civil War 44
Clarendon Park 181
Clemens, Roger 76
Coburn Gaming House 104
College of Basic Studies 64
College of Communications 64
college fees 70
colleges 59–70
    Babson 68
    Boston College 65
    Boston University 64–65, 175
    Brandeis 59, 67–68, 86
    Emerson 59
    Harvard 59, 60–61, 213–222
    MIT 59, 62–63, 223-225
    Northeast 65–66
    Radcliffe 61–62, 206-207
    Simmons 70
    Suffolk 66, 109
    Tufts 63–64
    Wellesley 66–67, 86
Collins, John F. 53
Columbia Redeviva 155
Columbus Park 153
Combat Zone 139
Combe, George 24
comedy clubs 59
Commercial Wharf 153
Commonwealth Avenue 167
Community Boating 190
Computer Museum 159
Concord 41, 231–234
Concord Baptist Church 180–181
Constitution Museum 131
Copley Place 171–172

Copley Plaza Hotel 171
Copley Square 170
Copley, John Singleton 83
Copp's Hill Burial Ground 125
Corinthian Yacht Club 257
Cotting, Uriah 163
Cotton, Rev. John 31
Cousy, Bob 77
Cranberry World 247
Cross Street 125
Curley, James Michael 50, 198
Cushing–Endicott House 167
Custom House Tavern 138
Cyclorama Building 181

D

da Verrazano, Giovanni 30
Davis, Bette 65
Dawes, William 41, 206
Declaration of Independence 146
DeMar, Clarence 79
Dickens, Charles 102, 141
Discovery 158
Dorchester 95
Dorchester Heights 42, 200
Downtown Crossing 137
driving 24–25
Dukakis, Michael 55
Durgin Park restaurant 147
Dyer, Mary 33, 113

E

East Cambridge 225–226
    Center for the Performing Arts 226
    Holy Cross Polish Church 226
    Sacred Heart Church 225
Eastern Point 263
Eastern Yacht Club 257
Eddy, Mary Baker 173, 211
Emerald Necklace 197–200
Emerson College 59, 191
Emerson, Ralph Waldo 23, 44, 144, 214, 219, 233, 234
Emmanuel Church 168
Enders, John 71
Endicott, John 31
Episcopal Divinity School 209
Essex 265
Everett, Edward 129
Exchange Place 138, 149
Exeter Street Theater 168

F

Falmouth 248, 252
Faneuil Hall 35, 42, 54, 146–147
Faneuil Hall Marketplace 95, 147, 149
Faneuil, Peter 35, 113
Fayette Street 184
Feast of the Assumption 119
Fenway 174–175
Fenway Court 86
Fenway Park 175

Fenway Victory Gardens 198
Fiedler, Arthur 115, 191
Filene's Basement 25, 137
First Baptist Church 168
First Continental Congress 41
fishing industry 31–32
Fitzgerald, Ella 65
Fitzgerald, John F. "Honey Fitz" 50, 121
Flat Side 101, 110
Fletcher School of Law & Diplomacy 64
Flower Lane 110
Fly Club 213
flying angel 119, 125
Flying Cloud 155
Flynn, Ray 55
Fogg Art Museum 86, 217
Fort Independence 200
Fort Putnam 225
Franklin Park 199
Franklin, Benjamin 145
Franklin Square 182–183
Franklin Street 138
Freedom Trail 95, 143
Frog Pond 112
Fruitlands Museums 237–238
Fuller Mansion 166
Fuller, Margaret 44
Fulton Street 153

G

Gage, General Thomas 41
Gardner, Isabella Stewart 86, 264
Garrison, William Lloyd 44, 104, 113
Geological & Mineralogical Museum 217
George III 39, 40
Georges Island 156
Gibson House Museum 166
Gilbert, Timothy 104
Gilman, Arthur 48
Gloucester 262
Gomez, Estevan 30
Goodwin Place 109
Goose, Elizabeth "Mother" 113
Gore Place 193
Gore, Rebecca Payne 193
Government Center 53, 141
Great Brewster Island 156
Great Fire (1872) 49
Gropius House 237
Gund, Graham 149

H

Hall, Captain Isaac 45
Hammond Castle Museum 262
Hamilton 266
Hancock, Ebenezer 148
Hancock, John 39, 41, 45, 105, 113, 231
Hancock, Thomas 35, 105
Hancock-Clark House 231
Hanover Street 122
Harbor islands 155–156
Harkness, Edward 61
Harkness Graduate Center 222
Harrison Gray Otis House 110

Hart Nautical Museum 223
Harvard 59, 60–61, 213–222
    Commencement 215
    establishment of 32
Harvard Bridge 191
Harvard Business School 213
Harvard Lampoon 213
Harvard Law Review 221
Harvard Law School 208, 221–222
Harvard Musical Association 107
Harvard Square, Cambridge 205
Harvard Square, Charlestown 129
Harvard Street 129
Harvard Village 237
Harvard, John 60, 129, 132
    statue of 213–214
Harwich 252
Hatch Shell 115, 191
Hawthorne, Nathaniel 44, 155, 168, 234, 258, 260
Hayden Planetarium 190
Hayden, Lewis 104
Haymarket 125
Head of the Charles Regatta 195
Higginson, Major Henry Lee 115
Holmes, Oliver Wendell 23, 102, 107, 130, 211
Homer, Winslow 87
Hooper Mansion 167
Hôtel Vendôme 167
House of Odd Windows 108
Hub of the Universe 23
Hunnewell Mansion 167
Hunt, William Morris 85
Hutchinson, Anne 137, 144
Hyannis 252
Hyannisport 252
Hynes Convention Center 170
Hynes, John 53

I

Immigrants
    Irish 49, 121
    Italians 50, 121
    Jews 50, 121
Immigration Restriction League 50
India Wharf 158
Institute of Contemporary Art 170
Ipswich 266
Irish, the
    immigration 49, 121
    and politics 50–51
Isabella Stewart Gardner Museum 86, 174–175

J

Jake Wirth's 140
Jamaica Pond 198
James II 34
James, Henry 102, 107
Jefferson, Thomas 42–43
Jewett Arts Center 67
John F. Fitzgerald Expressway 119
John F. Kennedy National Historic Site 199
John F. Kennedy School of Government 211
John Hancock Tower 170
John Harvard Mall 129

John Phillips House 107
Jones, Quincy 70
Jordan Hall 69
Jordan Marsh store 137
Joy Street 104

K

Kelley, John A. 79
Kenmore Square 175
Kennedy Library 200
Kennedy, John F. 53
Kerouac, Jack 236
King George's War 35
King's Chapel 87, 142
King's Chapel Burying Ground 144
King's Chapel Parish House 107
King, Martin Luther 64
Kipling, Rudyard 263
Kirkland, John 213
Kyoto, twinning with 159

L

Lake Waban 67
Land, Edwin 210, 221, 225
Larz Andersen Bridge 192
Larz Andersen Museum of Transportation 198
Lawrence 236
Lawrence, Captain James 157
Lebow, Fred 79
Lechmere Canal 190, 226
Lewis & Harriet Hayden House 104
Lexington 41
Lexington 231
Liberator, The 44
Lime Street 111
Lincoln 237
Lincoln Wharf 154
Lind, Jenny 108, 115
List Visual Arts Center 223
Little Brewster Island 157
Lock-Ober's Restaurant 140
Loeb Drama Center 208
Logan Airport 155, 156
Long Wharf 129, 155
Longfellow Bridge 190
Longfellow House 209–210
Longfellow Park 210
Longfellow's Wayside Inn 194
Longfellow, Henry Wadsworth 44, 102, 168, 208, 210, 211, 262
Louis Philippe 148
Louisburg Square 107, 115
Lovells Island 156
Lowell 236
Lyman House 193
Lynn Beach 257

M

Mackay, Charles 23
MacLaruin, Richard C. 224
Magnolia 262
Main Street, Charlestown 132

Majestic Theater 69
Manchester 261
Marblehead 257
Marlborough Street 166
Marriott Hotel 194
Massachusetts Bay Company 30, 129
Massachusetts Genealogical Society 168
Massachusetts General Hospital 71, 110
Massachusetts Institute of Technology 59, 62–63, 223–225
Massachusetts Spy 148
Massachusetts State House 105–106
Massasoit 29
Mather, Cotton 34, 61, 125, 216, 259
Mather, Increase 34, 125
Mayer, Jean 63
McKinley Square 138
McLauthlin Building 154
Meacham, George 165
medicine 71
Mercantile Wharf Building 153
Merrimack River 236
Minutemen National Historical Park 231
minutemen 41, 45, 231
MIT Bridge 191
MIT Museum 223
Mt Vernon 101
Mt Vernon Proprietors 106
Mt Vernon Street 107, 111
Mugar Memorial Library 64
Mugar Omni Theater 190
Munroe Tavern 231
Murray, Joseph 71
museums
    Armenian Library & Museum of America 193
    Cardinal Spellman Philatelic Museum 194
    Children's Museum 158–159
    Computer Museum 159
    Constitution Museum 131
    Fogg Art Museum 86, 217
    Fruitlands Museums 237–238
    Geological & Mineralogical Museum 217
    Gibson House Museum 166
    Hart Nautical Museum 223
    Isabella Stewart Gardner Museum 86, 174–175
    Larz Andersen Museum of Transportation 198
    MIT Museum 223
    Museum of American Textile History 236
    Museum of Comparative Zoology 217
    Museum of Fine Arts 83, 85, 87, 174
    Museum of Our National Heritage 231
    Museum of Science 190
    New England Quilt Museum 236
    Nichols House Museum 108
    Peabody Museum of Archaeology and Ethnology 217
    Postal Museum 194
    Rose Art Museum 86
    Sackler Museum 217
    Semitic Museum 217
    Transcendentalist Museum 238
    University Museums of Natural History 217
    Wellesley College Museum 86
music 115
Myopia Hunt Club 266
Myrtle Street 109

N

Nahant Island 257
Nantucket Sound 248
Napoleon Club 184
Nashoba Valley Winery 235
Neill, William C. 104
New Charles River Dam 189
New City Hall 141
New England Aquarium 157
New England Conservatory of Music 69, 115
New England Medical Center 64, 140
New England Quilt Museum 236
New Old South Church 171
Newbury Street 166
Newburyport 267
Newman, Robert 41
Newton 95
Nichols House Museum 108
Norman's Woe 262
North End 119–125
North Slope 108
North Square 122
Northeast University 65–66

O

Ocean Tank 157
Ocean Tray 157
Old Burying Ground, Cambridge 205
Old City Hall 144
Old Corner Book Store 144
Old Granary Burial Ground 45, 113
Old North Church 123–124
Old South Meeting House 145
Old State House 146
Old Sturbridge Village 238
Old West Church 110
Olmsted Historic Site 199
Olmsted, Frederick Law 197
Olympics 78, 79, 189, 190
Omphalos 205
Oneida Football Club 74
Opera Company of Boston 115
Orr, Bobby 78
Otis, Harrison Gray 106
Otis, James 35

P

Park Street Church 113
Park Street underground station 114
Parker House Hotel 141
Parkman, Francis 107
Parris, Alexander 149
Paul Revere House 122, 149
Paul Revere Mall 123
Paxton, William 87
Peabody Museum of Archaeology and Ethnology 217
Peddock Island 156
Pei, I.M. 53, 158, 170, 174, 200, 224
Peirce-Nichols House 261
Phillips School 104
Phillips Street 104, 109

Phipps Street Burying Ground 132
Phips, Sir William 259
Pickering Piano Factory 183
Pier 4 159
Pierce–Hichborn House 122
Pigeon Cove 265
Pilgrims 30
Pilot House 154
Pinckney Street 104, 108
Pioneer Village 261
Plum Island 267
Poe, Edgar Allen 24, 102
Pometacom 29
Pope Day 49
population 54, 95
Postal Museum 194
Prado 123
Prescott, Col. William 132
Primus Avenue 110
Prince, Rev. Thomas 137
Pro Arte Chamber Orchestra 115
Provincetown 250–251, 253
Prudential Center 53, 170
Public Garden 111, 165
Public Library 171
Puritan theology 32
Puritans 31

Q – R

Quincy 95
Quincy, Josiah 94
Quincy Market 85, 147, 149
racial tensions 44, 54
Radcliffe College 61–62, 206-207
Ratcliffe, Rev. Robert 142
Red Schoolhouse 194
Red Sox 74–76
Regis College 194
Revere, Paul 39, 41, 45, 83, 105, 113, 122, 123, 124,
    147, 174, 189, 231, 267
Richardson, Henry Hobson 149, 170, 215, 221
Ritz-Carlton Hotel 165
Robbins, Frederick 71
Rockport 264
Rocky Neck 263
Rogers, William Barton 62
Rollins Place 109
Rose Art Museum 86
Rose Kennedy Rose Garden 153
Rowe's Wharf 158
rowing 189, 195
Roxbury 54
Russell, Bertrand 23
Russell, Bill 77
Ruth, "Babe" 76

S

Sackler Museum 217
Sagamore Bridge 247
St Botolph Street 180
St Elsewhere 183
St Sauveur, Chevalier de 144
St Stephen's Church 123
Salem 31, 34, 258–261

Salem Street 125
Salt Street 148
Sandwich 249
Sargent, John Singer 87, 216
school busing 55
School Street 141
Scollay Square 53, 141
Second Harrison Gray Otis House 108
Semitic Museum 217
Sentry Hill Place 109
Sert, Josef Louis 220
Seven Years War 35
Sevens Pub 111
Shaker House 238
Shaw, Robert Gould 104
shortest street 184
Silber, John 64
Simmons College 70
slavery 44, 103, 104, 181
Sleepy Hollow Cemetery 234
smallpox epidemic 29
Smith Court 104
Smith, Captain John 30
Smith, John J. 104
Smith, Steve 70
Smoot, Oliver R. 192
Soldiers and Sailors Monument 114
Sons of Liberty 39
South Boston 85
South End 54, 179–184
South Slope 101, 106–107
South Station 179
Southwest Corridor 179–180
Spirit of '76, The 258
sport 60, 65, 74–79
Sports Museum of New England 192
Stamp Act 39
State Street 138
Stein, Gertrude 216
Stellwagen Bank 253
Stephen Higginson House 108
Stowe, Harriet Beecher 104, 144
Stuart Street 140
Stuart, Gilbert 87
students 59–70
Suffolk University 66, 109
Summer Street 137
swan boats 165
Swan Houses 107
Symphony Hall 174

T

Tarbell, Edmund 87
Tea Party Exhibit 158
tea tax 40
Telegraph Hill 114
Temple Street 109
textiles 43
The New England 168
The Vale 193
Theater District 140
Third Harrison Gray Otis House 107
Thoreau, Henry David 44, 234–237
Tobin Bridge 257
Townshend, Charles 40
trade 33, 35, 153

Transcendentalism 43
Transcendentalist Museum 238
Tremont Street 140
Tremont Temple 104
tribes
  Massachusetts 29
  Wampanoag 29
Trinity Church 48, 170–171
trolleys 114, 143
Tufts College 63–64

U

Union Boat Club 191
Union Oyster House 148
Union Park 179, 181–182
Union Street 148
Unitarianism 43
University Museums of Natural History 217
urban renewal 153
Usher House 154
USS Casin Young DD–793 131
USS Constitution 45, 129, 130, 155

V

Villa Victoria Housing Project 184
Vinegar Bible 125
Visitors Information Booth 114
visual arts 83–87
Vito Volterra Cultural Center 68
Voyager 158

W – Z

Walden Pond 235–237
Warren Tavern Club 132
Warren, Dr Joseph 39, 41
Washington, George 41, 206, 210, 213
Washington Street 137, 182
Waterhouse, Dr Benjamin 208
Watertown Square 193
Webster, Daniel 148, 191
Webster, Dr John 102
Weller, Thomas 71
Wellesley College 66–67
Wellesley College Museum 86
WERS-FM Radio 69
West Cedar Street 107
West Hill Place 112
whales 158, 253
White, Kevin 54
Widener Library 215–216
Williams, Ted 76
Willow street 107
Winter Street 140
Winthrop, John 29, 30, 55, 105, 112, 129, 144
Winthrop Square 132
witches 34, 259, 261
Woods Hole 252
World Trade Center 159
Wreck of the Hesperus 262
Yarmouth Street 180
Yastrzemski, Carl 76
zoo 199